D0913488

Admiralty Law
for the
Maritime Professional

Janis Schulmeisters, Esq.
and Justice John Ingram

The following admiralty texts, among other documents, have been used as references:

Admiralty Cases and Materials by Lucas and Schmidt, 2nd, 3rd and 6th ed. together with the Statute and Rule Supplement

Cases and Materials on Admiralty by Healy and Sharpe, 3rd ed. and 4th ed. By Healy, Sharpe and Sharpe

Admiralty and Maritime Law in the United States by Robertson, Friedell and Sturley. 2nd ed. together with the 2012 – 2013 Supplement

Admiralty and Maritime Law by Schoenbaum, 4th ed.

2005 Pocket Part of Schoenbaum's text

2007 Handbook of Maritime Laws and Forms by Healy Sharpe and Sharpe

Marine Insurance and General Average in the United States by Buglass, 3rd ed.

Ocean Marine Insurance by Flitner, 3rd ed.

Glossary of Maritime Law Terms by Tetley, 2nd ed.

Permission was received from BIMCO to include a copy of their Bill of Lading

Also permission was received from Lloyds to include their Salvage agreement

ISBN: 978-1-4834-3759-0 (sc)
ISBN: 978-1-4834-3758-3 (e)

Lulu Publishing Services rev. date: 10/13/2015

Contents

Introduction

Admiralty law is a specialty and ship's officers and shoreside management and executives (hereafter referred collectively as "Maritime Professionals") should be aware of the general principles of Admiralty/ Maritime Law because of the unique nature of Admiralty Law as it affects day to day operations in the industry as well as The BIG One (Maritime Disaster). A collision at sea can ruin your day but it will promote much litigation for years to come.

Senior U.S. District Judge Terry Haight (of Haight Gardner Poor and Havens' clan) recently spoke at the 225th Celebration of the U.S. District Court for the Southern District of New York (The Mother Court) and said this about admiralty law and the history of the Silver Oar which had been crafted by a silversmith in 1725 and served as the symbol of the Vice Admiralty Court of the Province of New York (predecessor court to the New York State Supreme Court).

Judge Haight said "There is something special about the oar. It is wholly fitting that the oar is the symbol of the law of the sea."

He went on to say:

"For the sea itself is eternally fascinating, and so are the ships and those who go down to sea in ships, who by their daring or distress, courage or cowardice, foresight or foolishness, triumphs or tragedy of navigation, give employment to admiralty judges and lawyers, thereby generating that equally fascinating body of law that we call admiralty."

It should be kept in mind that technically Admiralty pertains to the jurisdictional aspects of the law and maritime law relates to the body of the law that we know of as The General Maritime Law of the United States which includes case law (both federal and state). Federal Statutes and International conventions which affect such matters as the Rules of the Road, training and licensing of seafarers and pollution. Admiralty law does not concern itself with International Public Law such as Law of the Sea or Military Law as in the Uniform Code of Military Justice. Criminal law like medical malpractice has gone to sea and will be touched on in this text.

A short list of the areas that can effect every maritime venture includes:

1. The personification of a vessel is a very important and unique concept of admiralty.
2. An understanding of what is a "navigable" waterway can be important. Yes, there are water or river areas in the United States to which maritime law does not apply (intra state waters). It applies to many rivers and lakes, but for others there are significant differences.
3. The U.S. Law regarding shipowner's right to petition in The Big One (maritime disaster) for Exoneration from and Limitation of Liability to the value of the vessel after the casualty and the Special Fund for Personal Injury and Wrongful Death claimants and Maritime Professionals should be aware of Limitation.
4. The novel aspects of how vessels act on the water, which is different from how any craft on land acts, is important and has different requirements for the navigator.
5. Weather and its effect on shipping, hurricanes, typhoons and weather routing and duties of Ship's masters.

6. The Merchant Marine and its licensing and crew certifications and laws pertaining to maintenance and cure, Jones Act negligence, unseaworthiness and seafarer's rights to punitive damages for non payment of maintenance and cure and penalty wage claims.

7. Oil and chemical spills and pollution of the oceans and waterways and the consequences to ship's officers, pilots, shoreside management. The requirement for oil spill response plans incidents and the role of the U.S. Coast Guard as Federal on scene commander in spills within U.S. territorial waters.

8. Collisions, allisions, fires and strandings and the legal consequences thereof.

9. Cargo law - re international carriage of goods by sea and private carriage - including Harter Act and COGSA and its application to private carriage.

10. Charter Parties and dispute resolution primarily by arbitration in New York or London and the differences between the two systems and who are the arbitrators and what are their powers pursuant to the U.S. Arbitration Act and how arbitration awards are made into judgments and enforced - Enforcement of Arbitration Awards by the New York Convention on Arbitration.

11. Concepts regarding the ancient doctrines of Salvage and General Average.

12. Pilotage - Who is the Pilot? What is the Pilot's Role - Command or Control? Who is primarily responsible for licensing pilots who control foreign flag vessels and U.S. flag vessels engaged in foreign commerce? Compulsory pilotage and its true meaning. Who disciplines pilots (federal and state)? The Docking Master concept and regulations and licensing in some states and liability of Pilots and Pilot Associations.

13. Maritime Liens - What are they and why are they important? How are maritime liens extinguished? What is the priority of maritime liens in the distribution of proceeds from the Admiralty sale of a ship by a U.S. Marshal in Federal Court?

14. Marine insurance cases which are governed by state law except for issues which are defined by federal admiralty law. The United States does NOT have a Federal Maritime Insurance Act.
15. The law of Towage. Tugs not liable for negligence of Docking Masters. Duty of tug to tow and tow's warranty of seaworthiness to the tug. Towage and contracts of affreightment distinguished and impact of insurance.
16. Maritime liens for things such as salvage, crew wages, maritime torts and maritime contracts are important.
17. What is a vessel?

The above list is not meant to be exhaustive and there are a number of areas that will be touched upon including sovereign immunity and piracy and Coast Guard investigations and reporting of incidents and criminal investigations.

The basic idea is that the maritime professional whether shipboard or shoreside must have some idea about the impact of law on maritime commerce. One must have a general familiarity with the U.S. courts' system both state and federal and administrative agencies and where federal supremacy prevails and where the Savings to Suitors clause applies which permits litigants to sue in state courts where the state courts are competent to give the remedy. If the remedy is money, state courts have jurisdiction. If it is to arrest a ship *in rem* - the state courts cannot do so. The special attributes of maritime law as it applies to international transactions and its impact on daily business transactions and the myriad of incidents that occur on board ships must be understood by the maritime professional.

Most maritime law texts are written for law students or Proctors in Admiralty (maritime lawyers). For example, there is voluminous text on *The Law of Maritime Collision* by Professor Joseph Sweeney and Nicholas J. Healy, Esq. There are also similar texts on *The Law of Tugs,*

Towage and Collision and *The Law on Charter Parties, and Cargo Law* which are treaties by prominent admiralty lawyers which go into great detail re the applicable subjects. In addition, there are lengthy, scholarly law review articles on such subjects as the *Cruise Passengers' Rights and Remedies* or *The Fifth Amendment and Maritime Casualty Investigations* which are written by lawyers, judges and law professors and students. In addition, The Tulane Law School publishes a journal on maritime law. The maritime professional needs some of this pertinent information to have an appreciation of what might occur.

However, it is important for the reader who might wish to jump into the meat of maritime law and skip jurisdiction to understand both subject matter jurisdiction and personal jurisdiction. Subject matter jurisdiction refers to the courts' ability to hear a particular case. In the United States we do have federal and state courts which may have exclusive or concurrent jurisdiction to hear a maritime case. Personal jurisdiction refers to the court's authority over the person or entity and the *in rem* concept and attachment of assets of a defendant not found in the jurisdiction. State courts cannot arrest a vessel or its cargo to obtain jurisdiction over a party. An *in rem* action against a ship allows the federal court to exercise jurisdiction over the vessel and obtain security for any judgment without adjudication of liability.

In addition, it is essential to understand the concept of Navigable Waters of the United States. The term has a special meaning. It refers to interstate waters and waters that connect to and from the United States. Thus an incident on Lake George, a wholly land locked lake in New York State, is not subject to admiralty jurisdiction or federal maritime law. The U.S. Coast Guard does not patrol Lake George and local law enforcement police incidents on Lake George. A collision in the English Channel is within the admiralty jurisdiction of the U.S. District Court. Indeed a recent collision in the English Channel involving three non U.S. flag vessels was litigated in the Federal Courts in New York with various cargo claimants and vessel interests and the case was heard by a U.S. District Judge and governed by foreign laws and convention on collision which the United States had not signed on to. The term navigable waters has evolved over decades and problems occurred because much of our law evolved from England where most rivers were effected by the ebb and flow of the tides, something that did not exist on our Great Lakes and portions of interstate rivers such as the Mississippi River and Missouri River. We will touch, where applicable, on the origins and concepts that come from England and the consequences where relevant. For the most part, this text will consider maritime law as it applies throughout the United States. There had been conflicts between the common law courts in England and the admiralty courts for the right to hear cases. In English civil or common law courts, it was argued that only things that occurred at sea were to be heard by the Admiralty Judge and the rest by the common law courts.

Even the term admiralty comes from England. The word admiral comes from the Arabic word "Amir-al-bahr" meaning commander of the sea. The rank of Admiral in The Royal Navy (RN) was first used in 1500 and referred to a senior officer in the RN who was in charge of disciplining and administration of naval personnel. In the 1300's this individual assumed a judicial function. When our U.S. Constitution was enacted, admiralty referred to a court hearing cases arising from naval and marine matters. It should be noted that while England has an Admiralty Judge, in the United States we do not have Admiralty Judges. U.S. District Judges may sit in Admiralty when hearing a maritime case. State court judges hearing maritime cases are bound by the General Maritime Law of the United States and if there is a conflict between their state law and a principle of federal maritime law, they must apply the federal law.

Jurisdiction and the U.S. federal system

Lawsuits are handled in courts and an understanding is needed of the term "jurisdiction." It is the power and the right of a court to hear a particular case. There are two parts that have to be satisfied: (1) Whether that particular court may hear or handle that particular type of a case, and (2) Whether the court may fairly reach the party or parties over which the court will exercise its powers. Simply; jurisdiction is the court's right and ability to act. The first is called **subject matter jurisdiction**, and the second is the court's **jurisdiction over the parties or the res** (the "thing," e.g. the ship or its cargo.)

Elaborating on these requirements, we take the latter first. If the court cannot serve or reach the party, either actually or by way of some statute or "long arm" provision or accepted rule, any judgment it may issue concerning that party is invalid and is of no force and/or effect. This is the in personam or "personal" jurisdiction requirement. For example, a U.S. District Court cannot "reach" an Egyptian ship if it is in a port in Europe. On the other hand, if the ship is in New York Harbor, a federal court[1] in New York can reach that ship by issuing an order for the arrest of that ship. The ship is then in the court's jurisdiction area and can be "reached."

---

[1]   The term federal courts refers to the U.S. District Courts, U.S. Courts of Appeal and the U.S. Supreme Court.

Going to the second, the question is whether the particular court in question has the right to go and "reach" the party. The statute creating that court had to give it the right or "subject matter jurisdiction" to handle that type of a case. And this is where for the U.S. Court system, the United States Constitution and applicable statutes and court rules come in.[2]

Article III of the Constitution of the United States in relevant part provides:

> Section 1: The judicial Power of the United States, shall be vested in one Supreme Court, and in such inferior Courts as the Congress may from time to time ordain and establish. * * *
> Section 2. [1]: The Judicial Power shall extend to all Cases, in Law and Equity, arising under the Constitution, the Laws of the United States and Treaties made, or which shall be made, under their Authority; * * * (and) to all Cases of admiralty and maritime Jurisdiction. * * *

Section 9 of the Judiciary Act of 1789 provided:

> * * * The district courts . . . shall also have exclusive original cognizance of all civil causes of admiralty and maritime jurisdiction . . . saving to suitors, in all cases, the right of a common law remedy, where the common law is competent to give it . . .

Amended in 1949 and now contained in 28 U.S. C. § 1333 it provides:

> The district courts shall have original jurisdiction, exclusive of the courts of the States of:

---

[2]   The European, Asian and South American countries have their own rules, many of which are similar as the idea of courts reaching a foreign ship within its "reach" or jurisdiction have existed for centuries. Here we stay with the United States' rules and procedures.

> (1) Any civil case of admiralty or maritime jurisdiction, saving to suitors in all cases all other remedies to which they are otherwise entitled . . .

What is sometimes confusing is the "saving to suitors" language as it allows for the existence of laws used on this side of the Atlantic Ocean before the United States of America came into existence. Now that the States have turned into 50 states, that each have their separate statutes, this "savings to suitors" provision comes into play in many personal injury and cargo cases. Based on pre revolution law systems that permitted certain admiralty claims to be considered in local courts they can be tried in a state court if both parties agree, as the state court may be one of "general jurisdiction." This may, however, end with bizarre results as most state court judges are not familiar with maritime principles. It is the maritime lawyer's job to educate the state judges and many do. Therefore, Congress enacted the "removal" statute. This statute permits a defendant sued in a state court to "remove" or transfer the case to the federal court in the area. The statute provides in 28 U.S.C. §1441 subsection(a):

> Except as otherwise expressly provided by Act of Congress, any civil action brought in a State court of which the district courts of the United States have original jurisdiction, may be removed by the defendant or the defendants, to the district court of the United States for the district and division embracing the place where such action is pending.

This does not mean that every action is removable to a federal court, as a special provision provides that injured seamen "Jones Act" claims may not be removed. Also, there are the other situations where state law may be applicable. Suffice it to say here that with respect to seamen personal injury claims the plaintiff may maintain an action against his employer in a state court, and for many years many did, but in doing so the plaintiff gives up his *in rem* rights against the vessel for unseaworthiness. A Jones Act seaman's case cannot be brought *in rem*. A seafarer suit *in rem* against the ship for unseaworthiness in a federal court is an important right because it gives the seafarer jurisdiction and security for any judgment. Most seafarers do not proceed with an arrest because of the substantial costs that must be paid in advance to the U.S. Marshal's service.

There have been several recent cases holding that under the newly revised rewording of § 28 U.S.C. § 1441 remanding cases back to the state court where the defendant had removed the case on the ground that it was an admiralty case. *Cassidy v. Murray* 2014 WL 3723877 (D. MD July 2014), a recreational boat case. Indeed there are several lower federal court cases dealing with the subject of removal. Admiralty by itself is not reason to remove a case to federal court. Admiralty is not a federal question basis for removal. *Romero v. International Operating Co.*, 358 US 354, 372 (1959). The U.S. Supreme Court declined to expand the scope of federal jurisdiction under 28 U.S.C. §1331 to include "admiralty claims" out of concern that savings to suitors actions in state court would be removed to federal court and undermine the plaintiff's choice of forum. *Lewis*, 531 US at 455 (citing Romero 358 US at 371-72).

Removal must only occur where there is a federal question or diversity of citizenship and the amount in question is more than $75,000. If a federal statute is involved, it would be deemed a federal question. Thus many admiralty cases which do not involve federal question or diversity and jurisdictional amount will be remanded and more U.S. District Courts are doing just that. To be continued!

This brings us to the need for a brief discussion to understand the differences between the various court systems in the United States. In the United States we have two distinct types of legal systems or sets of laws: The federal system and the systems in each of the 50 States of the Union, plus one in the District of Columbia (the capital - Washington, D.C.) and the territories of the U.S. and the Commonwealth of Puerto Rico. Keeping in mind that the people and the disputes among them existed in the colonies and the colonial courts before 1776. Although for admiralty matters there was the British "Viceroy of Admiralty" who sat in New York (in a court that later became the United States District Court for the Southern District of New York) some seamen injury matters were handled by courts that became state courts.

In most cases we are dealing with the General Maritime Law of the United States and not American Law or American courts. Use of such terms are misnomers and erroneous and show a lack of understanding of the court systems in the United States. Indeed in a maritime casualty there may be civil claims under the GML and statutes of the United States such as the Limitation Statutes, 46 U.S.C. §30501-30512. In fact, a Judge sitting in admiralty may put on a different hat and sit in Criminal on the Maritime Manslaughter provisions of the United States Criminal Code and preside over a jury trial of a mariner for violation of federal criminal law arising out of the same casualty.

Just when everyone thought they knew what a vessel was, the U.S. Supreme Court came out with a new test for a vessel for admiralty jurisdiction and the bringing of an *in rem* action in *Lozman v City of Riviera Beach*, 133 S. Ct. 735 (2013). The Rules of Construction Act defines a vessel as including every description of watercraft or other artificial contrivance used or capable of being used, as a means of transportation on the water. 1 U.S.C. §3. Of course, that definition had engendered much litigation as to the term vessel. One federal judge whimsically wrote that under that definition a bathtub with three men in it would constitute a vessel. Also, the whale which swallowed Jonah could be deemed a vessel.

Lozman owned a 60 foot by 12 foot floating home. The home consisted of a house-like plywood structure with French doors on three sides, a sitting room, a bedroom, a closet, bathroom and kitchen along with a stairway leading to an upper level which had three office spaces. It did not have any engine or sails. An empty bilge space underneath the main floor kept it afloat.

He apparently docked at the City of Riviera Beach's Marina and failed to pay dockage fees. The City tried unsuccessfully to evict him. The City then brought an *in rem* action against the floating home in the U.S. District Court. Lozman moved to dismiss on the ground his floating home was not a vessel and that the court lacked admiralty jurisdiction. The District Court found it was a vessel and that it had jurisdiction and conducted a non jury admiralty trial and awarded the City $3,039.88 for dockage and nominal damages of $1.00 for trespass.

The Court of Appeals affirmed on the ground that it was a vessel capable of being moved over the water. The U.S. Supreme Court granted permission to appeal on grounds of conflict between Circuits on the meaning of the term capable of movement. In a somewhat humorous opinion, the Supreme Court reversed and said that it is not a theoretical application of the term capable, but a practical one. They said:

"Consequently, in our view a structure does not fall within the scope of this statutory phrase unless a reasonable observer, looking to the home's physical characteristics and activities would consider it designed to a practical degree to carrying people or things over the water."

Thus the Court lacked jurisdiction and the floating home should not have been arrested and sold pursuant to the admiralty sale. Surely, Mr. Lozman will sue the City for wrongful arrest. Thus, there is a new job for maritime experts to be "the Reasonable Observer" in a dispute over whether a thing is a vessel capable of moving people or things over the water.

A detailed discussion of the federal jurisdiction of maritime cases is not needed here. The following, however, should be noted.

1. There is a vast difference between the federal system and the legal systems of the various fifty states and the territories of Guam and the U.S. Virgin Islands and the Commonwealth of Puerto Rico.
2. To be able to sue in the federal court under diversity of citizenship or federal question jurisdiction (technical requirements for being able to invoke the help of the federal judiciary) the amount in controversy must be $75,000 or more.
3. The federal district courts are not courts of general jurisdiction, but their parameters are delineated by the statutes creating the court - a separate one for each court.[3]
4. One bringing an admiralty action in the federal court does NOT have to meet any jurisdictional amount requirement. This may sound as a small matter, but in the admiralty practiced, it is quite significant. Admiralty is not a basis for federal question.
5. Federal courts have admiralty *in rem* jurisdiction which state courts do not have. The *in rem* suit is unique in that one injured by or on the ship can sue the ship. This is a very important and a very significant provision, as we will see later, as it provides a method by which a claimant injured by or on the ship can obtain security for his claim even if the offending ship is a foreign flag ship that came to the American port on a one time voyage.
6. And, the question of politics is not to be ignored as some state court judges have to stand for re-election whereas federal judges are appointed for life.

---

[3]   For each district court there is a separate statute creating it. Today there are such courts in all 50 states, the District of Columbia and the territories such as the U.S. Virgin Islands, Guam and the Commonwealth of Puerto Rico.

7. A federal court sitting in admiralty is without a jury. A Jones Act case provides for trial by jury.

8. Most federal courts now have automatic disclosure rules and the federal discovery (or information disclosure) rules are usually broader than most state courts and there is a system for individual judge assignments and the cases proceed quicker. Under most U.S. District Court Local Rules - a very extensive Pre Trial Order (PTO) must be filed at least a month before the trial date. This extensive PTO helps both sides see the strengths and weaknesses of their cases and often prompts settlements.

What is an Admiralty case!?!

The road to what today, in the twenty-first century's beginning, is an admiralty case in American courts was rather tortured. Today we need a navigable waterway, a vessel and maritime nexus, but it took until 1995 for the case of *Jerome B. Grubart, Inc. v. Great Lakes Dredge & Dock Co.,* 513 U.S. 527, (1995) for the last case to come down and hopefully put the issue to rest. Indeed, in 2013 the U. S. Supreme Court gave a new guidance as to what is a vessel in *Lozman v. City of Riviera Beach,* 133 S.Ct. 735 (2013) affirming that a houseboat that could not be used for navigation, and was not so used was not a vessel. Before that the basic definition of a vessel had been – anything used or capable of being used to transport on the water was a vessel, such as a canoe or a barge.

All waters in the United States are not "navigable waters of the United States." While many large lakes are not, many smaller ones may be. The development in our law to distinguish them took about one hundred fifty years. The beginnings of our laws find their origins in England, so do the disputes as to what is and what belongs in admiralty. The vestiges of admiralty came from England, where the dispute between admiralty and civil law had raged for centuries. One must keep in mind that all navigable waters of the British Isles are waterways that connect to the Atlantic Ocean or the North Sea or the English Channel and are affected by the ebb and flow of the tide. The idea that tidal effect is necessary for admiralty came over to the United States before the courts realized that in the United States there are many waters used by ships that are not affected by tides. As strange as it may seem, it took over a century for the courts to recognize this. The second aspect in this dispute is the question of what type of tort and/or contract cases belong in admiralty. Keep in mind that most agreements concerning shipments over the water have always been made on land. An early erudite opinion was issued in 1815 by then Circuit Judge Story who eventually became a Supreme Court Justice.

The story is told that his 79 page opinion was delivered within two weeks of oral argument in the case of *De Lovio v. Boit*, 7 F. Cas. 418 (No. 3776) (C.C.D. Mass 1815) leading to the speculation that he had earlier prepared his discourse on admiralty jurisdiction and was just waiting for the appropriate case to publish it. In that case the vessel ESPERANZA, a Spanish flag slaver trading between West Africa and Havana, owned by Spaniard De Lovio living in Havana, Cuba, left Havana in March and was captured by British warships in June 1812 and sold by a vice-admiralty court in July in Sierra Leone. De Lovio's friends in Boston had persuaded several underwriters to insure the voyage. The underwriters signed the policy containing the "lost or not lost" provision in October, not knowing that the voyage was already over. When the suit was filed in 1815 the underwriters moved to dismiss on the grounds there was no admiralty jurisdiction and the District Judge dismissed the action. Judge Story sitting in admiralty on the Circuit court of Massachusetts reversed and set forth his views on the Constitution's Article III thus:

> On the whole I am, without the slightest hesitation, ready to pronounce that the delegation of cognizance of "all civil cases of admiralty and maritime jurisdiction" to the courts of the United States comprehends all maritime contracts, torts, and injuries. **The latter branch is necessarily bounded by locality; the**

former extends over all contracts, wherever they may be made or executed, or wheresoever may be the form of the stipulations) which relate to the navigation, business, or commerce of the sea. [Emphasis mine.] The next inquiry is, what are properly to be deemed "maritime contracts." Happily in this particular there is little room for controversy. All civilians and jurists agree, that in this appellation are included, among other things, charter parties, affreightments, marine hypothecations, contracts for maritime service in the building, repairing, supplying and navigating ships; contracts between part owners of ships, contracts and quasi contracts respecting averages, contributions and jettisons; and what is more material to our present purpose, policies of insurance. * * * There is no more reason why the admiralty should have cognizance of bottomry instruments, as maritime contracts, than of policies of insurance. Both are executed on land, and both intrinsically respect maritime risks, injuries and losses.

However, it was not until 1871 that the Supreme Court came fully around to this view when finally in *Insurance Co. v. Dunham*, 78 U.S. 1 (1870) it said:

> The learned and exhaustive opinion of Justice Story, in the case of De *Lovio v. Boit* . . . (1915) affirming the admiralty jurisdiction over policies of marine insurance, has never been answered, and will always stand as a monument to his great erudition... We are of the opinion that the conclusion of Justice Story was correct.

Note that the great erudition talking about torts and injuries held it to be "bound by locality," which he reiterated in 1833 in *Thomas v. Lane*, 23 F. Cas. 957, 960 (No. 13,902) where he said:

> In regard to torts I have always understood, that the jurisdiction of the admiralty is exclusively dependent upon locality of the act. The admiralty has not, and never (I believe) deliberately claimed to have, any jurisdiction over torts, except such as are maritime torts, that is, such as are committed on the high seas, or on waters within the ebb and flow of the tide.

This ebb and flow of the tide language caused many difficulties over the next century and a half.

In *The Thomas Jefferson*, 23 U.S. 428 (1825) the wages of a seaman for a voyage on the Mississippi above the effect of tide was the issue and it was held that there was no admiralty jurisdiction because the claim was for wages earned above tidal waters.

In *Peyroux v. Howard*, 32 U.S. 175 (1837) the litigation was for the payment for repairs to the vessel PLANTER, a vessel whose voyages on the Mississippi were on the waters that **sometimes** were affected by the tide, namely New Orleans, and therefore was held to be within admiralty.

In *The Orleans v. Phoebus*, 36 U.S. 175 (1837) it was an action to sell a vessel and to partition (divide among the owners) the proceeds. The boat was employed only on the Mississippi, and **may** have touched tidal waters, but substantially operated not on waters affected by the ebb and flow of the tide, and it was held not to be within admiralty jurisdiction.

In *Waring v. Clarke*, 46 U.S. 441 (1847) it was a libel *in rem* to recover damages for injuries as a result of a collision in an area of the Mississippi about 95 miles above New Orleans "within ebb and flow of tide." The court's language is notable.

> It is the first time that the point has been distinctly presented to this court, whether a case of collision in our rivers, where the tide ebbs and flows, is within the admiralty jurisdiction of the courts of the United States, if the locality be, in the sense in which it is used by the common law judges in England, *infra corpus comitatus.*

[*Infra corpus comitatus = Within the body (territorial limits) of the county. In English law, waters which are infra corpus comitatus are exempt from the jurisdiction of admiralty*].

> Our conclusion is, that the admiralty jurisdiction of the courts of the United States extends to the waters, as far as the tide flows, though that may be *infra corpus comitatus*; that the case before us did happen where the tide ebbed and flowed *infra corpus comitatus*, and that the court has jurisdiction to decree upon the claim of the libellant for damages.

There was a dissent by Justice Woodbury complaining that it was 203 miles up river above the sea.

Because of such views, still not giving in to the whole concept, in 1845 was passed An Act Extending The Jurisdiction Of The District Courts To Certain Cases, Upon The Lakes And Navigable Waters Connecting Same:

> Be it enacted . . . That the district courts of the United States shall have, possess and exercise the same jurisdiction **in contract and tort,** arising in, upon, or

concerning **steamboats and other vessels of 20 tons burden and upwards** enrolled and licensed for the coasting trade, **and at the time employed in business of commerce and navigation between ports and places in different States and Territories upon the lakes and navigable waters connecting said lakes**, as is now possessed and exercised by said courts in cases of like steamboats and other vessels employed . . . **upon the high seas or tide waters within the admiralty jurisdiction of the United States**. . . .

There was still a difficulty in *The Genesee Chief v. Fitzhugh*, 53 U.S. 443 (1851) which involved a collision on Lake Ontario. The steamer sunk a sailing vessel and the sailing vessel's owners sued the Steamer *in rem*. There was an objection to admiralty jurisdiction on the grounds there are no tides on the Great Lakes. The court now explains how times have changed from the establishment of the United States and the time the Constitution was adopted when all 13 colonies were on major rivers that were to some extent affected by tide. Now, in1851, there are questions of international law, questions of prize matters, and commerce among states and other nations. But the court notes that it is not commerce alone as that would make it "arbitrary." It also notes that in England tidal waters and "public lands" concepts merged, whereas, in U.S. there are many "public rivers" that are navigable and therefore "public navigable waters" that are not affected by tide. It then struggled to say:

> It is the decision in the case of *The Thomas Jefferson*, 23 U.S. 428 (1825) which mainly embarrasses the court in the present inquiry. . . But at the same time we are convinced that, if we follow it, we follow an erroneous decision into which the court fell, when the great importance of the question as it now presents

itself could not be foreseen; and the subject did not therefore receive that deliberate consideration which at this time would have been given to it by the eminent men who presided here when that case was decided. For the decision was made in 1825, when the commerce on the rivers of the west and on the lakes was in its infancy, and of little importance, and but little regarded compared with that of the present day. * * *

[And then the Court makes the distinction (not really an excuse) by saying.]

> The case of **Thomas Jefferson did not decide any question of property**, or lay down any rule by which the right of property should be determined. If it had, we should have felt ourselves bound to follow it notwithstanding the opinion we have expressed. For every one would suppose that after the decision of this court, in a matter of that kind, he might safely enter into contracts, upon the faith that rights thus acquired would not be disturbed. In such a case, *stare decisis*[4] is the safe and established rule of judicial policy, and should always be adhered to. For if the law, as pronounced by the court, ought not to stand, it is in the power of the legislature to amend it, without impairing rights acquired under it. **But the decision referred to has no relation to rights of property.** [Emphasis mine]

Sixteen years later the court again wrestled with an admiralty tort jurisdiction issue. In *The Plymouth*, 70 U.S. 20 (1865) the steamer FALCON anchored alongside a wharf caught fire due to negligence

---

[4] Stare Decisis is "to stand by things decided" – the doctrine of precedent whereby a court must follow the decision of an earlier court on the same issue.

of its crew and the wharf and warehouse and valuable property were destroyed. The wharfinger sued FALCON's owner and attached another vessel owned by FALCON's owner. The Supreme Court upheld the motion to dismiss for lack of admiralty jurisdiction on the grounds of the **LOCALITY** rule. The court discussed the argument of a "mixed case" such as the tort having been committed partially on land and partially on the navigable water. But then goes on to say that the "mixed" cases are contract cases, because in contract cases the locality is not important; - either it is a maritime contract or it is not. Also, "personal wrong" cases are not like this one, for example, where one entices a minor on shore to commit a wrong on the vessel. It goes on to say that in tort, the locality is important, namely, that the wrong and injury complained of must have been committed wholly upon the high seas or navigable waters, or, at least the substance and consummation of the same must have taken place upon these waters to be within the admiralty jurisdiction, then adding:

> A trespass on board a vessel, or by the vessel itself, above tide waters, when that was the limit of jurisdiction, was not of admiralty cognizance. The reason was, that it was not committed within the locality that gave it the jurisdiction. The vessel itself was not important. * * * The jurisdiction of the admiralty does not depend upon the fact that the injury was inflicted by the vessel, but upon the locality – the high seas, or navigable waters where it occurred. 70 U.S. at p. 22

This "locality" language over the years gave the jurisdictional question many difficult problems.

Finally in 1948 **The Extension of Admiralty Jurisdiction Act** *was passed to partly fix the problem. Originally contained in 46 U.S.C. § 740 it was reworded and now, following the 2006 rewriting and* *renumbering of 46 U.S. Code, states in § 30101 entitled Extension of Jurisdiction to Cases of Damage or Injury on Land:*

(a) In General –
The admiralty and maritime jurisdiction of the United States extends to and includes cases of injury or damage, to person or property, caused by a vessel on navigable waters, even though the injury or damage is done or consummated on land.

(b) Procedure -
A civil action in a case under subsection (a) may be brought *in rem* or *in personam* according to the principles of law and rules of practice applicable in cases where the injury or damage has been done and consummated on navigable waters.

(c) Actions against the United States –
(1) Exclusive Remedy – In a civil action against the United States for injury or damage done or consummated on land by a vessel on navigable waters, chapter 309 or 311 of this title, as appropriate, provides the exclusive remedy.
(2) Administrative Claim – A civil action described in paragraph (1) may not be brought until the expiration of the 6-month period after the claim has been presented in writing to the agency owning or operating the vessel causing injury or damage.

Returning to the development of admiralty jurisdiction, the locality rule caused several apparent anomalies. For example:

In 1963 we had the "unseaworthy coffee bean" in *Gutierrez v. Waterman S.S. Corp.*, 373 U.S. 206 (1963). Coffee beans spilled on dock from broken bags of coffee just **unloaded** from the ship (probably due to the longshoremen having used hooks in handling the burlap bags) and Gutierrez slipped on the beans on the pier's apron and was seriously injured. Admiralty jurisdiction was upheld. However, eight years later in *Victory Carriers, Inc. v. Law,* 404 U.S. 202 (1971) the cargo was being assembled on the pier or dock, **not yet being loaded on board the vessel moored at the dock.** When plaintiff, Law, was injured by a defective forklift on the dock used to move the cargo it was held by the majority that maritime law does not govern longshoremen accidents caused by defective equipment of longshoreman's employer!!! There was a vigorous dissent by Justices Douglas and Brennan – unable to distinguish between loading and unloading.

The next year brought the beginning of what the requirements for admiralty jurisdiction now seems to be.

In the eighteen year development that follows, first came *Executive Jet Aviation, Inc. v. City of Cleveland*, 409 U.S. 249 (1972). Here the airplane took off from the Cleveland airport, ran into a flock of seagulls and crashed in Lake Erie, a navigable waterway of the United States. It was held that there was no admiralty jurisdiction because there was no relationship whatsoever between the crash and traditional maritime activity even though the place of injury was on a navigable water – Lake Erie. The Supreme Court went on to explain that for maritime jurisdiction to exist there must be a **maritime nexus,** a connection to traditional maritime activity. This did away with the strict "locality" rule – first established in 1815 in the *De Lovio* case.

Ten years later, the maritime commerce connection was expanded in *Foremost Insurance Co., v. Richardson*, 457 U.S. 668 (1982). Here the case dealt with a collision on a navigable waterway between a water skier and a small fishing boat. The court upheld admiralty jurisdiction for the sake of **uniformity** in maritime litigation because uniformity is needed in applying the rules for preventing collisions on navigable waters.

Eight years later in *Sisson v. Ruby*, 497 U.S 358 (1990) the fire was on a pleasure boat in a marina when the clothes dryer on the pleasure boat caused a substantial part of the marina to burn with many other private boats being destroyed. The court recognized the commercial activity (or potential interruption to or potential interference with maritime commerce) by the fire, because pleasure boating is a very substantial maritime activity in the world.

These three cases over an eighteen year period provide for the need to have a vessel on navigable waters involved in a maritime activity. The reason these cases went to the Supreme Court were the desire by at least one party to invoke the admiralty's right or ability to limit liability to the value of the vessel after the casualty.

Another five years later came the icing on the cake in *Grubart v. Great Lakes Dredge & Dock Co.*, 513 U.S. 527 (1995). [Below – Great Lakes Dredge & Dock Co. v. City of Chicago, 3 F. 3rd 225 (7th Cir. 1993).] Here the flooding of downtown Chicago was brought into admiralty. It started with work on a pier on the Chicago River. The pier owner had his pilings replaced. The work damaged by weakening the tunnel under the Chicago River and when the tunnel's walls broke the river flooded the city and caused enormous damage. The dredge owner petitioned for limitation of liability, something only available in admiralty.

As noted, all four cases at the bottom of the inquiry had the desire to invoke admiralty jurisdiction so the party liable could limit its liability. **– Hence the need for understanding admiralty jurisdiction,** and the new wrinkle in Maritime Law decided by the Supreme Court in *Lozman v. City of Riviera Beach* noted above.

This text deals with limitation of liability, *in rem* principles, ship arrests, navigable water concepts and other matters as the text progresses. But now, at least the student should understand why the development of and an understanding of admiralty jurisdiction concepts is important in maritime business.

The special attributes of admiralty

As noted earlier, the question of admiralty jurisdiction keeps coming up as the world changes or as new situations come up. Here we consider a few of the special attributes that apply to maritime business, practice and litigation. While the subjects are treated in more detail later on, here we touch upon a few of the special attributes:

1-   The "personification of the vessel" or *in rem* claims and proceedings.
2-   Vessel "arrest" procedures and letters of undertaking.
3-   The limitation of liability procedures in general terms.
4-   The need for several types of marine insurance and advisability for other types.
5-   The types of relief available in admiralty.

1   *The in rem principles or personification of the vessel.*
In every day situations if one is involved in a car accident, the one who feels he has been injured makes a claim against and sues the other driver or the other car's owner and probably his insurance company. Will he ever think of suing the car? – No. The car is an inanimate object and did not do anything wrong. The driver did the wrong. In maritime situations it is not different in how it happens but there is a great difference as to what happens after the accident. It is the assignment of the blame to the vessel, or the "guilty" vessel against which a claim can be made. Did the ship do anything? Of course not. Those navigating

the vessel did the wrong, but the ship physically caused the injury or damage. For example, if a ship is brought alongside a dock too fast and damages the dock was the ship responsible, or was the one in charge of the docking maneuver? Or if a ship proceeds up a river too fast causing wash damage to a marina along the shore; or a ship's falling boom injures one of the seamen due to the fault of the officer in charge of the operation; or the ship coming into a collision with another due to the pilot's fault; or the cargo being damaged because it was not properly secured by the stevedore at the loading port and the officer did not see the improper securing.

In each one of these situations, and many others that you may imagine, the vessel itself will be liable *in rem*. The ship, the thing or "the *res*" is liable. And this *in rem* liability continues with the vessel, even if it is sold to a new owner and continues for the time the right to sue the ship continues, which would be a period of "laches" or a statute of limitations, no matter where the ship goes.

Why do we have such a principle? Because the maritime business is unique and until the relatively recent invention of the cell phone, the internet and other modern gadgets, a sailing ship or a tramp steamer could be here today and gone tomorrow, and if during the stay here an accident caused serious damage to a local here the injured person could be out of luck trying to catch the foreign ship's owner in the foreign country. And what chance would a stevedore living in the Bronx, New York have in getting justice from a ship registered in Shanghai if the ship never comes back to New York Harbor? Such problems have existed for centuries.

Thus, we have the "personification of the vessel" for both, tort and contract claims. This means that the injured party can sue the ship and the ship can be held to be liable, up to its full value for the injury resulting from the activity. It gives the injured party redress where the ship's owner is in a foreign country. With this theory comes another illustration or limitation. For an *in rem* claim to exist the claim has to rise to the level having the effect of a **maritime lien.** That is the phrase that is used to make *in rem* claims against the vessel. An exhausting list really can not be made, but a brief listing of the type of claims should suffice. A claim having the effect of rising to a maritime lien exists when:

1- The claim is for a tort committed on the vessel. This includes injuries to persons on the ship such as slipping on oil spilled on the deck, falling due to a defective stairway or any other personal injury due to a defective condition or the fault of an officer or co-worker.

2- A tort committed by the vessel. This includes injury to a dock, injury to another vessel in a collision, injury to someone on land by something the ship does, such as causing a fire that spreads to the dock, striking a buoy or other navigational aid, dropping or dragging an anchor on a pipeline or cable or any other thing that causes damage or injury to someone or something not on the vessel.

3- Damage to cargo carried on the ship for any variety of reasons, such as unseaworthiness, improper loading, failure to properly carry (discussed at length later) failure to properly care for, damage caused by a collision, almost any other reason for damage to cargo on board the vessel.

4- Salvage claims. This is a claim for payment of the service rendered to a ship in peril.

5- Pilotage fees, docking fees, tugboat assistance costs.

6- Supply of necessaries such as fuel, mooring lines, repairs, food etc.

7- Charter claims; all types starting with bareboat, time, voyage charters, late arrivals, failure to arrive, etc.

8- Breach of agreements to carry.

9- Vessel mortgage claims.

10- Almost any other type of claim where the activity on the ship or by those engaged in the operation of the ship have caused a loss to another engaged in a maritime activity or on shore.

The above is just a brief listing as it is not possible to imagine all the things that can happen with ships. The importance, however, is that it must be within the admiralty jurisdiction for the personification principles to come into play which means that: (a) it must involve a vessel; (b) it must take place on navigable waters; and (c) must have the maritime nexus.

2   Vessel "arrest" procedures

While the procedure will be explained in more detail later, suffice it here that it permits a party to arrest a ship in the Federal Court. What does arresting a ship mean? It is an admiralty procedure under the Federal Rules of Civil Procedure where the claimant starts a lawsuit in the court that has jurisdiction over the geographic area where the ship is at that moment. The claimant (plaintiff) asks the court to order the ship held in port until the legal action can proceed. When the judge signs that order and it is served by the marshal on the ship it means that the ship will not be permitted to depart until appropriate arrangements are made to have financial security in the court for the injured person's claim and a release order is signed by the Federal Judge. The procedure is very expensive requiring initial outlay of substantial funds, which, however, will be recovered if the claim is real, approximately $25,000 for the first week and similar expenses every following week. It is not a procedure to be used lightly as "arresting" a vessel keeps it from operating and the owner loses money every minute the ship is not operating. On the other hand it gives the locally injured person the ability to obtain security for his claim, even though the rights associated with the claim or the amounts due will be negotiated or litigated later. Furthermore, damages will be awarded against the claimant, to the shipowner, if it is determined that the arrest was wrongful. Again, money – yes, it costs money to run a ship.

3   *Availability of limitation of liability to shipowners*

Covered in greater detail later, it is a procedure protecting the shipowner from unlimited liability when one of his employees causes a major disaster – *as long as the owner was not at fault or "in privity" with the one committing the wrong.* The reasoning for this procedure is to encourage investment in shipping. As the discussion of the development of the cases from *Executive Jet* to *Grubart, supra,* shows, the reason the parties were seeking to have the cases treated under admiralty jurisdiction were so that there would be the ability to invoke the limitation of liability statutes. And that really was the real issue in bringing the cases to the Supreme Court, because statutes limiting liability for wrongs committed by those operating a conveyance or machinery do not exist on land.

4   *The need for marine insurance*

The operation of a ship is big business. Similarly, the operation of a small sailboat can become big business if a friend joining for a ride suffers serious injuries due to a stupid mistake.[5] One must keep in mind that the ocean, no matter how beautiful, is a very unforgiving place and is not friendly to those who make mistakes. The navigable waters are demanding and unforgiving, whether on the ocean or on a river, and often the amounts involved are large. Therefore insurance for injury to the vessel, injury to crew members and passengers, injury to the cargo and injury to the environment all can decimate the business very rapidly. Realizing that injuries do happen – methods of insuring against

---

[5] The 2006 amendments to 46 U.S. Code changed the limitation of liability provisions by excluding pleasure yachts and several others from this special maritime procedure. For the former law see, *Foremost v. Richardson,* 457 U.S. 668 (1982). But now compare 46 U.S. Code § 30506 (a) excluding yachts, fishing vessels and some other small craft from the limitation amount set forth in § 30505. This change will bring on other litigation as most likely it was not intended to include large "mother" fishing vessels.

such losses exist. A detailed examination of the Hull, Protection and Indemnity, War Risk and Pollution control policies are covered later. Suffice it here to say that insurance is a necessity for maritime business.

5   *Types of relief available in admiralty*

Over the years there has been the statement that an "admiralty court is a court of equity." Today that phrase, although still used really means very little. In fact, today there are no special "admiralty courts" as such. The federal courts used to have "separate" admiralty judges, or special situations where federal judges "sat in admiralty" and the Southern District of New York once was one of the busiest "admiralty" courts. That all changed with the 1966 amendment to the Federal Rules of Civil Procedure merging civil and admiralty practices, and more recently, within the last two decades with the individual case assignments. Thus, while the language still is being used for courts "sitting in admiralty" that really is not so. Does the foregoing mean that admiralty rules have been abandoned – A RESOUNDING NO!!! While most district courts still have special admiralty practice rules, now all federal courts and all federal judges may and do hear admiralty matters. There are, however, a number of special procedures that are used when one deals with an admiralty matter. Therefore, let us look at some of the more individualistic types of relief available in admiralty.

First of all, most of the forms of relief available in general civil practice are available in and apply in admiralty, such as:

A   Basic tort liability (we still need the duty, the breach of that duty, and causal relationship between that breach and the resulting damage).

B   In contract cases we also have the breach of the contract principles, the old offer, acceptance, consideration, substantial performance, anticipatory breach, cover and all the other rules applicable in contract cases.

C   The equitable relief comes into play when we get to talk about unjust enrichment.

For example in *Archawski v. Hanioti*, 350 U.S. 532 (1956) it was a suit for the return of passage money. It was a contract for transportation on water which certainly is a maritime contract. But then plaintiff added "fraud" and now the court had a problem which it resolved on the basis of unjust enrichment. And, the federal district court has the power to give equitable relief. [It is doubtful that the same situation would come up with modern cruise travel.]

However, the court can grant in admiralty other equitable relief, such as specific performance. In *Marine Transit Corp v. Dreyfus*, 284 U.S. 263 (1932) the barge sank and the cargo owner sued the barge owner. The barge owner claimed that the charter contract called for arbitration and sued for specific performance to arbitrate. The barge owner resisted paying the arbitration fee and the court held that (1) the contract was within admiralty, (2) within the arbitration statute, and (3) the admiralty court had power to order specific performance. [It has to be remembered that "specific performance" – the court ordering you to do something – is a very special remedy by reason of the Constitution's provision against personal servitude.]

D   Punitive damages are available in admiralty. In *Protectus Alpha Nav. Co. v. North Pacific Grain Growers, Inc.*, 585 F. Supp. 1062 (D. Or. 1084) a bulk grain vessel caught fire while moored at the dock. Fire fighting progressed well, when the dock foreman ordered the ship away to the middle of the river, where shoreside water power was not accessible by firefighters and the ship burned to total loss. The court awarded $7 million general damages, $2 million interest and $500,000 punitive damages. Punitive damages can be awarded in cases of shipowner not timely paying a crewmember's wages, or not paying maintenance and cure and more recently in pollution situations. However, under the federal law there is no set rule as to how punitive damages are to be calculated. As a result of the Exxon Valdez spill the question of how punitive damages are to be assessed went to the Supreme Court and the court reduced the $2.5 billion award to $507.5 million, punitive damages being closer to the actual damages – close to 1.1 ratio. However, all the judges could not agree on one assessment rule. Thus, while punitive damages are allowed in admiralty cases there is no rule of how they are to be assessed. The court in its various opinions by the justices reviewed the rules used in many states, but could not agree on one rule. In *Exxon Shipping Company v. Baker,* 554U.S. 471(2008) [Overruling and vacating 472 F.3d 600 and 490 F.3d 1066] the Supreme Court created a new Maritime Rule – that punitive damages may not exceed compensatory damages in cases where the spilling conduct was not activated for the purpose of inflicting injury.

E   Interest is usually awarded in admiralty. In *City of Milwaukee v. Cement Div. National Gypsum Co.,* 115 S.Ct. 2091 (1995) it was reiterated that the prevailing party in admiralty receives interest, unless there are great reasons why the court should deny it. IT IS REIMBURSEMENT FOR THE LOSS AND LOSS OF THE USE OF THE MONEY – it is not punitive, just *restitutio in integrum,* which means that the court will try to place the party back in the situation it was before the wrongdoer injured him. Although the percentage of interest to be awarded has changed over the years, today it is related to the Treasury-Bill interest. In suits against the U.S. government the interest is set by statute at 4% after judgment. As between private parties interest runs from the date of the injury, except that interest is not awarded for pain and suffering.

IV

Admiralty and Maritime Law in the United States – generally

The American maritime civil law dealing with tort and contract aspects is made up of the statutes passed by Congress that deal with maritime matters (including the regulations issued in accordance with the authority given by the statutes) and what is commonly known as the General Maritime Law. Within the last few decades criminal aspects have also entered the admiralty field in greater degrees, particularly in oil spilling situations.

The General Maritime Law includes both, maritime contract law and maritime tort law with all the attributes that apply to contract and tort law. Clearly, the basic principles and theories have existed for centuries, just as maritime commerce and relations between the participants. In *East River Steamship Corp. v. Transamerica Delaval, Inc.,* 476 U.S. 858 (1986) considering the application of products liability in admiralty, the Supreme Court said:

> With admiralty jurisdiction comes the application of substantive admiralty law. (citation omitted) Absent a relevant statute, The General Maritime Law, as developed by the judiciary, applies. *United States v. Reliable Transfer Co.,* Inc., U.S. 397 (1975). Drawn from state and federal sources, The General Maritime

Law is an amalgam of traditional common-law rules, modifications of those rules, and newly created rules. * * * This Court has developed a body of maritime tort principles . . . .

As to contracts, as noted before, the general maritime law covers charters, salvage contracts, marine insurance contracts, repair contracts, towage contracts and other similar agreements. Regarding torts, again we have maritime personal injuries that include negligence, intentional misconduct, vicarious liabilities and product liabilities.

Maritime negligence is no different than land based negligence in most situations. The basic tort principles and requirements still apply:

1   There has to be a **duty** that the actor has.
2   The actor **breaches** that duty by either a wrongful act or failure to act when he should have acted.
3   There has to be a **causal relationship** between the breached duty and the injury.
4   There is a resulting **injury** or **damage** from the breach.

This is the same as in any other negligent tort case. For mariners the important thing is to note that many of the maritime principles that have existed continue to exist.

With respect to **duty** in maritime matters we have some additional concepts. The basic one still exists, the need to act reasonably under the circumstances (the same as on land). Then we also have the myriad of regulations that apply in maritime commerce regarding training, equipment, maintenance of the equipment, the need to know how to use the equipment, the knowledge necessary to do the job properly (such as licensing of officers, certification of crew members, familiarity with equipment etc.) and a term that applies to maritime only

– unseaworthiness, or its counterpart – seaworthiness.[6] When dealing with seamen injury cases hereafter it will be seen that for a seaman to recover on the theory of unseaworthiness he only needs a scintilla of evidence of the vessel's unseaworthy condition that caused the injury.

Except for those special situations that apply to crewmembers, the duty in admiralty is still to act reasonably under the circumstances and requires one to be aware of what should be **foreseeable**. The thing that sometimes is baffling is the extent to which a small mistake may cause a very significant damage later on. The sea is very unforgiving and always exacts a toll for a mistake.

The aspects of maritime tort liability that have to be considered include:

1   Vicarious liability
2   Causation rules
   A   Cause in fact
   B   Proximate cause
   C   Superseding cause
   D   Avoidable consequences
3   Comparative fault
4   Passengers and visitors as distinguished from crew members
5   Product liability in admiralty
6   Ryan indemnity and contribution

---

[6] Unseaworthiness is a concept that has two distinct meanings in admiralty. The basic standard of fit for the intended voyage is quite obvious. The other concept comes into play when we deal with vessel crew member injuries where the term has a practical meaning that expands the seaman's rights in injury situations. The concept has been noted in many cases. To mention a few see, *Mitchel v. Trawler Racer, Inc.* 362 U.S. 539 (1960); *Martinez v. Sea-Land Services, Inc.*, 763 F.2d 26 (1st Cir. 1985).

Vicarious liability.

This deals with situations where the fault of one is imputed to the other. The most common is the fault of an employee imputed to the employer. This is similar to the delivery truck driver's fault being imputed to the owner of the business who employed him when a third party is injured. Sometimes it can also be by a regulation, such as a building contractor being liable if a scaffold falls and someone is hurt – by regulation in New York. In maritime cases the fault of a ship's master or officer or fellow employee is almost always imputed to the ship *in rem*. While it may not be imputed to the shipowner *in personam,* in all cases the practical point is that if the ship has been arrested due to an *in rem* claim the court can, or will, go ahead and sell the ship unless the owner appears and defends or posts a letter of undertaking for the release of the vessel. Thus, practically the shipowner has to deal with it to avoid the ship being sold out from under him.

For example, if several seamen are seriously injured on board a vessel due to a mate's or engineer's fault and their collective damages aggregate, say $10,000,000, the shipowner or his insurer have to pay these claims, or at least give security until the actual amounts are determined by the court, in order to keep the ship from being sold to pay for those liabilities. While this may sound simple, in real situations it is quite involved. Marshal's fees and expenses during the arrest period have to be paid in advance and they can be quite expensive. On the other hand, if the claims are real it is worth going through those expenses.

Causation rules

Here the question is the relationship(s) between the negligent act and the damage to the injured party. Was it *a cause in fact,* or was it a *proximate cause,* or was it a *contributing cause,* was there a *superseding cause,* or as shown later in seamen injury cases did the owner's negligence cause in the slightest degree the injury. How do we determine if the cause of the injury (or other relative occurrence) is actually a "cause in fact?" The usual analysis deals in terms of "but for." *Moser v. Texas Trailer Corp.*, 623 F.2d 1006, 1013 (5th Cir. 1980). But for the happening of x the injury would not have happened. "Foreseeability" is said to be the touchstone of "proximate cause." *W. F. Magann Corp. v. Tug Delilah*, 434 F. Supp. 517 (E.D. Va. 1977) and cases on pages 523 – 524. What it really comes down to is whether, intentionally or unintentionally, the doing of the act or the failure to take the precaution led to the consequences or injury. And the connection has to be **real.** *See Fournier v. Petroleum Helicopters, Inc.*, 665 F. Supp. 483, 485 (E.D. La. 1987) where the landing of the helicopter on the water was held not to be the cause of later developed back problems. But there has to be a limit. Arguing that if one had not been born he would not have been injured sounds ridiculous. But what is the cut off point? The problem does not have a clear answer. There is, however, a case that tries to explain it. In *Petition of Kinsman Transit (or Buffalo Bridge cases)*, 338 F.2d 708 (2d Cir. 1964) the ship had been moored for the winter on Buffalo River, a common practice for Great Lakes ships being tied up for the winter season. It broke free from its moorings during the spring thaw, when ice was running in the river and the ship careened down the river and eventually lodged sideways at a bridge causing an artificial dam together with the ice that was running in the river. The result was that the river ran out of its banks and land on both sides of the river flooded for several miles on both sides. The land owners sued the shipowner for the flood damage. Judge Friendly of the Second Circuit Court of Appeals wrote the opinion saying that there must come a point in the causation chain when it no longer is "foreseeable" that the initially negligent act would cause the damage.

The *superseding cause*, came into play after a rather unfortunate case in the Second Circuit involving the vessel Ponce De Leon. Following the case of *United States v. Reliable Transfer*, 421 U.S. 397 (1975), which established the proportionate fault rule, in the Ponce De Leon case it was held that a district judge's adjudged percentage of the apportionment of fault (say 30/70 or 90/10 or 80/20) was subject to a "clearly erroneous" standard on appeal.[7] A clearly erroneous standard is one where the appeals court says that the district judge was obviously ("clearly") wrong in determining the facts or reaching a conclusion based on the facts shown by the record. While possible in factual determinations, it really is not possible in the division of damages situations. If fault assessment of 75/25 might be held clearly erroneous a division of 70/30 might not be. Or, 60/40 or some other percentage. It just is not practically possible and therefore no appeals court would touch such allocation on "clearly erroneous" ground. BUT, there had to be a way of letting the one whose fault was so insignificant that it would not be fair to hold him liable to let him off the hook. The Supreme Court came up with the *superseding cause* in *Exxon Co. v. Sofec, Inc.,* 517 U.S. 830 (1996). Such a ruling requires that:

1   The intervening or superseding cause, force or occurrence must bring about a result or harm that is **different** from the one that was originally happening; and
2   The intervening or superseding cause must <u>not</u> be a normal result or consequence from the original act of negligence.

The *Exxon v. Sofec* case dealt with a tanker breaking from its mooring in Hawaii during a storm. For the next hour or so the ship's master and officers concerned themselves with retrieving the broken fuel hose while

---

[7] In *Getty Oil Company v. SS Ponce De Leon,* 555 F.2d. 328 (2d. Cir 1977) Getty company's ship was anchored properly at the edge of the anchorage. There was dense fog and the PONCE DE LEON was coming in. Eventually it struck the anchored vessel. The District judge assigned 15% liability to the anchored vessel on the grounds that it saw the approaching vessel on radar and could have let out its anchor chain to avoid the collision. While the case was being appealed the district judge died and the Second Circuit did not want to send the case for a new re-trial. Thus the "clearly erroneous" rule became firmly established as there had been an earlier 5th Circuit decision to the same effect.

the ship kept drifting ***without anyone noting the ship's position with respect to the nearby land for well over an hour*** and when the officers finally decided to check the position of the drifting vessel it was too late and the ship went onto the rocks and was totally lost. The court held that the negligence of the master and officers was a superseding cause and the owner of the mooring buoy which broke was not responsible for the vessel's grounding.

The next one – **avoidable consequences** - is really nothing other than acting reasonably under the circumstances being aware of all the relevant facts that one can reasonably ascertain under the circumstances. *Kermarec v. Compagnie Generale Transatlantique,* 358 U.S. 625 (1959).

Comparative fault

Sometimes called "proportionate fault" is the rule that if both parties participating in the activity (or if there are three or even four) are both or each partially at fault for the resulting injury. In such a case the liability for the resulting damage will be apportioned among the participants according to their respective degrees of fault. For example, if two ships collide and both have made mistakes, the court will decide the degree of fault of each, say 20% fault on A and 80% fault on B. This rule was established for maritime collision and stranding cases in the case of *United States v. Reliable Transfer,* 421 U.S. 397 (1975). Prior to that for the last century the rule had been "half damages" meaning that the court would not try to assess the degree of fault of the participants, as long as both had done something or failed to do something which resulted in helping the occurrence take place. The old half damages (Solomonic) rule had been criticized for many decades.

This leads to settlement of cases on so called "cross liabilities." This means that if A suffered $2 million damages and B suffered $4 million in damages and the liabilities are assessed as A being 70% at fault and B 30% the outcome would be:

A's damages $2 million
B's damages $4 million
Total damages $6 million

As A has to pay 70% of $6 million, A's liability is $4.2 million, and as A itself suffered $2 million, A has to pay to B $2.2 million. (The converse for B is 30% liability or $1.8 million and as it suffered $4 million, subtracting its own $1.8 million it receives from B $2.2 million.)

The same situation applies in injury or other situations where only one suffered damage but both parties were at fault. The percentage of the liability of the one being hurt will be applied to the entire damages amount. Thus if A and B were both at fault for A's damages amounting to $2 million and B the defendant was negligent to the extent 60% and A for 40 %, A will receive only 60% or $1.2 million.

Passengers, visitors and other workers

They are not on the same level as seafarers - members of the crew. The crewmember's easier burden was briefly mentioned earlier. That is a special crew member situation elaborated on in the chapter dealing with seamen which gives them the "warranty of seaworthiness," which does not apply to the harbor workers, visitors and passengers. Still the basic rules of negligence apply: duty, breach of that duty, damage or injury and causal relationship between the breach and the injury, with proof of proximate causation. *Kermarec v. Compagnie Generale Transatlantique,* 358 U.S. 625 (1959). In *Chandris, Inc. v. Latsis,*515 U.S. 347 (1995) the port engineer joined the ship on its voyage before entering the shipyard for the annual repair period working on proposed repair work. He was injured and claimed to be a seafarer - a crew member as ship's crew members are entitled to free medical care. The court found that since he had not signed articles and really was a shore worker he was not entitled to the status of a seaman.

Products liability

As the case of *East River Steamship Corp. v. Transamerica Delaval, Inc.,*476 U.S. 858 (1986) shows, product liability is a theory that applies in admiralty. The basic rule is that to recover on this theory the plaintiff must prove:

1   The defendant manufactured or sold the product
2   The product was unreasonably dangerous or defective when it left the defendant's possession
3   The defect caused the plaintiff's injury.

Note that if the damage is to the product itself there can be no recovery for economic loss as a result of the defective product.

How can a product be "unreasonably dangerous?" Firstly, the design could have defects. Second, even if it is not negligently designed it can be unreasonably dangerous if the risks inherent in the product are greater than a reasonable buyer would expect, and the gravity of the harm outweighs the potential utility of the product. In *Brown v. Link Belt Division of FMC,* 666 F.2d 110 (5th Cir. 1982) plaintiff Brown was employed by Shell as an operator on Shell's offshore oil platforms. Shell, which had sent Brown to the platform to change a valve, arranged for the crew-boat APACHE to take Brown back to his base platform. Everyone agreed that on this particular night the weather and sea conditions in the vicinity were aptly described as heavy winds, rain and high seas. The captain of the APACHE informed Shell that the seas were too rough to attempt to transfer Brown from the platform to the ship. Shell's dispatcher on a nearby platform, who knew the existing conditions, directed the captain to attempt the transfer. The normal method of transfer, and the one used here, was to have the crane on the platform lower the employee in a personnel basket to the deck of the transfer vessel. As Brown was being lowered, the cable began to unwind rapidly.

The rapid descent of the personnel basket and the erratic motion of the ship caught in the high waves resulted in the basket crashing onto the deck of the APACHE injuring Brown. However, the court did not hold the company liable because:

> Here, * * * Shell and the plaintiff, himself a crane operator, knew well how cranes operated in transporting personnel. Moreover, the record is clear that Shell and the plaintiff were both aware of the dangerous sea conditions existing at the time of the accident. In sum, the degree of knowledge possessed by Shell and the plaintiff were such that the trial court properly concluded that reasonable minds could not differ that FMC's failure to warn was not a cause in fact of the accident.

The court went on to explain:

> In *Hunt v. City Stores, Inc.,* 387 So.2d 585 (La. 1980) the Louisiana Supreme Court outlined the proof required in a products liability suit. The plaintiff must prove that the product was defective, i.e. unreasonably dangerous in normal use; that the product was in normal use at the time the injury occurred; that the product's defect caused the injury; and that the injury might have been anticipated by the manufacturer. In defining unreasonably dangerous, a balancing test is mandated:

if the likelihood and gravity of harm outweigh the benefits and utility of the product, the product is unreasonably dangerous. Likelihood of harm here is tied to the factor of the crane's use in severe weather. Implicit in the district court's ruling is that the likelihood and frequency of such use, and therefore resultant harm, was slight when compared to the unquestioned utility of the crane. We agree that reasonable minds could not differ that this was so, and that the crane was not unreasonably dangerous to normal use. We affirm the directed verdict for Link-Belt. So, the question of what constitutes "unreasonably dangerous" will depend on the proofs and an understanding of the industry. Sometimes the decisions on the same facts may differ in different parts of the country.

Ryan indemnity and warranty of workmanlike performance

Ryan Stevedoring Co. v Pan Atlantic Steamship Corp., 350 U.S. 124 (1956) first came about as a case to extricate the American shipowner from what had become known as the "Sieracki seaman" liabilities created by the Supreme Court in 1946 to give the harbor worker relief from the then outdated provisions of the 1927 Longshore and Harborworkers' Compensation Act. More on the LHWCA later, when we deal with harbor worker situations. A short history, of the evolution will assist in understanding the issues. When the LHWCA was first enacted in 1927 its purpose was to create compensation for the harbor workers and establish stability in that part of the industry. It attempted to reduce litigation between the worker and the employer. It did not work out that way because the Act did not provide for inflation. The idea had been that the injured harbor worker would receive compensation regardless of fault and would not have to engage in extensive litigation, and the fact that the employer paid compensation would protect the employer from all other suits. Unfortunately, the failure of the Act to provide for inflation ruined the situation. Within a few years the compensation payments provided for in the Act were not enough and soon became just a mere pittance. As courts do not change things quickly it took until 1946, by which time the harbor worker's compensation really was just a pittance that a New York law firm (really two brothers) brought a case arguing that the longshoreman should also be entitled to the "warranty of seaworthiness" like seamen when they made a claim against the shipowner or ship if the injury took place on the ship. In *Seas Shipping v. Sieracki,* 328 U.S. 85 (1946) the court used the book, *Two Years Before the Mast* by Dana to analogize a harbor worker's job to that of a seaman. The court used the chapter in this book where the crew members loaded skins on the west coast of the United States by carrying the skins through the breakers to a boat standing just past the breakers for delivery to the sailing ship anchored further out, by saying that the crew was doing the "traditional" work of loading the ship, hence the longshoremen also do the "traditional work of the seamen."

Why is this significant or important?

Well, as we will see later, members of the crew of a ship are entitled to the *warranty of seaworthiness* from the shipowner, which is a *species of absolute liability,* or liability without fault. What it means is that if there is some kind of a defect on the ship that is causally connected to the injury, the shipowner is absolutely liable to the injured person and contributory fault of the injured will only proportionately reduce damages. What then happened became a real anomaly. After the *Sieracki* decision there was almost no harbor worker injury case where he did not recover from the ship. Either the hatch boards were wobbly, or they were improperly stacked causing the man to fall, or the cargo came into the ship too fast or something else was not exactly right on the vessel. The injured harbor worker almost always recovered.

So, the shipowner's lawyers went to work and came up with what eventually became the **Ryan doctrine.**

In *Ryan Stevedoring Co. v Pan Atlantic Steamship Corp.,* 350 U.S. 124 (1956) the harbor worker was injured due to his fellow worker's fault. The shipowner argued that he had engaged the harbor worker's employer, the Stevedore company, as the expert who knew how to do the job, and when his worker made a mistake this was "a breach of warranty of workmanlike service" and therefore the Stevedore should indemnify the shipowner for the monies the shipowner had to pay to the injured harbor worker for the injury caused by the ship's "unseaworthiness" even though the condition was caused by another harbor worker. The Supreme Court agreed and henceforth the "round robin" of the harbor worker injuries came into existence. Eventually a stop was put to it by the 1972 amendments to the Longshoremen and Harborworker's Compensation Act (to be discussed later) BUT the theory of ***the breach of the warranty of workmanlike service*** remains in our admiralty law. And, this theory now continues not only in injury situations but also in some cargo damage cases. What is significant about a true *indemnity* case is that the one who impleads a third party and obtains indemnity can recover attorney fees for the indemnity suit (not for defending the initial complaint against him).

V

Seamen, their obligations and rights and those of the shipowner

The life of a seaman has never been easy. He or she is away from the family for months on end and not so long ago for periods of years. To gain an insight in what it was during the sailing ship era one can read *Two Years Before the Mast* by William Dana written in the early1800's and Jack London's *Seawolf.* Those are not romantic novels, rather they show the harsh life of seamen, and the reasons for quite a few of our rules and statutes enacted for the benefit of seamen, albeit only in the 20th century. With the modern container ships and mammoth tankers, the days when ships stayed in port for weeks are gone. Still, many of the difficulties for the individuals remain. Less than one hundred years ago the American seaman had very few rights. And the same situation existed for seamen of all the maritime nations. In 1903 the Supreme Court decided the case of *The Osceola,* 189 U.S. 158 where it was admitted that the seaman Patrick Shea was injured because the captain wrongfully had ordered that the gangway be rigged when the ship approaching port was still in stormy seas and thus the captain's order was clearly negligent. The Supreme Court's opinion clearly states that it looked at the maritime laws of ten maritime nations and found them all to similarly keep the seaman from recovering for his injuries. Referring to English law our Supreme Court stated:

> In English courts, the owner is now held to be liable for injuries received by the unseaworthiness of the vessel,

> though not by the negligence of the master who is
> treated as a fellow servant of the owner. . . . Beyond this,
> (the need for seaworthiness) however, we find nothing
> in the English law to indicate that a ship or its owners
> are liable to an indemnity for injuries received by the
> negligence or otherwise in the service of the ship.

The case is oft cited for other propositions, namely that an injured seaman is entitled to be repatriated at the owner's expense, to receive wages to the end of the voyage and maintenance and cure – namely all necessary medical services. And this is really quite understandable as the ruling people in most countries up to the beginning of the twentieth century were the wealthy business men or royalty.

Today it is different as a result of the changes that started with railway workers in the United States in 1906. As a result of the much publicized injuries and deaths of railroad workers Congress passed the Federal Employers' Liability Act, 45 U.S. Code §§51 – 59. This statute abolished the old type defenses and gave the railroad workers a right to receive compensation for work related injuries. A bit of history is in order.

For centuries the wealthy owner of the ship and later of the railroad had several <u>absolute</u> defenses to the injured workers' claims that kept the owner free of liability. The first was the "assumption of risk" which meant that the worker assumed the risks involved in doing the job and therefore if he was injured, the employer was not liable or responsible. It was a complete defense. The second was the defense used in the *Osceola* case, the fellow servant rule. Namely, if a fellow servant caused your injury, like the captain's negligent order in that case, the owner was not liable and the injured person received nothing. The third was the "contributory negligence" rule, again a complete defense for the employer or shipowner. The slightest mistake by the injured person contributing to his injury barred all recovery. And, to crown these defenses the fourth provision was that if the injured person did have a claim (let us say the injury was due to the ship's unseaworthiness) the claim died with him and his dependents received nothing. Going through literature one can find evidence that in the east to west passages around Cape Horn or through the Strait of Magellan in sailing ships they usually lost one or two crew members overboard due to the rough seas in those waters. For the railroad workers, of course, it was the nineteenth century.

But it was the railroad workers who first caused enough publicity to bring the attention of the American Congress so that it created a statute for their benefit. It was the Federal Employers' Liability Act (FELA) that started to equalize the situation, for lack of a better term, or to provide some compensation for the worker.

The first section of FELA, 45 U.S.C. § 51 entitled Liability of Common Carriers by Railroad, in Interstate or Foreign Commerce, for injuries to Employees from Negligence; Definition of Employees, provides:

> Every common carrier by railroad while engaging in commerce between any of the several States or Territories * * * shall be liable in damages to any person suffering injury while he is employed by such carrier in such commerce, or, in case of the death of such employee, to his or her personal representative, for the benefit of the surviving widow or husband and children of such employee; and, if none, then of such employee's parents; and, if none, then of the next of kin dependent upon such employee, for such injury or death resulting in whole or in part from the negligence of any of the officers, agents, or employees of such carrier, or by reason of any defect or insufficiency, due to its negligence, in

> its cars, engines, appliances, machinery, track, roadbed, works, boats, wharves, or other equipment.[8]

This was a drastic change in the relationship between the wealthy employer and the worker. Where previously the employer had the defenses of assumption of risk, fellow servant negligence and contributory negligence being complete bars these defenses were abolished (specifically in the other sections) and the claim did not die with the individual if the injury killed him.

The other very important point is the degree of liability or burden of proof by the injured worker. Whether the injury resulted "in whole or in part from the negligence of any of the officers, agents, or employees" of the railroad. This does away with the requirement that the injured person prove that the railroad's negligence was the "proximate cause" of the injury. As long as there is the slightest fault by any employee of the railroad or any of its equipment, the injured worker recovers. The only reduction is for the percentage of the injured person's own contributory fault.

This change in the degree of liability is very important as it also applies to seamen and their claims against the vessel or shipowner once the Jones Act in 1920 made these statutes applicable to seamen. Before the Jones Act the seaman did not recover anything as shown by the 1918 Supreme Court ruling in *Chelentis v. Luckenbach Steamship Co.,* 247 U.S. 372 (1918). For two more years the seamen got nothing.

The industry has been fighting this continuously for a hundred fifteen years and in 2011 it tried it again. On June 23, 2011 the Supreme Court decided *CSX Transportation, Inc. v. McBride,* 131 S.Ct. 2630 (2011). McBride was a locomotive engineer ordered to operate rail

---

[8] See the appendix for the other sections.

car "switching" or moving of individual rail cars. McBride protested that the configuration was unsafe as it required constant use of hand operated independent brake but was ordered to use it as is. About ten hours into the job he injured his hand while using the brake. Despite several operations he never regained the full use of his hand. The issue brought to the Supreme Court was the judge's charge to the jury.

The railroad wanted the court to instruct the jury that CSX's negligence "was a proximate cause" of the injury. Instead the judge's charge was that the defendant railroad was liable "if (d)efendant's negligence played a part - no matter how small – in bringing about the injury. . ."

As the dissent in the case notes, as early as 1837 "proximate cause" had to be shown to establish liability, see *Waters v. Merchants' Louisville Ins. Co.,* 36 U.S. 213 (1837). And the industry has been so arguing for over a hundred years. Particularly, in 1957 the Supreme Court took two cases, one for a railroad worker and the other for a seaman on this same issue: *Rogers v. Missouri Pacific R. Co.,* 352 U.S. 500 (1957) [for a railroad worker] and *Ferguson v. Moore McCormack Lines, Inc.,* 352 U.S. 521 (1957) [for a seaman]. As the *CSX Transportation v. McBride* in the year 2011 shows, the industry has not stopped making its arguments.

For seamen this came about in 1920 with the passage of the Jones Act, formerly 46 U.S. Code § 688, now contained in 46 U.S. C.§ 30104 which states:

> *Personal injury to or death of a seaman*
> A seaman injured in the course of employment or, if the
> seaman dies from the injury, the personal representative
> of the seaman may elect to bring a civil action at law,
> with the right of trial by jury, against the employer. Laws
> of the United States regulating recovery for personal

injuries to, or death of, a railway employee apply to an action under this section.[9]

Accordingly today a seaman who is a member of the crew of a vessel when injured or is deceased is entitled to:

1   Sue the employer under the Jones Act for negligence and have his case tried to a jury, either in State or a Federal court. *O'Donnell v. Great Lakes Dredge & Dock Co.,* 318 U.S. 36 (1943).[10]

2   Receive maintenance and cure, repatriation and wages to the end of the voyage regardless of fault for the injury. *The Osceola,* 189 U.S. 158 (1903); *Harden v. Gordon*, 11 Fed. Cas. 480 (C.C.D. Me. 1823); Even if the injury is his own fault he is entitled to these, *Koistinen v. American Export Lines,* 83 N.Y.S. 2d 297 (N.Y. City Ct. 1948).

3   He can sue the ship *in rem* and obtain security for his claim joining both, the Jones Act and the unseaworthiness claims because his injury claim rises to the level of a maritime lien, giving him the right to arrest the vessel and thus ensure the ability to collect his eventual judgment, but the arrest can only be in a federal action in a federal court. However, if the suit is only for negligence under the Jones Act it cannot be brought *in rem* unless caused by willful or gross misconduct.

4   He can sue the shipowner for unseaworthiness under The General Maritime Law. *Mitchell v. Trawler Racer*, 362 U.S. 539 (1960) and in such a lawsuit he can also allege negligence on the part of the shipowner or other fellow servants.

---

[9] The reference is to FELA, 45 U.S.C. §§ 51 – 60 contained in the appendix.

[10] Keep in mind that only in the Federal court can he make an *in rem* claim against the vessel and obtain security. When the shipping companies were being "reduced" in the 1990's more than one seafarer found that his State court action practically disappeared as he had no "security" against a steamship company going into bankruptcy.

Unseaworthiness, or the "breach of warranty of seaworthiness" regarding seamen injuries is a species of absolute liability or liability without fault. *Seas Shipping Co. v. Sieracki,* 328 U.S. 85 (1946); *Mitchell v. Trawler Racer,* 362 U.S. 539 (1960); *Vargas v. McNamara,* 608 F.2d 15 (1ˢᵗ Cir. 1979). Today the injured seaman will join both the unseaworthiness and negligence claims in the same lawsuit. It is important to note that a defect in the ship, even if it is a passing situation as in *Mitchell v. Trawler Racer Inc.,* gives the injured seaman a real edge in the claim against the shipowner and the ship *in rem.*[11]

For a seaman to have these rights he must be a member of the crew. Usually this means that he has signed articles for a foreign voyage or a coastwise voyage where articles sometimes are not signed. While all the other type of claims cannot be listed they do include claims for: injuries with all the applicable compensatory and consequential damages, lost wages, earned wages, wrongful discharge, tortuous interference with maritime employment rights and in case of an injury on the job for unearned wages to the end of the voyage, plus maintenance and cure. The latter two can become quite important.

Employment on board a ship is a maritime contract. 46 U.S.C. § 10101 defines a seaman as "an individual . . . engaged or employed in any capacity on board a vessel." In most ocean voyages seamen are required to sign articles. Section 10301 of 46 U.S. Code notes that seamen status applies to all international voyages and all inter-coastal voyages but not to voyages where the crew shares in the profits, as often is the case on fishing type of vessels.

---

[11] When we discuss the history of the Longshoremen cases prior to the 1972 amendments of the Longhore and Harbor Worker Compensation Act we will note how following the *Sieracki* decision in 1946 and then the *Ryan Stevedoring Co. v. Pan Atlantic Steamship Corp.,* 350 U.S. 124 (1956) the relationships in the industry between the harbor worker injured on the ship due to a "defect" created by his co-workers and the ship and the stevedore became a round-robin of litigation until the 1972 amendment of the statute.

And, pursuant to 46 U.S.C. § 10302 the maritime contract (referred to as "Shipping Articles" or "agreement " which is the formal agreement between the seamen and the ship's owner (via the captain) must contain the following provisions:

(a)   The owner, charterer, managing operator, master, or individual in charge shall make a shipping agreement in writing with each seaman before the seaman commences employment.

(b)   The agreement shall contain the following:
    (1) the nature, and, as far as practicable, the duration of the intended voyage, and the port or country in which the voyage is to end.
    (2) the number and description of the crew and the capacity in which each seaman is to be engaged.
    (3) the time at which each seaman is to be on board to begin work.
    (4) the amount of wages each seaman is to receive.
    (5) regulations about conduct on board, and information on fines, short allowance of provisions, and other punishment for misconduct provided by law.
    (6) a scale of the provisions that are to be provided each seaman.
    (7) any stipulation in reference to advances and allotments of wages.
    (8) other matters not contrary to law.

(c)   Each shipping agreement must be signed by the master or individual in charge or a representative of the owner, charterer, or managing operator, and by each seaman employed.

(d)   The owner, charterer, managing operator, master, or individual in charge shall maintain the shipping agreement and make the shipping agreement available to the seaman. And, when applicable it should state the partial payments due the crew on wages.

And with respect to wages 46 U.S.C. § 10313 is very strict as to when wages are to be paid. Without quoting or paraphrasing the section it is clear that during the voyage a seaman is entitled to "draws" in every port and at the end of the voyage to be paid within 24 hours after the cargo is discharged or within four days after the seaman is discharged. The penalty for not paying wages under subsection (g) of the section becomes very expensive to the shipowner: - "2 days wages for each day payment is delayed." In the 1980's a company tried to test this statute and lost. In *Griffin v. Oceanic Contractors Inc.,* 458 U.S. 564 (1982) the Supreme Court dealt with non-payment of 412.50 from April 1976 until final judgment in 1982 and affirmed the amount due at $302,790.40.

The above illustrates how the statutes read today. It took, however, a number of years for the situation to reach this point. Today it is clear that if a seaman is injured on board a vessel, **regardless of who was at fault,** he is entitled to (1) Repatriation to his home port; (2) Full medical care until absolute cure or reaching "maximum cure;" and (3) Maintenance during his convalescence. Initially the "maintenance" was intended to keep him / her in satisfactory room and board during convalescence. More recently, however, the seamen unions have included in the labor contract a specific sum ($40 or $50 per day or some other sum) and the courts have held that union agreements are enforceable on the basis of labor relations law.

Still, the law of repatriation, wages to the end of the voyage, medical care and maintenance are due in all cases – regardless of fault. *The Osceola,* 189 U.S. 158 (1903); *Chelantis v. Luchenbach Steamship Co.,* 247 U.S. 372 (1918).

And, there are a number of cases dealing with seamen engaged in consumption of alcohol and then being injured, or being engaged in what sometimes is called "frolic and banter" and being injured. Even if the seaman is at fault himself he is still entitled to repatriation, medical care and maintenance and wages to the end of the voyage. However, willful injury can be a ground for withholding maintenance and cure. Example – seaman drunk and riding on top of subway car and sustaining injury.

When the injury is caused by the shipowner or a "fellow servant" the other claims come into play. Now the injured has a claim for pain and suffering, an amount for the injury, lost wages during convalescence, lost future wages, reduction in future employment if that is a result, and any other relevant claim.

Thus the next thing to consider is the **seaman status.** Who is a seaman and who is entitled to the benefits of a seaman.

1   the individual must be contributing to the function of the vessel and
2   the individual must have a kind of a permanent connection to the vessel.

These two criteria usually suffice. Where they cause problems is when the individual performs work that may also be that of another class of workers, such as harbor workers. If such differences arise in your work you probably will have to obtain legal advice. For the purposes of our discussion several criteria will help:

1   Did the individual sign articles – if yes, he certainly is a seaman.
2   Did he aid in the mission of the ship – yes, again. It depends on the type of ship.

Certainly a hairdresser and musician are seafarers on a passenger vessel. Certainly, a cook or a steward is a seaman on every ship that goes to sea.

Here you must keep in mind that this section applies ONLY to suits by seamen against their employer. Again another reason why the seaman status is important. The individual must be a member of the crew of a vessel!!!!

Still, the law of repatriation, wages to end of voyage, medical care and maintenance are due **in all cases regardless of fault.** *The Osceola,* 189 U.S. 158 (1903); *Chelentsis v. Luchenbach Steamship Co.,* 247 U.S. 372 (1918).[12]

And, there are a number of cases dealing with seamen engaged in consumption of alcohol and then being injured, or being engaged in what sometimes is called "frolic and banter" and being injured. If the seaman is at fault himself he is still entitled to repatriation, medical care and maintenance and wages to the end of the voyage. When the injury is caused by the shipowner or the fault of "fellow servant" the other claims come into the picture such as pain and suffering, lost future wages, lost or reduced future employment because of a disability, contributory fault, future pain, etc.

The problem comes up in cases like *Chandris v. Latsis*, 515 U.S. 347 (1995). The reason the plaintiff wanted to be a seaman is because that

---

[12]   Also, it must be noted that the rights given to a seaman are not limited to injuries on board the vessel. He is entitled to the rights he has even if he is injured while on shore leave, as long as he is a member of the crew. There is a case where a seaman on shore leave met a friendly person and was hoping for a romantic interlude, when her brother, a much larger person came out of the next room. The seaman retreated to the balcony and jumped not realizing the house was on a cliff and he broke both legs. The company claimed that as the injury was due to his own fault they did not owe him anything. The court ruled that nevertheless the shipowner had to repatriate him, pay his wages to the end of the voyage and all medical expenses and maintenance. *Koistiner v. American Export Lines,* 83 N.Y.S.2d 297 (N.Y. City Ct. 1948). Similarly, during World War II the seaman returning to his ship in Naples during a blackout fell into a drydock as a result of having partied quite a bit. He was entitled to repatriation and all medical and wages to end of the voyage.

way he would get free medical care until complete cure and maintenance. In fact he was a port engineer for the fleet and although at the time of the injury he was on board the ship, he did NOT aid in navigation, rather his presence on board was in aid of preparing the ship for its next shipyard repair period. In *Archer v. Trans/American Services, Ltd.*, 834 F.2d 1570 (11th Cir. 1988) the seaman returned from leave – went to the office on June 21st and was told to report to the ship on the 23rd the sailing day. On June 22nd he was injured in car accident on shore. Was he entitled to crewmember's status and receive maintenance and cure and medical? Yes. He was held to be a member of the crew.

The bottom line here is that it is a fact intensive inquiry to see in which of the slots it fits. Also, as you will see later, generally speaking (and there are exceptions) if one is a harbor worker he is not a seaman. The distinction is important because the remedies and entitlements are different. That having been said, let us turn to the applicable statutes and their development.

In the modern context where vessels stay away from home port for long periods and union rules require personnel changes even though the ship is not at the home port the question arises as to when the seaman becomes a member of the crew. The *Archer v. Trans/American Services, Ltd.*, 834 F.2d 1570 (11th Cir. 1988) reasoning was applied in a case where the seaman was sent by air from New York to join the vessel in Egypt. He arrived in Cairo and was being taken by taxi to the ship. The taxi crashed and he was seriously injured. The claim was that he had not yet joined the ship because theoretically the captain could have refused to sign him as a crew member. The court held that as the company had sent him to join the vessel and it was now expected that he would join the crew and therefore he was entitled to repatriation, wages to end of voyage and all medical expenses plus maintenance. Similarly, a seaman returning from partying in Naples during World War II fell into a drydock which was not lit due to a blackout. He was still entitled to repatriation, maintenance and cure all medical and wages to the end of the voyage. *Warren v. United States,* 340 U.S. 523 (1951).

Also, a discussion is needed about the Supreme Court's decision in *Miles v. Apex Marine Corp.,* 489 U.S. 19 (1990) and its effect on maritime recoveries. While the case discussion deals with the Death on the High Seas Act it has a profound influence on seamen injury cases in that it is the leading case on the type of damages a seaman, or ones claiming through a seaman, can get from the seaman's employer – only pecuniary damages. This means that survivors of seamen cannot recover from the employer for loss of consortium, or mental anguish or loss of companionship to children.

In the "modern" world this is a very unfair decision. Initially thought to make "uniform" the recoveries for seamen from the employer shipowner the unfairness of this ruling was further illustrated when Congress, following a serious air crash (TWA 800) in 2006 amended the Death on the High Seas Act (now contained in 46 U.S.C. §§ 30301 – 30307) by adding a new section § 30307 for commercial aviation accidents. This section permits recovery of "nonpecuniary damages" for survivors of air crash victims if the crash is 12 or more miles from shore. Thus, the spouse and children of a seaman killed at sea cannot recover for loss of society, companionship or sex but survivors of air crash victims can. The Miles case also noted that punitive damages cannot be awarded in Jones Act seamen cases against the shipowner. This has led several courts to clearly distinguish *Miles* by permitting spouses of seamen to recover nonpecuniary damages when the wrongdoer is not the seaman's employer but a third party. Also there is a movement afoot to amend the Act, but that is still a ways off.

Longshoremen and other harbor workers

Longshoremen have been loading and unloading ships for centuries and for most of that time the distinction between those who follow the sea and those who work "the long shore" has been noted. I seem to recall an article written about half a century ago by an insurance company's executive criticizing the Supreme Court's 1946 case of *Seas Shipping v. Sieracki,* 328 U.S. 85 (1946) by a reference to the shore workers during the Roman Empire several thousand years ago. And, people working on ships in port get hurt.

Without going through a tortured history, it is known that in 1927 Congress passed the Longshore and Harbor Workers' Compensation Act (LHWC). 33 U.S.C. § 901 et. seq. It was a good beginning but it did not take care of the problem. It limited the stevedore employer's liability to his employees to the amounts set forth in the statute and made that the employee's exclusive claim against the employer. These amounts were not tied to inflation and very soon became inadequate. Today the awards are quite generous and much greater than State workers compensation awards.

Even though the idea of proportionate fault and doing away with contributory negligence being a bar had existed for some time, as shown by *Max Morris v. Curry,* 137 U.S. 1 (1890), where it was found that an injured harbor worker's claim was not to be thrown out by his contributory fault (the court not deciding whether it would be "proportionate fault" or "divided damages") the problem pervaded in admiralty because the case of *Halcyon Lines v. Haenn Ship Ceiling & Refitting Corp.*, 342 U.S. 282 (1952) kept bothering the courts, where it was held that there is to be no contribution among joint tort-feasors in admiralty. This reasoning, when one looks at the dates of some of these decisions, is difficult to grasp. As shown later by *United States v. Reliable Transfer Co.*, 421 U.S. 397 (1975) proportionate fault rule now exists in all admiralty areas. However, for an understanding of the present day LHWCA some of the history is necessary.

As noted above, the 1927 LHWC did not solve the problem and by mid 1940's it was sorely inadequate for the injured harbor worker. So, their lawyers looked for a "solution." And, as New York Harbor was a very active place, with many, many harbor worker injuries, it fell upon New Yorkers to find the solution. The answer was the case of *Seas Shipping v. Sieracki,* 328 U.S. 85 (1946). To make a long tortuous story short the Supreme Court held that longshoremen had been doing "the traditional work of seamen" [relying on a chapter in William Dana's *Two years Before the Mast,* where on the west coast the skins were carried through the surf by the crew members] and held that longshoremen are entitled to the "warranty of seaworthiness" the same as crew members of ships!!!

This opened flood gates of litigation by harbor workers against shipowners. The books are full of cases where the longshoremen in opening hatches piled the hatch-boards haphazardly and then one of them stepped on the pile, fell and was injured and sued the ship for "unseaworthiness" and recovered because "unseaworthiness" is a species of absolute liability. This continued until shipowners' lawyers came up with the *Ryan* doctrine, first discussed in *Ryan Stevedoring Co. v Pan Atlantic Steamship Corp.*, 350 U.S. 124 (1956). The shipowner claimed that any fault on the part of the stevedore as the injured man's employer was a breach of the stevedore's warranty of workmanlike service or performance. As a result of this theory when the harbor worker sued the ship for unseaworthiness the ship would commence a third party indemnity action against the harbor worker's employer for indemnity and counsel fees. **The theory of the LHWCA's protection of the harbor workers' employers contemplated in the 1927 act was completely destroyed.** The employer paid the compensation award and also paid the shipowner what it paid to the injured employee. At the end of the day the harbor worker in effect indirectly received from his employer, by way of the vessel obtaining indemnity from the stevedore employer, whatever the jury would give him. From industry standpoint this was untenable.

The situation continued for some seventeen years until the Longshore and Harbor Workers' Compensation Act (LHWCA) was amended in 1972. This time inflation was considered and the round-robin litigation stopped. The idea of the statute was to provide reasonable compensation to the injured harbor worker, to have his employer, the Stevedore, available for reasonable taking care of the employee and to limit the stevedore's liability in injury situations. Also, it abolished the harbor worker's right to claim "unseaworthiness" as the basis of his claim against the vessel.

The major sections of the LHWCA are set forth in the appendix. Here we deal with the practical aspects of the relationships. It must be remembered that the industry and transportation methods are changing. In the 1960's and 1970's most cargo ships were still the so called "break bulk" vessels. This meant that the vessel had from four to seven hatches with cargo working gear at each hatch. Each hatch had a lower hold, a lower tween deck and an upper tween deck space, with cargo being stowed on each level and secured by the stevedores. In the twenty-first century there are very few such break bulk vessels. The majority of cargo is transported on container vessels where the vessel carries several thousand containers, all secured and carried in a number of layers. For certain types of cargoes, such as pipes, construction gear, etc. the old type break bulk ships are still used, but those are relatively few.

Also, the work of the longshoreman has drastically changed. Although there is authority that the first container vessel was created in early 1950's, by 1960's and 1970's the break bulk vessels still dominated the ocean trade. But things rapidly changed thereafter and by 2009 ninety percent of non-bulk cargo moved in container vessels.[13] Where several decades ago the longshoremen had to secure the cargo in the hold or packed or re-packed the containers before they were loaded on the vessel, in 2010 and subsequent years most containers are loaded and sealed inland or at the terminal or the pier. Or the container arrives fully loaded. The harbor workers are employed only to load the containers onboard the container vessel with mechanical equipment. However, as some break bulk type of vessels still exist, the "old" relationships are treated here.

First we must distinguish between the harbor worker and the seaman, and here we make reference to the statutory definitions with practical applications. Section 902 of the LHWCA containing definitions specifies, among other things, the following:

1- The injury refers to any injury associated with employment as a harbor worker.
2- The "employee" is any person engaged in maritime employment of loading or discharging vessels, repairing ships, building ships or breaking up ships, but DOES NOT include office workers, secretaries or security personnel. (Pier guards are not harbor workers.)

---

[13] See Wikipedia history of containerships at http//en.wikipedia.org/wiki/ containerization#history.

3- Individuals employed by marinas, clubs and other recreational facilities are not included in the act. [Initially this was not so stated and all clubs and marinas were in a quandary as they could not afford the higher premiums for coverage under the Act for their employees; particularly the summer help in the clubs, as the statute requires the existence of benefits procured by the employer for all employees or "harbor workers."]

4- The master or any member of the crew of a vessel is NOT an employee under this statute.

5- An "employer" is one whose employees are engaged, in whole or in part, upon navigable waters of the United States (including adjoining pier, wharf, dry dock, terminal, way, marine railway or other adjoining area customarily used by an employer in loading, unloading, repairing or building of vessels).

6- Disability is incapacity due to injury on the job.

7- Compensation is the allowance payable to an employee pursuant to the statute.

8- Wages means the money rate at which an employee is compensated. [Note that fringe benefits are NOT included. For seamen fringe benefits are part of the damages a seaman is entitled to receive from his employer in case the employer was at fault, but only if employer is at fault.]

9- "National average weekly wage" means the national weekly earnings of production or nonsupervisory workers on private nonagricultural payrolls.

[This is now tied to the national weekly wage which includes changes due to inflation. It is hoped that this way the payments will remain reasonable.]

Other definitions are in the appendix. The above gives an idea of what the statute covers.

- Section 903 entitled "coverage" explains that the statute applies to injuries on navigable waters of the United States and adjoining piers, wharves or vessel repair or building facilities.

- It also notes that injury due to intoxication does not deny coverage unless it was "solely" the cause of the injury.

- Section 904 – provides the insurance for the worker.

(a) In effect it provides that for an employer to be engaged in longshore operations he must provide evidence of insurance for his employees, or qualify as a self-insurer.

(b) Compensation will be paid to the injured harbor worker irrespective of fault as a cause for the injury.

Section 905 - This is the section that changed the round-robin litigation that existed for some seventeen years. It is **the crux of the 1972 amendments** and provides:

(a) Employer liability; failure of employer to secure payment of compensation

The liability of an employer prescribed in section 904 of this title **shall be exclusive** and in place of all other liability of such employer to the employee, his legal representative, husband or wife, parents, dependents, next of kin, and anyone otherwise entitled to recover damages from such employer at law or in admiralty on account of such injury or death, except that if an employer fails to secure payment of compensation as required by this chapter, an injured employee, or his legal representative in case death results from the injury, may elect to claim compensation under the chapter, or to maintain an action at law or in admiralty for damages on account of such injury or death. In such action the defendant may not plead as a defense that the injury was caused by the negligence of a fellow servant, or that the employee assumed the risk of his employment, or that the injury was due to the contributory negligence of the employee. For purposes of this subsection, a contractor shall be deemed the employer of a subcontractor's employees only if the subcontractor fails to secure the payment of compensation as required by section 904 of this title.

(b) Negligence of vessel

In the event of injury to a person covered under this chapter **caused by the negligence of a vessel**, then such person, or anyone otherwise entitled to recover damages by reason thereof, **may bring an action against such vessel as a third party in accordance with the provisions of section 933 of this title, and the employer shall not be liable to the vessel for such damages directly or indirectly and any agreements or warranties to the contrary shall be void.** If such person was employed by the vessel to provide stevedoring services, no such action shall be permitted if the injury was caused by the negligence of persons engaged in providing stevedoring services to the vessel. If such person was employed to provide shipbuilding, repairing, or breaking services and such person's employer was the owner, owner pro hac vice, agent, operator, or charterer of the vessel, no such action shall be permitted, in whole or in part or directly or indirectly, against the injured person's employer (in any capacity, including as the vessel's owner, owner pro hac vice, agent, operator, or charterer) or against the employees of the employer. **The liability of the vessel under this subsection shall not be based upon the warranty of seaworthiness or a breach thereof at the time the injury occurred. The remedy provided in this subsection shall be exclusive of all other remedies against the vessel except remedies available under this chapter.**

This subsection (b) has changed the way ship or cargo operations are performed. Before this section became law deck officers took an active role in supervising the loading and discharging of the cargo. This refers to the break bulk type of a ship. But then came *Scindia Steam Navigation Co., Ltd. V. De Los Santos,* 451 U.S. 156 (1981). Here the question was when should the ship's officers intervene with what the longshoremen were doing. The basic idea is that the shipowner has turned the vessel over to the stevedore, an expert in loading and discharging ships who knows how to do its job. The bottom line was that if the officers saw something that was so improvident that they should interfere, then they must do so. But that creates a problem as it can be claimed that the officer's action contributed to the accident and the injury, and the ship again can be held to be at fault. Thus, the modern approach, at least in the United States, is that the officers do not interfere, unless they see something really dangerous. Of course, with the recent container vessels such interference is practically nonexistent as the loading and discharging of containers is mechanized.

Accordingly, the bottom line at this point is that the shipowner engages the stevedore to load and unload the vessel and the stevedore does so. One basic requirement is that all equipment that is part of the vessel must be in proper working order when the vessel's cargo spaces are being turned over to the stevedore. Of course, there are exceptions but the above is the usual mode of operation. Certainly if the shipowner is aware of a hidden danger, it must advise the stevedore. Normally, a stevedore will not work a ship if it is aware of a dangerous condition. Prior to the turnover a shipowner must correct any dangerous condition or the stevedore will not work. This is known as "fix or quit."

VII

Wrongful Death and Death on the High Seas

Little repetition is necessary that under the common law the claim for wrongful death died with the individual and that a "survival" statute is necessary to preserve the civil claim against the wrong doer. For maritime wrongs the statute was passed in 1920, the Death on the High Seas Act initially contained in 46 U.S.C. §§ 761 – 769. With the recent rewriting of 46 U.S. Code the sections have been renumbered and are contained in sections 30301 – 30308. The relevant parts provide:

CHAPTER 303 - DEATH ON THE HIGH SEAS

Sec. 30301. Short title
This chapter may be cited as the "Death on the High Seas Act".

Sec. 30302. Cause of action
When the death of an individual is caused by wrongful act, neglect, or default occurring on the high seas beyond 3 nautical miles from the shore of the United States, the personal representative of the decedent may bring a civil action in admiralty against the person or vessel responsible. The action shall be for the exclusive benefit of the decedent's spouse, parent, child, or dependent relative.

Sec. 30303. Amount and apportionment of recovery

The recovery in an action under this chapter shall be a fair compensation for the pecuniary loss sustained by the individuals for whose benefit the action is brought. The court shall apportion the recovery among those individuals in proportion to the loss each has sustained.

Sec. 30304 Contributory negligence

In an action under this chapter, contributory negligence of the decedent is not a bar to recovery. The court shall consider the degree of negligence of the decedent and reduce the recovery accordingly.

Sec. 30305. Death of plaintiff in pending action

If a civil action in admiralty is pending in a court of the United States to recover for personal injury caused by wrongful act, neglect, or default described in section 30302 of this title, and the individual dies during the action as a result of the wrongful act, neglect, or default, the personal representative of the decedent may be substituted as the plaintiff and the action may proceed under this chapter for the recovery authorized by this chapter.

Sec. 30306. Foreign cause of action

When a cause of action exists under the law of a foreign country for death by wrongful act, neglect, or default on the high seas, a civil action in admiralty may be brought in a court of the United States based on the foreign cause of action, without abatement of the amount for which recovery is authorized.

Sec. 30307. Commercial aviation accidents

(a) Definition. - In this section, the term "nonpecuniary damages" means damages for loss of care, comfort, and companionship.

(b) Beyond 12 Nautical Miles. - In an action under this chapter, if the death resulted from a commercial aviation accident occurring on the high seas beyond 12 nautical miles from the shore of the United

States, additional compensation is recoverable for nonpecuniary damages, but punitive damages are not recoverable.

(c)   Within 12 Nautical Miles. - This chapter does not apply if the death resulted from a commercial aviation accident occurring on the high seas 12 nautical miles or less from the shore of the United States.

Sec. 30308. Nonapplication
STATE LAW- This chapter does not affect the law of a State regulating the right to recover for death.
INTERNAL WATERS – This chapter does not apply to Great Lakes or waters within the territorial limits of a State.

At this juncture it is also necessary to note that the "Jones Act" dealt with in chapter V is something that applies in cases of death on the high seas. You will recall that the Jones Act, originally contained in 46 U.S.C. § 688 and now in § 30104 includes recoveries by those affected by a seaman's death (previously dealt with in chapter V).

There are a few points that need to be noted:

1   DOHSA applies "beyond a marine league" from shore. One marine league is equal to three nautical miles.

2   In *Moragne v. States Marine Lines,* 398 U.S. 375 (1970) the wrongful death was applied to a longshoreman inside the three nautical miles. The court just felt that it would be inequitable not to give a recovery inside the marine league, hence such a recovery was allowed under The General Maritime Law.

3   Note that DOHSA allows for nonpecuniary damages in air-crash accidents at sea. This does not help seamen because of *Miles v. Apex.*

4   There is one exception for nonpecuniary damages in admiralty – in *Yamaha Motor Corp. v. Calhoun,* 516 U.S. 199 (1996)

nonpecuniary recovery was allowed for a 12 year old child dying on a jet ski on navigable waters. She was not a "seaman" and thus *Miles* did not apply.

In 2010 proposals were submitted in the Senate to permit nonpecuniary damages also to seamen and those claiming under them but so far the change has not been passed.

VIII

Suits against the Government

Our system, being based on the English system, still entertains the old English phrase that "the King can do no wrong." While many State writings still use this archaic phrase on occasion, only (by my last checking) the State of Pennsylvania officially has said that this is nonsense as there are no kings in the United States. The basic theory as to suing the government still persists, only it is called "Sovereign Immunity." This means that one (any citizen) may not sue the government unless the government has "consented to be sued" or practically speaking has passed a statute that permits one to sue the government. Initially, when some government employee or government action egregiously hurt some citizen the remedy was to ask your congressman to put in a private bill for compensation. But that, of course, only helped the wealthy or someone whose case was taken up by the public - really a very unsatisfactory situation.

So, after World War I the idea that the government should be suable for admiralty wrongs came into existence. The first was the Suits in Admiralty Act passed in 1920, initially contained in 46 U.S.C. §§ 741 - 752. The second government's waiver came in March 1925 when the Public Vessel's Act was passed, 46 U.S.C. §§ 781-790 and the third, albeit only partially, came in 1948 in the previously discussed Admiralty Extension Act contained in 46 U.S.C. § 741. For non-admiralty claims against the government there is the Federal Tort

Claims Act. Its procedures in some respects are different as it contains an administrative claim procedure . The three sets of statutes for claims against the government, quoted in part hereafter, point up several important factors.

1   The first upholds the principle that the government can only be sued when, where and how it has given its consent.

2   The statutes waiving sovereign immunity are strictly construed. This means that the party suing the government must comply with all the requirements, otherwise the court just does not have jurisdiction to entertain the lawsuit

3   The time limits for admiralty suits against the government have a DIFFERENT statute of limitations from private litigation. Where private parties have three years for torts and six years for contracts before the statute of limitations expires with the government it is TWO YEARS from the time the cause of action arose, and in Admiralty Extension Act cases (vessel on navigable waters causes damage on land) practically speaking only one and a half years, as it first requires an administrative claim, which can drag out for six months before a suit may be instituted.

And there are some other C.F.R. regulations that require an administrative claim before an action may be commenced.

4   The next point is that any suit against the government in admiralty must be brought in a federal court. And for suits against Public Vessels the venue provisions can be very important. In cases where the government's ship is in a United States port the suit must be brought where the vessel is located when the suit is filed, regardless of where the wrongful act took place.

5   The interest against the government in admiralty is 4% by statute and does not vary with Treasury bill rate changes as it does in the private sector.

6 It is also important to note that the proper party defendant is "The United States of America" not the Navy, not the Coast Guard nor some other government department or agency. If it is an agent (private steamship company) that has been operating the government's vessel for the government and the agent's employees commit the wrong, or breached the contract, the proper party defendant still is the "United States of America." [There are a number of cases on the books where the attorney thought that he could and should also sue the private agent company and sadly found out that if he let the statute go against the United States he was out of luck.] In fact, when a claimant joins the government's agent as a party, the government's lawyer will move to dismiss the case against the agent.

7 Also, as the waiver of sovereign immunity is by statute, for the period set by the statute, the parties or their lawyers (including the Attorney General) may not extend it. [Among private litigants it is possible to give "extensions of time to sue" and private parties may give such "extensions" to the government's counsel, but IT DOES NOT WORK THE OTHER WAY AGAINST THE GOVERNMENT!!!. Thus, if a government agent tells you that he will give an extension of time to sue the government he either does not know what he is talking about or is trying to lull you into a false sense of security.

8 There are several areas where C.F.R. regulations have been passed affecting the time to sue, by way of a prerequisite requirement for an administrative claim. That requirement must be complied with as in most cases it is jurisdictional. This means that if you, the claimant, have not complied and the time to do so has passed you are out of luck. The only way that a time to sue the government can be extended is by an act of Congress, signed by the President. In other words - no way no how!!!

Now let us look at the statutes as re-written in 2006. Although the language in some of the sections is a bit different from the wording originally enacted, there do not appear to be any substantive changes and the old precedents apply. There still is the difference between the Suits in Admiralty and Public Vessels Act. The PVA still has the «old» venue provision stating that if the public vessel is in port the action must be brought in that district. Also, the PVA still maintains the «reciprocity» provision regarding suits by foreigners. Namely, if a foreign national sues the United States for a wrong done by a public vessel of the United States he must prove «to the satisfaction of the court in which the action is brought that the government of that country, in similar circumstances, allows nationals of the United States to sue in its courts.» There are several cases where the foreign nationals were denied recovery because their country did not permit suits by Americans. See *Blanco v. United States*, 775 F.2d 53 (2nd Cir. 1985).

The **Suits in Admiralty Act** (formerly 46 U.S.C. §§ 741-752 now is chapter 309 or 46 U.S.C. §§ 3091 - 30918) in relevant parts provides:

§ 30902. Definition
"In this chapter, the term 'federally-owned corporation' means a corporation in which the United States owns all the outstanding capital stock.

§ 30903. Waiver of immunity
(a)   IN GENERAL.--In a case in which, if a vessel were privately owned or operated, or if cargo were privately owned or possessed, or if a private person or property were involved, a civil action in admiralty could be maintained, a civil action in admiralty *in personam* may be brought against the United States or a federally-owned corporation. In a civil action in admiralty brought by the United States or a federally-owned corporation, an admiralty claim *in personam* may be filed or a setoff claimed against the United States or corporation.

(b) NON-JURY.--A claim against the United States or a federally-owned corporation under this section shall be tried without a jury.

§ 30904. Exclusive remedy

If a remedy is provided by this chapter, it shall be exclusive of any other action arising out of the same subject matter against the officer, employee, or agent of the United States or the federally-owned corporation whose act or omission gave rise to the claim.

§ 30905. Period for bringing action

A civil action under this chapter must be brought within 2 years after the cause of action arose.

§ 30906. Venue

(a) IN GENERAL.--A civil action under this chapter shall be brought in the district court of the United States for the district in which--
    (1) any plaintiff resides or has its principal place of business; or
    (2) the vessel or cargo is found.
(b) TRANSFER.--On a motion by a party, the court may transfer the action to any other district court of the United States.

§ 30907. Procedure for hearing and determination

(a) IN GENERAL.--A civil action under this chapter shall proceed and be heard and determined according to the principles of law and the rules of practice applicable in like cases between private parties.
(b) IN REM.--
    (1) REQUIREMENTS.--The action may proceed according to the principles of an action in rem if--
        (A) the plaintiff elects in the complaint; and
        (B) it appears that an action *in rem* could have been maintained had the vessel or cargo been privately owned and possessed.

(2) EFFECT ON RELIEF *IN PERSONAM*.--An election under paragraph (1) does not prevent the plaintiff from seeking relief *in personam* in the same action.

§ 30908. Exemption from arrest or seizure

The following are not subject to arrest or seizure by judicial process in the United States:

(1) A vessel owned by, possessed by, or operated by or for the United States or a federally-owned corporation.

(2) Cargo owned or possessed by the United States or a federally-owned corporation.

§ 30909. Security

Neither the United States nor a federally-owned corporation may be required to give a bond or admiralty stipulation in a civil action under this chapter.

§ 30910. Exoneration and limitation

The United States is entitled to the exemptions from and limitations of liability provided by law to an owner, charterer, operator, or agent of a vessel.

§ 30911. Costs and interest

(a) IN GENERAL.--A judgment against the United States or a federally-owned corporation under this chapter may include costs and interest at the rate of 4 percent per year until satisfied. Interest shall run as ordered by the court, except that interest is not allowable for the period before the action is filed.

(b) CONTRACT PROVIDING FOR INTEREST.-- Notwithstanding subsection (a), if the claim is based on a contract providing for interest, interest may be awarded at the rate and for the period provided in the contract.

§ 30912. Arbitration, compromise, or settlement

The Secretary of a department of the United States Government, or the board of trustees of a federally-owned corporation, may arbitrate, compromise, or settle a claim under this chapter.

* * *

§ 30914. Release of privately owned vessel after arrest or attachment

If a privately owned vessel not in the possession of the United States or a federally-owned corporation is arrested or attached in a civil action arising or alleged to have arisen from prior ownership, possession, or operation by the United States or corporation, the vessel shall be released without bond or stipulation on a statement by the United States, through the Attorney General or other authorized law officer, that the United States is interested in the action, desires release of the vessel, and assumes liability for the satisfaction of any judgment obtained by the plaintiff. After the vessel is released, the action shall proceed against the United States in accordance with this chapter.

§ 30915. Seizures and other proceedings in foreign jurisdictions

(a) IN GENERAL.--If a vessel or cargo described in section 30908 or 30914 of this title is arrested, attached, or otherwise seized by judicial process in a foreign country, or if an action is brought in a court of a foreign country against the master of such a vessel for a claim arising from the ownership, possession, or operation of the vessel, or the ownership, possession, or carriage of such cargo, the Secretary of State, on request of the Attorney General or another officer authorized by the Attorney General, may direct the United States consul residing at or nearest the place at which the action was brought--

(1) to claim the vessel or cargo as immune from arrest, attachment, or other seizure, and to execute an agreement, stipulation, bond, or undertaking, for the United States or federally-owned

corporation, for the release of the vessel or cargo and the prosecution of any appeal; or

(2) if an action has been brought against the master of such a vessel, to enter the appearance of the United States or corporation and to pledge the credit of the United States or corporation to the payment of any judgment and costs in the action.

(b) ARRANGING BOND OR STIPULATION.--The Attorney General may--

(1) arrange with a bank, surety company, or other person, whether in the United States or a foreign country, to execute a bond or stipulation; and

(2) pledge the credit of the United States to secure the bond or stipulation.

(c) PAYMENT OF JUDGMENT.--The appropriate accounting officer of the United States or corporation may pay a judgment in an action described in subsection (a) on presentation of a copy of the judgment if certified by the clerk of the court and authenticated by--

(1) the certificate and seal of the United States consul claiming the vessel or cargo, or by the consul's successor; and

(2) the certificate of the Secretary as to the official capacity of the consul.

(d) RIGHT TO CLAIM IMMUNITY NOT AFFECTED.--This section does not affect the right of the United States to claim immunity of a vessel or cargo from foreign jurisdiction.

* * *

The **Public Vessels Act** (formerly in sections 781 - 790) now is in Chapter 311, of 46 U.S.C. §§ 31101 - 31113 in relevant parts provides:

§ 31102. Waiver of immunity

(a) IN GENERAL.--A civil action in personam in admiralty may be brought, or an impleader filed, against the United States for--

(1) damages caused by a public vessel of the United States; or

(2) compensation for towage and salvage services, including contract salvage, rendered to a public vessel of the United States.

(b) COUNTERCLAIM OR SETOFF.--If the United States brings a civil action in admiralty for damages caused by a privately owned vessel, the owner of the vessel, or the successor in interest, may file a counterclaim in personam, or claim a setoff, against the United States for damages arising out of the same subject matter.

§ 31103. Applicable procedure

A civil action under this chapter is subject to the provisions of chapter 309 of this title except to the extent inconsistent with this chapter.

§ 31104. Venue

(a) IN GENERAL.--A civil action under this chapter shall be brought in the district court of the United States for the district in which the vessel or cargo is found within the United States.

(b) VESSEL OR CARGO OUTSIDE TERRITORIAL WATERS.--If the vessel or cargo is outside the territorial waters of the United States--

(1) the action shall be brought in the district court of the United States for any district in which any plaintiff resides or has an office for the transaction of business; or

(2) if no plaintiff resides or has an office for the transaction of business in the United States, the action may be brought in the district court of the United States for any district.

* * *

§ 31106. Exoneration and limitation

The United States is entitled to the exemptions from and limitations of liability provided by law to an owner, charterer, operator, or agent of a vessel.

§ 31107. Interest

A judgment in a civil action under this chapter may not include interest for the period before the judgment is issued unless the claim is based on a contract providing for interest.

* * *

§ 31110. Subpoenas to officers or members of crew

An officer or member of the crew of a public vessel may not be subpoenaed in a civil action under this chapter without the consent of--

(1)   the Secretary of the department or the head of the independent establishment having control of the vessel at the time the cause of action arose; or

(2)   the master or commanding officer of the vessel at the time the subpoena is issued.

§ 31111. Claims by nationals of foreign countries

A national of a foreign country may not maintain a civil action under this chapter unless it appears to the satisfaction of the court in which the action is brought that the government of that country, in similar circumstances, allows nationals of the United States to sue in its courts. [See *Blanco v. United States*, 775 F.2d 53 (2nd Cir. 1985) noted earlier.]

§ 31112. Lien not recognized or created

This chapter shall not be construed as recognizing the existence of or as creating a lien against a public vessel of the United States.

The foregoing provisions clearly set forth the situations where admiralty suits may be brought against the government. If one has a claim there should not be any fear in starting such a suit as the Federal Government has set up several offices for dealing with such matters and bringing such an action does not create any personal adverse situations or repercussions.

The one thing to be noted is that the Suits in Admiralty Act deals with various maritime claims, such as cargo damage, general average, salvage and injury claims. The Public Vessels Act applies if a government vessel is involved, be it an aircraft carrier or a small Army Corps of Engineers vessel or the Coast Guard's buoy tender or ocean going cutter. As long as it is a government vessel that was involved, the PVA is the applicable statute.

IX

Maritime Liens

Maritime liens are the special attribute of maritime law necessary by reason of the type of business that is maritime commerce. Here we start with a bit of history. The British case of *Harmer v. Bell*, 13Eng. Rep. 884, is a historically leading decision by the Privy Council in 1852. The facts can be summarized as follows.

In January 1848 Scottish steamship BOLD BUCCLEUGH ran down and sunk English sailing ship WILLIAM in the Humber River. WILLIAM's owners brought *in rem* action against the BOLD BUCCLEUGH in Scottish court but that vessel had left the jurisdiction. In January 1849 WILLIAM's owners brought another suit in Scottish court of Sessions, arrested the vessel and released it on bail (what we would call a letter of undertaking in our maritime practice). In June 1849 the vessel was sold to Harmer, who introduced an affidavit saying he knew nothing of the collision or the claim. WILLIAM's owners disputed the affidavit. In August 1849 the BOLD BUCCLEUGH entered Humber River and WILLIAM's owners arrested her in an action in the High Court of Admiralty and moved to dismiss the earlier Scottish action. Vessel's owners objected to dismissal of the Scottish action and the arrest. Admiralty's Judge Dr. Lushington (a famous British Admiralty judge) gave judgment for WILLIAM's owners. On appeal, Court of Common Pleas held for WILLIAM's owners explaining. A maritime lien does not include or require possession. The right of the lien travels with the thing no matter into whose possession the vessel comes. Not at all like the usual land liens. A maritime lien is a claim or privilege upon a thing to be carried into effect by legal process. Then referring to American Justice Story's comment in 1831 which says that Admiralty enforces the right *in rem*.

> A maritime lien is the foundation of the proceeding *in rem*, a process to make perfect a right inchoate from the moment the lien attaches; and whilst it must be admitted that where such a lien exists, a proceeding *in rem* may be had, it will be found to be equally true, that in all cases where a proceeding *in rem* is the proper course of action, where a maritime lien exists, which gives a privilege or claim upon the thing, to be carried into effect by legal process. This claim or privilege travels with the thing, into whosesoever possession it may come. It is inchoate from the moment the claim or privilege attaches, and when carried into effect by legal process by a proceeding *in rem*, relates back to the period when it first attached.

This brings us back to our first chapter on jurisdiction and claims against the "personified" ship, or a claim *in rem* against the ship itself. Thus, it is very important that we understand the following points:

1. If a claim rises to the level of a maritime lien it is one that allows you to arrest a ship. Why is this important? Because when you may arrest a ship you have the ability to obtain security that you hold while you litigate even if the ship then leaves.

2. This maritime lien goes with the ship even if the ship is sold seven or more times over. Thus, if you have a claim that rises to a maritime lien and the ship runs away you may catch it in a foreign

port or when it comes back or goes to another port where you can catch it.

3   There are basically two types of maritime liens:

    a   Ones created by the general maritime law

    b   Ones created by statute, such as the modern Ship Mortgage Act.

4   **Keep in mind that an *in rem* claim against a vessel in the United States can only be enforced in a Federal Court – State courts do not have *in rem* jurisdiction.**

[The British case mentioned at the beginning of this section started in a British admiralty court!!!]

The usual maritime type liens that have existed for years include claims for seamen's wages, tort claims, breach of contract claims (cargo damage, charter breaches), claims for necessaries, claims based on repairs to the vessel, salvage claims, maritime contract claims and mortgage claims. Also, the costs for enforcing these claims will be enforced.

There is no statute that sets the priority of maritime liens. Case law and admiralty procedure, however, give an indication of some of the case law developed priorities. Before listing the priorities, a brief comment is necessary as to how a maritime lien is enforced. Enforcement requires the commencement of an action in which the court has jurisdiction over the *res*, the ship. That is done by filing a complaint (or having a complaint on file in court) when the ship is within the court's jurisdiction.

[In the "old days" one could file a complaint and not proceed with the case for months awaiting the ship's arrival. For the last twenty or so years, this is no longer possible because of the "individual judge assignments" where the federal judges keep an eye on their calendars and do not permit cases to sit on their docket without processing of the lawsuit. Thus, today in the United States one has to either arrest the vessel right away, or catch it in another U.S. port.]

The procedure, without going into all the details, requires:

1   That the ship be in the jurisdiction, namely in the town within that particular federal court's jurisdiction.
2   That a complaint be filed.
3   That an order be obtained from the federal judge directing the arrest of the vessel be obtained, which requires the lawyer to go to the judge and show him the complaint and show that the complaint alleges a claim that rises to the level of a maritime lien. At that point the judge will sign the order (that the lawyer has previously prepared and gives to the judge to sign) directing the Marshal to arrest the vessel.
4   A certified check for the Marshal to defray the arresting and keeping costs of the vessel for about one week, which, depending on the jurisdiction, can be from $25,000 to $30,000. [These were the amounts in the New York, New Jersey area a few years ago].
5   The arresting party must be able to keep advancing to the Marshal the weekly expenses, usually up to 6 or 7 weeks, unless the shipowner gives a **letter of undertaking** for the amount demanded in the complaint plus costs. The amount is negotiable, and can be reduced by the judge. **If the vessel has to be sold and the shipowner does not give a *letter of undertaking* then the arresting party may have to shell out as much as $100,000 to $150,000 before the ship is sold.**

This amount the plaintiff will get back fully when the ship is sold, but he must be able to shell out that money – or do not bother to go through the arrest procedure.

Of course, if you have a substantial claim and it is meritorious, and the value of the vessel is substantial and the ship is an operating vessel then the owner will probably give a letter of undertaking (usually by a P & I club) within a day or two of the arrest and the initial outlay by the plaintiff will not be large as the Marshal will return the excess money upon release of the vessel.

To go through these procedures one needs an attorney familiar with admiralty procedures. (Ones who usually do not practice admiralty law most likely will not be able to get this done in time in the modern days when ships have very quick turnaround times.)

The ability to enforce a maritime lien is a very powerful admiralty tool.

Maritime liens priorities

As noted before, the priorities of maritime liens are not specifically set forth. Case law has developed the following priorities:

first party that gets paid

1   The Marshal's *custodia legis* expenses (the cost of keeping the ship – the $70,000 - $100,000 mentioned before) come off the top of the money received following the sale and are paid to the arresting attorney relatively soon after the sale is confirmed.

2   Seamen wage claims and maintenance and cure payments come next.

3   Salvage and general average expenses (topics to be discussed *infra*) come next, and possibly recent pilotage and towage costs.

4   First preferred ship mortgages are usually next. [You can see that the preferred mortgage is not at the top, as often is in land and real estate situations.]

5   Maritime tort claims. These include such claims as collision damage, personal injury claims, negligent towage (although there is authority to the contrary holding that these would be contract claims), and minimal authority for holding that cargo could be

considered a "tort" claim, although they generally are considered to be contract claims.

6   Maritime Contract claims or liens. These are the lowest and usually in cases where an older ship is being sold they get nothing. [I have had several situations where I represented the cargo claimant, and in those cases I never recovered anything on the basis of the cargo damage claims when the relatively old ship was sold at a Marshal's sale. There just was not enough money received in the sale.]

For mortgage type of liens detailed statutory requirements were enacted with the 1988 statute. They are too detailed for this presentation. However, for a brief view of them several statutory excerpts are given here.

46 U.S.C. § 30101 Definitions
In this subtitle--

(1)   "documented vessel" means a vessel documented under chapter 121 of this title (46 U.S. Code);
(2)   "foreign vessel" means a vessel of foreign registry or operated under the authority of a foreign country;
(3)   "public vessel" means (except in chapter 315 of this title) a vessel that is owned, demise chartered, or operated by the United States Government or a government of a foreign country;
(4)   "recreational vessel" means a vessel--
      (A) operated primarily for pleasure; or
      (B) leased, rented, or demise chartered to another for the latter's pleasure;
(5)   "seaman" means a master or a crewmember of a vessel in operation;
                              * * *
(6)   "vessel of the United States" means a vessel documented under chapter 121 of this title, numbered under chapter 123 of this title, or titled under the law of a State.

46 U.S.C. § 31301 Commercial Instruments and Maritime Liens
Definitions
In this chapter—

(1)   "acknowledge" means making--
      (A) an acknowledgment or notarization before a notary public or
          other official authorized by a law of the United States or a State
          to take acknowledgments of deeds; or
                              * * *
(2)   "mortgagee" means--
      (A) a person to whom property is mortgaged; or
      (B) when a mortgage on a vessel involves a trust, the trustee that
          is designated in the trust agreement;

(3)   "necessaries" includes repairs, supplies, towage, and the use of a
      dry dock or marine railway;
(4)   "preferred maritime lien" means a maritime lien on a vessel--
      (A) arising before a preferred mortgage was filed under section
          31321 of this title;
      (B) for damage arising out of maritime tort;
      (C) for wages of a stevedore when employed directly by a person
          listed in section 31341 of this title;
      (D) for wages of the crew of the vessel;
      (E) for general average; or
      (F) for salvage, including contract salvage; and

(5)   "preferred mortgage"--
      (A) means a mortgage that is a preferred mortgage under section
          31322 of this title; and
      (B) also means in section 31325 and 31326 of this title, a mortgage,
          hypothecation, or similar charge that is established as a
          security on a foreign vessel if the mortgage, hypothecation,
          or similar charge was executed under the laws of the foreign

country under whose laws the ownership of the vessel is documented and has been registered under those laws in a public register at the port of registry of the vessel or at a central office.

46 U.S.C. § 31322 Preferred mortgages

(a) A preferred mortgage is a mortgage, whenever made, that—
  (1) includes the whole of the vessel;
  (2) is filed in substantial compliance with section 31321 of this title;
  (3) (A) covers a documented vessel; or
      (B) covers a vessel for which an application for documentation is filed that is in substantial compliance with the requirements of chapter 121 of this title and the regulations prescribed under that chapter;

* * *

(b) Any indebtedness secured by a preferred mortgage that is filed or recorded under this chapter, or that is subject to a mortgage, security agreement, or instruments granting a security interest that is deemed to be a preferred mortgage under subsection (d) of this section, may have any rate of interest to which the parties agree.

* * *

A preferred mortgage under this subsection continues to be a preferred mortgage even if the vessel is no longer titled in the State where the mortgage, security agreement, or instrument granting a security interest became a preferred mortgage under this subsection.

* * *

46 U.S.C. § 31325 Preferred mortgage liens and enforcement

(a)   A preferred mortgage is a lien on the mortgaged vessel in the amount of the outstanding mortgage indebtedness secured by the vessel.

The bottom line with respect to maritime liens is that they are very specific to maritime matters, they are very powerful, albeit sometimes very expensive to enforce, and really require a lawyer familiar with maritime matters.

X

Carriage of Goods

International commerce has existed for centuries. Of course it includes the shipment of goods from one country to another and often across the seas. While some of the earlier rules were contained in the Hammurabi codes, here we start with the American ocean shipping statutes, the Harter Act of 1893, previously contained in 46 U.S.C. §§ 190 – 196, now, since October 2006 contained in 46 U.S.C. §§ 30701 – 30707. As amended in 2006, these sections do not contain all the rules. The main cargo statute, the Carriage of Goods by Sea Act of 1936 still is the mainstay of the American cargo law. Previously contained in the "old" 46 U.S.C. §§ 1300 – 1312 and now as part of 46 U.S.C. § 3071 it remains the basic American law on cargo shipments and the relationship between the ocean carrier and the shipper of the cargo.[14]

In 2008 the United Nations adopted a convention to modernize the law affecting international transportation of goods. It deals with the relationships between the shipper of cargo and the carrier. The convention was opened for signature in Rotterdam in 2009 and it became known as the "Rotterdam Rules." As of June 2015 there are

---

[14] The reason why as of 2015 there still exists a dichotomy of citations affecting cargo law is that at the time Title 46 was rewritten in 2006 it was thought that most countries would quickly adopt the "Rotterdam Rules" hoping the world's ocean shipping rules would finally be made uniform. It did not happen. As of 2015 the twenty needed countries still have not ratified the convention. Also, the United States has not adopted the Rotterdam Rules.

strong suggestions that the convention may be adopted by the United States, but that has not yet happened. Accordingly, here are considered the existing American statutes and cases. The Rotterdam Rules are included in the appendix and can be dealt with if and when they are adopted.

The second problem with the Rotterdam Rules is that they are written in the form of European statutory system where the Rules are intended to take care of all situations. That really cannot exist and the American case precedent rules still will have to be considered.

As the court decisions construing the relationships between the cargo owner (shipper) and the "carrier" or the vessel's owner or operator were decided during the last seventy plus years here we continue to deal with what used to be the major sections in the American Carriage of Goods by Sea Act (COGSA) Sections 1303 and 1304. The reason the old section numbers are used is that most texts as of 2013 still refer to the "old" sections and the court references still refer to these old numbers.

In the appendix we have the text of COGSA, as the statute appears in § 30701 today under the heading of the "revised" Harter Act but really is identical to the COGSA wording. As the volume of American law and texts deal with the "old" sections 1303 and 1304 we start with these two sections as they set forth the duties and exemptions of the "carrier" – the ship and its owner. They explain the basic relationships if the carrier has complied with the first due diligence requirement to make the ship seaworthy at and prior to the commencement of the voyage.[15]

Note that the due diligence "permission" – for lack of a better term, applies only to subsection (1), NOT (2) of the old section 1303. The duty to properly load, handle, stow and carry is absolute.

---

[15] Now they are subsections 3 and 4 of § 30701.

The first two subsections contain the crux of the statute. They provide:

(1) The carrier shall be bound, before and at the beginning of the voyage, to exercise due diligence to--
- (a) Make the ship seaworthy;
- (b) Properly man, equip, and supply the ship;
- (c) Make the holds, refrigerating and cooling chambers, and all other parts of the ship in which goods are carried, fit and safe for their reception, carriage, and preservation.

Then it continues:

absolute duty, not due diligence

(2) The carrier shall properly and carefully load, handle, stow, carry, keep, care for, and discharge the goods carried.

(3) After receiving the goods into his charge, the carrier, or the master or agent of the carrier, shall, on demand of the shipper, issue to the shipper a bill of lading showing (the marks and numbers and other usual information).

Note that the need to exercise only "due diligence" applies to the commencement of the voyage. Why so? Because as an international voyage continues, and as most did in 1936 when the statute was first enacted, additional cargoes were loaded for discharge in further ports. And for those the owner in the home port had no real control. The owner at home could only exercise the real "due diligence" when the voyage commenced at the home port, or just before it commenced.

The bill of lading is the prima facie evidence of the receipt by the carrier of the goods as therein described.

The carrier cannot make any agreement relieving the carrier or the ship from liability for loss or damage to or in connection with the goods,

duty to properly, load, stow, and carry is absolute to ship owner arising from negligence, fault, or failure in the duties and obligations the carrier is required by the statute to provide.

The next section is the one that protects the carrier from liability if (and only if) the carrier has complied with the basic requirement of due diligence to make the ship seaworthy and to properly load and care for the cargo. The relevant extracts of § 1304 provide:

Rights and immunities of carrier and ship

>   *Unseaworthiness*
>   (1) Neither the carrier nor the ship shall be liable for loss or damage arising or resulting from unseaworthiness unless caused by want of due diligence on the part of the carrier to make the ship seaworthy, and to secure that the ship is properly manned, equipped, and supplied, and to make the holds, refrigerating and cool chambers, and all other parts of the ship in which goods are carried fit and safe for their reception, carriage, and preservation in accordance with the provisions of paragraph (1) of section 1303 of this title. Whenever loss or damage has resulted from unseaworthiness, the burden of proving the exercise of due diligence shall be on the carrier or other persons claiming exemption under this section.

>   *Uncontrollable causes of loss*
>   (2) Neither the carrier nor the ship shall be responsible for loss or damage arising or resulting from--
>   (a) Act, neglect, or default of the master, mariner, pilot, or the servants of the carrier in the

navigation or in the management of the ship; *[The usual carrier's excuse.]*

(b) Fire, unless caused by the actual fault or privity of the carrier;

* * *

(q) Any other cause arising without the actual fault and privity of the carrier and without the fault or neglect of the agents or servants of the carrier, but the burden of proof shall be on the person claiming the benefit of this exception to show that neither the actual fault or privity of the carrier nor the fault or neglect of the agents or servants of the carrier contributed to the loss or damage.

These provisions, (2) (a) and (b) and (q) require the comment that one must keep in mind they apply only to the relationship between the vessel's interests and the interests of the cargo that the vessel carries on that voyage. So, what is meant by the neglect of "master, mariner or pilot" "in the management of the ship?" And why is the "carrier" excused from liability? It is the industry's allowance to the one investing in international commerce for faults one can not control. Practically this means that if a ship winds up in a collision due to the fault of the master or one in charge of navigation at the moment, the owner of the ship will not be liable to the cargo that is damaged <u>on his ship</u>. Does it mean that the cargo is completely out of luck? – No. It can still recover from the other vessel if both vessels were at fault. And there have been many such situations. For example, there was absolutely no reason why the two passenger liners ANDREA DORIA and STOCKHOLM should have collided off Nantucket in 1956. The ocean was empty and there was no reason for them to be passing relatively close. The captains wanted to give their passengers a "view" of the other big ship. What nonsensical idea for passing so close in the empty ocean. The result was the loss of the ANDRA DORIA and a number of her passengers. That aside, however, the cargo on the ANDREA DORIA could not recover from her owners as the vessel owner was relieved due to her master's "error in navigation."

Similarly in other major casualties where there was a fire on the ship that damaged its cargo. Particularly in the days of wooden ships, when a fire in the galley could result in extensive damage. The vessel's owner on shore had no control over the occurrence, unless the owner was in actual "fault" or "privity."

And, then subsection (5) is the one that for many years has been the subject of extensive litigation. It provides:

> *Amount of liability; valuation of cargo*
> (5) Neither the carrier nor the ship shall in any event be or become liable for any loss or damage to or in connection with the transportation of goods in an amount exceeding $500 per package lawful money of the United States, or in case of goods not shipped in packages, per customary freight unit, or the equivalent of that sum in other currency, unless the nature and value of such goods have been declared by the shipper before shipment and inserted in the bill of lading. This declaration, if embodied in the bill of lading, shall be prima facie evidence, but shall not be conclusive on the carrier. * * *

This provision embodies the business relationships in regular commercial shipping situations. Obviously if the shipper declares the value of its cargo as being say two million dollars the freight rate for the package or container will be much higher than if the value were declared to be, say, two thousand dollars. And this is where the situation described in *Norfolk Southern Railway Co. v. Kirby*, 543 U.S. 14 (2004) comes up. For an understanding of the case an elaboration of the rules and practices associated with bills of lading is necessary.

A Bill of Lading is the document the carrier issues once it accepts and loads cargo on the vessel. It is a commercial document and several different copies of it are in the appendix as in a number of European countries the extensive American Bill of Lading form is not used. Also, now many shipments, if not most, are "intermodal" shipments. This means the container is packed inland, brought to the ship by rail or truck and at the other side of the ocean similarly brought inland for initial opening inland. Usually on one piece of paper the bill of lading contains the following:

A On the front of the document
   The shipping company's name
   The name of the shipper
   The name and usually the address of the consignee (the receiver of the cargo)
   A description of the goods in general terms
   The "marks and numbers" – the identifying code of the goods
   The value of the goods
   The freight rate
   Any other specific notation that is necessary for the particular cargo

2 On the back of the document

The various clauses that apply to the shipment. These can be anywhere from about 10 to 25 different paragraphs in small print. All these clauses are part of the contract of carriage.

It is very important to understand that all the matters stated on the Bill of Lading, its front and the back, are part of the agreement between the shipping company and the owner of the cargo shipped.

Also it must be understood that the Bill of Lading serves at least three and possibly four purposes:

It is the receipt given by the ship for the cargo delivered to it.
It is the document of title – the proper holder of it is the owner of the cargo.
It is the contract off carriage – the terms of the shipping agreement.
It may be a negotiable instrument. Many are not negotiable instruments, but others are.

Today many shipments of cargo, if not most, are "intermodal" and are covered with an intermodal bill of lading. This means that the cargo is loaded in the container inland, say Omaha, Nebraska, and then delivered by truck or rail to the loading port, say Elizabeth, New Jersey, where it is loaded on a container vessel going to Europe. In Bremerhaven it is unloaded and trucked to a town in the middle of Germany where it is opened for the first time. The terms of that bill of lading apply to all the parts of that voyage.

Here follows a brief description of some of the clauses on the back of the bill of lading that have been the subject of extensive litigation over the years.

The Clause Paramount This deals with the law applicable to the relationship in question. If the shipment is to or from the United States COGSA applies.

Period of responsibility clause Provides that the carrier is responsible only for the time the goods are on the vessel - "tackle to tackle" per COGSA. However, if the company has its own terminal it will be responsible after receipt of the cargo at its pier. This has changed in modern shipping as most shipments are by containers that most likely were stuffed inland and will be unstuffed somewhere in the middle of the country to which it is sent. Still the clause may apply, depending on the facts of the case.

Discharge and delivery This clause usually provides that the carrier may start discharging as soon as the vessel arrives.

Lighterage This usually states that lighterage is for the account of the merchant (namely the cargo shipper or owner). However, all bills of lading usually incorporate COGSA provisions until delivery of cargo because they are more favorable to the shipowner. In cases where that has not been done the carrier may regret it as shown hereafter in the *Ultramar* case. A good illustration comparing the "old" Harter Act and COGSA is *United States v. Ultramar Shipping Co., Inc.,* 685 F. Supp. 887 (S.D.N.Y. 1988); aff'd. 854 F.2d 1315 (2d Cir. 1988) where the government brought the action to recover cargo lost when a lightering vessel ran aground, capsized, and sank. The grain had been shipped in a large bulk carrier which could not enter the port of Chalna, Bangladesh. Lighters were used to bring the cargo into port while the bulker stayed anchored off shore. The lighter CHERRY LAJU was not covered by the bill of lading, the basic shipping agreement having been made on a private contract agreement that did not incorporate COGSA. The CHERRY LAJU, an old Victory ship, used as a lighter capsized because the grain was not properly secured as it usually is on long ocean voyages, viz. the short 40 mile run from the anchored mother ship to the river entrance. The court applied the "old" Harter Act as the grain had left the rail of the mother ship, requiring "proper delivery" under the Harter act. It stated:

> The Harter Act also presently applies during the time period following discharge of cargo from the ship and prior to its delivery; this coverage during the unloading period continues until proper delivery has been made to a fit and customary wharf. * * * Thus, the Court

finds and concludes that discharge occurred when the stevedore unloaded the wheat from the ULTRAMAR into the CHERRY LAJU and the other five vessels. Accordingly, this Court concludes that the Harter Act controls the obligations of defendants during the period between discharge from the ULTRAMAR and delivery at Chalna. This view is consistent with the decision in *Isthmian Steamship Co. v. California Spray-Chemical Corp.*, 290 F.2d 486, 488-89 (9th Cir. 1961), in which the Court applied the Harter Act to lighterage between Alexandria, Egypt and quays at which deep draft vessels such as the carrier's could not dock. See also, *Central Trading Co. v. Dong Myung*, 361 F. Supp. 302, 304 (S.D.N.Y. 1973).

Both to Blame Clause
Deals with liabilities in a ship collision case and ascribes liability to the carried cargo in proportion of the carrying ship's fault. In United States such a clause is invalid, but in many European countries it is enforceable.

The New Jason Clause
This deals with general average situations. Covered in more detail later, General Average is an age old principle where in situations where the vessel is in serious danger sacrifices are made to save the voyage. All parties participating in the voyage have to pay for the expenditures made to save the voyage.

The Himalaya Clause
(Often called the rights and immunities of All Servants and Agents of the Carrier clause.)
Initially designed for situations where the steamship company either had its own stevedoring subsidiary or had a corporate relationship

to its stevedores, it has been extended to all kinds of "agents" of the carrier. Basically, it permits the ocean carrier's agent to take advantage of the steamship company's right to the various COGSA exceptions and immunities even though the injury happens on shore. It is now prevalent in through bill of lading situations. Thus, in 2004 the Supreme Court let the railroad take advantage of the clause. It was a shipment of computer parts from inland in Australia to the port then by ship to Norfolk where it was put on a railroad for final destination in Alabama. The damage was done when the train derailed after leaving Norfolk, and the question was whether the Railroad (as "agent of the carrier") can take advantage of the $500 per package limitation given to the shipowner if the shipper does not declare the value of the cargo. As all the through bills of lading involved in that case contained the Himalaya clause and COGSA the court gave the railroad that protection. *Norfolk Southern Railway Co. v. Kirby,* 543 U.S. 14 (2004). This case, however, has been seriously questioned and seriously distinguished by the Second Circuit Court of Appeals in *Sompo Japan Insurance Company of America v. Union Pacific Railroad,* 456 F.3d 54 (2d. Cir. 2006). The Second Circuit Court of Appeals (one of the most respected appellate courts in admiralty matters for many, many years) points out in a 25 page opinion that the Supreme court in *Kirby* did not consider the Carmack Amendment 49 U.S.C. § 10501 which deals with transportation on railroads and limitation of liability provisions similar to those in COGSA and holds that the Himalaya clause of the through Bill of Lading (being a contractual agreement situation – albeit an adhesion clause) is trumped by the statute in the Carmack amendment. As of this time there are still a number of lawyer written arguments debating whether *Kirby* is correct or whether *Sompo* is correct. Frankly, this dispute is a bit beyond this course, but if any student wishes he can find the text of the *Kirby, Sompo* and a few other cases on line. The bottom line here is that the economic decision whether to declare the value of each package (which is an economic decision between the cargo owner and his underwriter) is one that has to be discussed by the shipper with his cargo underwriter.

The main point here is that it is the <u>economic decision</u> by the shipper and his underwriter whether to declare the true value of the shipped cargo. Or, who bears the risk of loss, the shipper and his underwriter if true value is not declared, with the advantage of a lower freight rate, or the vessel's owner and his underwriter if the value is declared and the higher freight rate is paid.

With the Rotterdam Rules, if and when they become part of our legal system it will be some time until the basic rules can be summarized. Why? Because they are written in the European system style believing they have anticipated and provided for every possible occurrence. I doubt that can be done. The difficulty will be in finding out exactly which sections apply to any particular set of facts as the rules have very, very many cross references among the sections and chapters. Look at the appendix and you will see what I mean.

XI

Charter parties - the contracts for renting ships

A "charter" of a ship is the renting of the ship. It is similar to renting a car, either for one voyage, several voyages, a definite period of time or for an extended period of time. The three basic ship charter forms are: the bareboat or demise charter, the time charter or the voyage charter. The critical differences are the duration and the control the owner retains or gives up. As in all other contract situations, the parties can agree on all the terms in their agreement. Today the charter forms are available on the internet and the parties can clearly see what are the terms of their agreement. Some thirty or forty years ago, before the internet and before the "fax" became available world-wide, it was very important for the chartering broker to be intimately familiar with the terms of the various charter party forms as agreements were often made with relatively short cable exchanges where the terms of the charter were sent in abbreviated form where the brokers had to know exactly what each abbreviation meant in the chartering world.

By reason of the nature of maritime business the three different types of charters are for particular business situations. The first the "Demise" or "Bareboat" charter as the term implies provides that the charterer or renter takes the vessel bare and at the end of the charter returns it in the same condition as he received it, less ordinary wear and tear. And, yes, ships do wear down. If nothing else, the steel wastes with age, the motors may need re-wiring, the radar may need new solenoids or screens, or whatever, the gyro may need overhauling, the turbine may need replacement blades, the diesel may need a new cylinder liner, etc., etc. Whatever it may be, the charterer provides his master and chief engineer, his crew, his stores, pays for the fuel, does ordinary repairs, or casualty repairs, keeps the ship in class and does everything a prudent owner of a ship would do, including the taking out of the usual marine insurance on the vessel, such as Hull, P & I and War Risk insurances. The law looks at him as the "owner pro hac vice." This also gives him the right to take advantage of the limitation of liability statutes, which other type of charterers can not. Demise charters usually run for many years, sometimes as long as 20 years, as some companies use this form of charter as a financing tool.

The other two charters are Time and Voyage charters. As their terms imply, one is for a stated period of time and the other for one or more specific voyages. In the last few decades companies have also used Time charters as financing tools and the ship is time chartered from the owner, who financed building the ship, to his subsidiary, the operating company. It must be kept in mind that a time charterer may not take advantage of the limitation of liability statutes.

The basic attributes of a Time Charter are:

1   The owner engages and hires his crew.
2   The owner supplies and victuals the vessel. Sometimes the charterer pays for fuel.
3   The owner supplies the Master, who is an agent of the charterer for some purposes only, usually with reference to the loading and discharging of cargo.
4   The owner performs all repairs to the vessel.
5   The owner obtains all insurance, although the charterer may also take out charterer's liability insurance.

6   The owner's master and crew remain in charge of the vessel's navigation.

7   The charterer has use of the full reaches of the vessel's cargo carrying capacity for his cargo.

8   The charterer tells the ship what cargo to load, when, where and at what ports to call. The owner's master however remains in charge of navigation. Here arise some charter disputes, where the owner's captain decided to take a longer, slower, in his opinion safer, route. This, of course, costs the charterer more money as he may have contemplated ten voyages during the period and now gets only nine.

There are many clauses in these type of charters dealing with what speed the ship can make in what kind of weather, how much cargo it can carry, what trading warranties it must comply with, a requirement that the vessel always must be afloat (as there are many ports where it is well known and accepted that during low tide the vessels sit on the bottom), when will it be drydocked and for how much time, what situations will cause "off hire" periods, what allowances are made for routine voyage repairs, etc., etc. A copy of such a Time charter is separately copied in the appendix for your perusal.

The third or last type of charter is the "Voyage" charter. This can be for either one voyage, say New Orleans to Capetown, or for seven consecutive voyages within a range, say Gulf coast ports to ports on the west and south costs of Africa, again with stipulations that the ship will always be afloat (meaning the ship will not be ordered to berth where she may lay on the bottom during low tide, unless that is normal practice in that port.) Here the full control of the ship's operation remains with the shipowner's master and his decisions and prerogative as to what is safe operation of the vessel. The charterer basically hires the ship's cargo carrying capacity, for the type of cargo agreed, during the period of the charter, for loading and discharging at the agreed ports.

So, what are the problems in chartering situations and how are they usually resolved. One important factor is the economic market. If a company makes a three year charter agreement for carrying grain from U.S. Gulf ports to the East Coast of Africa, say Mozambique a profitable period is probably anticipated. There was a time, however in the 1990's when Mozambique got its rice and grain growing industry in order and no longer needed as much of these grains as it had for decades before. The market shrank and the chartered vessels were not needed as much. But the charterer has a contract for using the vessel for several years. All of a sudden operational "difficulties" arise.

Most, if not all time and voyage charters have provisions for settling disputes by arbitration. It all gets back to the terms of the original agreement. Where did you agree to arbitrate the disputes that you may have anticipated; in which country and with which arbitration panels. The main point here is that these questions must be thought about before one enters into the chartering agreement.

Another approach may be in not starting the charter. In *Sunskar Ltd. V. CDII Trading,Inc.,* 828 F. Supp. 2d 604 (S.D.N.Y. 2011) the agreement was to carry ore from Mexico to China and the real issues were whether there was an agreement to charter the vessel and whether disputes were to be settled by arbitration. The court found in favor of an existing agreement and directed arbitration. In its discussion the court also found that the arguing that the company's official may not have had authority to act may not be used as "if the principal has created the appearance of authority" he may nevertheless bind the company, citing *Highland Capital Management LP v. Schneider,* 607 F.3rd 322, 328 (2nd Cir. 2010). Also, if the basic agreement makes a specific reference incorporating the other agreement and the arbitration clause contained in it, arbitration most likely will be compelled. *Glencore Ltd. V. Degussa Engineered Carbons L.P.,* 848 F. Supp. 2d 410 (S.D.N.Y. 2012).

Within the last few decades the practice of settling maritime contractual type disputes by arbitration has substantially increased. Yes, arbitration is faster and cheaper. But, as in most maritime matters, you must obtain the advice of experienced maritime counsel.

XII

Towage and Pilotage

Towage with respect to ocean going vessels has drastically changed within the last few decades by reason of extensive use of bow and stern thrusters. However, it still is a very important part of maritime law as towage of barges up and down the rivers and more and more towage in the oceans has become the practice in the industry. One of the initial questions with respect to tug and barge situations is whether the agreement is one of towage or "contract of affreightment." If it is a contract of affreightment, then the tug and the barge act like a unit and it is an agreement between the shipper of the cargo and the tug – barge flotilla (or their owner or operator) as the carrier or ship. In that situation the tug and the "integrated barge flotilla" become the bailee of the cargo and we go back to the Harter and COGSA situation. If it is a question of a pure towage contract then the responsibilities and liabilities between the tug and the tow are based on whether the tug was negligent. Also, it should be noted that for a towage contract to exist a writing is not necessary. Writings became the order of the day when the tug assistance was coupled with pilotage and still exists with ships that do not have bow and stern thrusters. In the "old days" when ocean going vessels needed tugs to help them dock alongside a wharf the question of the docking master's mistakes became a big issue. Where today such a docking master can talk with the assisting tug with his VHF or local walkie-talkie or cell phone, not that many years ago it was done by whistle signals: such as one short to push, two short to pull three to stop, short and long to do something else, etc. In those cases the possibility of a mix-up was not unheard of. As damage to the large ship in hitting the dock could be very substantial the tug - docking pilot relationship could become very expensive. So, they came up with the theory of the "borrowed servant." This meant that when the docking pilot went on board the large ship to direct the docking of the ship he became the "servant" of the ship (although not a crew member) and if he made a mistake the ship's interests could not sue his real employer the tug company. The agreement was contained in the tug boat's tariff and also in the "pilotage ticket" that the ship's captain had to sign before the pilot started giving the docking orders. [And there are cases holding that even if the captain had not signed the ticket, as it was the custom in the port that everyone knew the tug owner was still protected.] The important distinction in these situations was that if the mistake was made by the docking pilot the ship could not sue the tugboat company. If the mistake was by the man left in charge of the tug (such as pushing when he should have pulled or the like) then the ship's interests could sue the tug company. The validity of this type of agreement and relationship was approved by the Supreme court in *Sun Oil Co. v. Dalzell Towing*, 287 U.S. 291 (1932). [To illustrate how things have changed, Dalzell Towing, one of the big towboat companies in New York Harbor in its day, went out of business some 30+ years ago.] The procedure for this type of docking still exists for ships that do not have bow and stern thrusters and require tugs to help them dock.

The idea of a pilot becoming the "borrowed servant" of a ship also still exists with harbor pilot situations, even though pilotage may be compulsory. Keep in mind that if the pilot makes a mistake (regardless of any contract clause that may exist) and the ship winds up in collision or causes damage to some other entity the ship still will be liable *in rem* to the injured third party and the claim rises to the level of a maritime lien.

As mentioned earlier, these usually are towage contracts where the tug's liability is based on tort principles. Over the years tug companies have tried to limit their liability by certain contract clauses, usually attempting to exculpate the tug company's liability for mistakes made by tug captains. While basic contract law permits exculpatory provisions, where public necessity comes in, the courts will sometimes step in. [In England, particularly in London, it is understood that when a ship is being towed up the Thames River if the tug makes a mistake the ship is still liable and must indemnify the tug.] In the United States we have many rivers that have very heavy tug / barge traffic. And a number of tug companies tried to exculpate themselves from liabilities for mistakes by their tug crews. Eventually the question went to the Supreme Court and the basic rule was laid down in *Bisso v. Inland Waterways Inc.,* 349 U.S. 85 (1955). The long and the short of it is that absolute exculpatory clauses by tug boat companies are not valid in the United States. If the tug company wishes to contract away its negligence (which many wish to do) it must give a different cheaper towage rate where the tug company remains liable for tort. In New York Harbor there are such dual rates for towage that have existed for years. Towage of oil barges in the barge canal above Albany, where banging the barge against locks and docks is quite common there are agreed provisions where the tug company is excused from liability. Sometimes the industry deals with these situations by providing in the contract for the taking out of insurance and naming the other on its insurance policies.

Also, you must keep in mind that in a towage situation the *Ryan* warranty of workmanlike service (discussed above in longshoremen injury cases) can apply to towage situations. *James McWilliams Blue Line, Inc. v. Esso Standard Eastern,* 245 F.2d 84 (2d Cir. 1957); *Tebbs v. Baker Whitley Towing,* 407 F.2d. 1055 (4th Cir. 1969).

Collision – Rules and cases for preventing collisions

The rules for preventing ship collisions have existed for several centuries and are followed by all countries whose ships sail the seven seas. This presentation is not intended for the teaching of the rules of the road that all deck watch officers and captains are required to learn and obey whenever they are in charge of the navigation of a ship. However, the Rules (or cases where their violation has led to an accident) are a very significant part of the maritime law and therefore many of them are copied in the appendix and hereafter are presented to you in some of the more significant relationships where their violations have resulted in major casualties. While this is not a set of instructions for their learning, an understanding of them and the consequences for failing to comply with them is noted. The rules are divided in several parts: the general application, how the ships should be operated when vessels are near each other, what kind of signals they should or must give and what kind of lights they must display at night, as knowledge of these factors make it possible for navigators to act in a proper manner. Read over the rules set forth in the Appendix to see the type of matters they cover.

Here we look at some of the more common ones that a seaman must be aware of (even though all licensed deck officers must be intimately familiar with all of them).

What is very important is the application of what is known as the "Rule of the Pennsylvania." It goes back to a collision between a sailing ship and a steamer shortly after the Civil War. The steamer was held to have violated the speed in fog rule as it then existed as a result of which it struck and sunk the sailing ship. The court went on to explain the consequences of one violating the rules for preventing collisions. The Supreme Court in the case of *The Pennsylvania,* 86 U.S. 125 (1873) stated:

> The liability for damages is upon the ship or ships whose fault caused the injury. But when, as in this case, a ship at the time of a collision is in actual violation of a statutory rule intended to prevent collisions, it is no more than a reasonable presumption that the fault, if not the sole cause, was at least a contributory cause of the disaster. In such a case the burden rests upon the ship of showing not merely that her fault might not have been one of the causes, or that it probably was not, but that it could not have been. Such a rule is necessary to enforce obedience to the mandate of the statute.

This rule has been carried over to many areas in the law where violation of a statue is causally related to the resulting injury. For example, in a seaman injury situation if the injury was due to a failure to have a certain type of a safety harness, the rule of the Pennsylvania applies. Although there are situations where the casualty has been caused by "inscrutable fault" or an "Act of God" such situations are rare indeed. Usually, maritime collisions or casualties occur because someone has violated one or more of the rules designed to prevent collisions or other casualties. While it is not necessary to review a great number of collision cases, a review of some will help in understanding the importance of the need to strictly follow the rules.[16] First, however, here are some of the basic rules.

With respect to the United States, the same as for other nations, there are some rules that apply to the waters of the particular nation because of the peculiarities of that nation's waters. For the United States we have the "Inland Rules." That is because there are peculiarities with such rivers as the Mississippi, Missouri, Ohio, Colorado and other rivers that require specific provisions. Similarly, for the Rhine River in Germany there are certain special requirements. Here we will note that such differences exist, but will limit our discussion to the "International Rules" that apply "to all vessels upon high seas and in waters connected therewith navigable by seagoing vessels." The same Rule 1 goes on to provide that governments may make additional rules to take care of matters on their inland rules.

Another, no longer "new" but developed within the last half century are the Traffic Separation schemes. Thus we have special rules for approaching busy harbors and areas of high traffic, such as the English Channel, the Gibraltar and New York Harbor, to mention a few. The next point is Rule 2 that makes all rules applicable to all situations, what used to be called the "General Prudential Rule," which provides:

> (a) Nothing in these Rules shall exonerate any vessel, or the owner, master, or crew thereof, from the consequences of any neglect to comply with these

---

[16] In my 36 years of practicing admiralty law, 32 of which were with the Department of Justice's New York office where I was familiar with all the cases that were handled there, only two collision situations came about where only one vessel was held to be at fault. One was the SEAWITCH – ESSO BRUSSELS disaster where it was the failure of the steering gear at the inopportune moment resulting in over 40 deaths and great financial losses. The other was a collision in the Straits of Malaca where the other ship's captain was asleep in his cabin leaving an inexperienced seaman on the bridge by the automatic steering system.

Rules or of the neglect of any precaution which may be required by the ordinary practice of seamen, or by the special circumstances of the case.

(b) In construing and complying with these Rules due regard shall be had to all dangers of navigation and collision and to any special circumstances, including the limitations of the vessels involved, which may make a departure from these Rules necessary to avoid immediate danger.

Next, Rule 3 provides a number of definitions, and here we have the definition of the word "vessel:" as "every description of water craft . . . used or capable of being used as a means of transportation on water."

Of course, the other definitions are just as important, but this one illustrates why in the beginning we spent time on finding out what navigation and navigable waters meant. It means that the rules apply equally to a canoe and an aircraft carrier. The reason other craft are specifically described, including such terms as "length" "breadth" "restricted visibility" and others because these are special situations involving the association with navigation, oceans and rivers that are different from the normal occurrences on land. You must learn these definitions.

Rules 4 and 5 state that the rules apply "to any condition of visibility" and that

> Every vessel shall at all times maintain a proper look-out by sight and hearing as well as by all available means appropriate in the prevailing circumstances and conditions so as to make the full appraisal of the situation and of the risk of collision.

- Have proper lookout to avoid getting in collision

This rule 5, or its violation, have been the cause for many if not most collisions and casualties.[17]

Rule 6 lists a number of factors to be considered in determining "safe speed." The difference between good visibility and foggy conditions bring out different considerations. And with the advancing technology the application of a number of considerations, factors or reasonable interpretation of rules enter the picture. For example, before radar was invented and for quite a few years after that invention the rule was that in restricted visibility one was allowed to proceed at such speed that the vessel could be stopped in half the distance of visibility. While quite a reasonable rule it was honored more in the breach as when one encountered fog in the ocean the idea of stopping just was not a practical approach. Yet, that is what the rules required and if one violated that rule and wound up in a collision the consequences were dire. Such areas as the Strait of Gibraltar had a significant number of collisions. Also, as late as the 1960's there were many "old timers" who experienced difficulties with the relative motion concept required for proper use of a radar. Today there is ARPA which calculates most of the possibilities for the navigator. Thus, the "modern" approach for subsection (b) of Rule 6 regarding the use of radar and some of its limitations, such as not detecting small vessels or the effects of ice and the state of the sea. Here, the best guide is experience and total familiarity with the equipment one has onboard.

---

[17] Without giving the case, an example came with a pilot bringing a ship into Rhode Island harbor on a clear day when there should not have been any problems. Just before the ship sheered out to the channel the pilot was pouring himself a cup of coffee. He also added milk and sugar and then stirred the cup, while facing away from the forward direction. The coffee was being poured at the precise time when the side of the channel depth was reduced and the slight right rudder that was being carried drove the ship out of the channel – because the pilot had not kept a "proper lookout," albeit for less than a minute.

The next Rule 7 entitled "Risk of Collision" clearly points out that the theory and practical considerations and attendant facts all deal with the need to carefully consider what **will be happening,** not what exists at any particular moment. At any precise moment it is already too late. The Rule starts with subsection (a) which states:

> Every vessel shall use all available means appropriate to the prevailing circumstances and conditions to determine if risk of collision exists. If there is any doubt such risk shall be deemed to exist.

The other parts of the rule specify use of radar equipment, visual bearings and other relative facts. Always the "constant bearing and decreasing range" have been the first hand notification of potentially dangerous situation. But then consider two or three vessels approaching the same pilot station at the same time. Yes, the risk clearly exists. It is the other considerations or factors that permit the vessels to safely be dealt with.

And the next Rule 8 deals with specifics in general terms (really a misnomer). One needs to study Rule 8 and most likely memorize it verbatim. Clearly any rule cannot specify how to act in every situation, but the statements in this rule are very good guides for how one must act. If one examines court decisions in collision cases one will find that in each collision most likely several of the guides in Rule 8 have been violated or sufficient attention was not paid to it.

The next two rules of the first part are Rule 9 dealing with "Narrow Channels" and Rule 10 with the earlier mentioned Traffic Separation Schemes that apply to not only the United States but also the International Maritime Organization's traffic separation schemes. Again these are important Rules that the navigator must study and master. After World War II ended in 1945 the nations also started to work closer on international maritime maters and the International Maritime Organization (IMO) became much more recognized and utilized in international commerce. The ship's officer and the shore-side employee must become familiar with the Rules applicable to his or her particular area of service.

Here we next briefly consider what has been labeled as Section II of the COLREGS referring to the "Conduct of Vessels in Sight of One Another," Rules 11- 18. It is really important to note the difference in the Rules when the persons on one vessel can see the other vessel. **This does not mean seeing the other ship's dot or signal on the radar.** It means – **seeing the other ship visually with your eyes.**

The foregoing may sound a bit simple but it is not. It really means seeing the other vessel. But how about patchy fog, when at one point you see the other ship and then you do not. It is a problem. And it goes back to the Definitions – Rule 3; Lookout Rule 5; Safe Speed Rule 6; Risk of collision Rule 7; and actions to void collision Rule 8. **They all continue to react with each other.**

So, on to Rule 12 – Sailing vessels. Here we need to know two things: These rules apply **only** to two sailing vessels, as if one vessel is under power that is the one that must keep out of the way of the sailing vessel. And here it depends on the direction of the wind and whether it is over you vessel's port or starboard side. Here I would only add: if you are qualified to be in charge of a sailing vessel, you certainly should know these rules by heart.[18]

Rules 13 through 17 specify which vessel has the obligation to give way, or to have the right of way in overtaking, meeting and crossing

---

[18] Does it happen that individuals owning sailboats in inland waters, such as the Long Island Sound, take out their boats not knowing the rules? Sure. Still, you as the mariner must know how to deal with approaching dangerous situations.

situations. Again, these are situations where the one in charge of navigation needs to know what he is doing. What these rules do not deal with are the characteristics of the vessel involved. Those factors are considered in other areas, but not as a part the COLREGS. Yet, they are very, very important as the lack of such understanding will cause collisions.

Here the factors not mentioned in the statute include the maneuvering characteristics of the vessels. One must keep in mind that a ship does not turn or move as a car. The turning of the wheel does not make the ship turn right away. There are, however, certain general factors that must be kept in mind. For example, depending on the construction of the vessel, a ship proceeding at full sea speed will travel along its original path between three to four times its length if the rudder is put over hard right or hard left. This means that if a ship is say 600 feet long it will travel 1,800 to 2,400 feet along its original course line before it starts to leave it. Thus, if one intends to get out of the other ship's way, say in a crossing situation where your ship is the burdened vessel, and wishes to do that at a moderate rate of turn, the motion should be started before the two ships are within more than a mile of each other, and most likely earlier. Anything less than that is plain arrogance or stupidity. And there are a number of cases where that was the real cause of the disaster. What comes to mind is the well-known collision between the ANDREA DORIA and the STOCKHOLM in July 1956. These were two ocean liners that were meeting off Nantucket in the open ocean. For some stupid reason they decided to pass each other closely, possibly wishing to show the passengers the other ship. They had no business being that close. The result was the collision in which a number of people died and the ANDREA DORIA sank.

The main point here is that the one in charge of the navigation of the ship must be timely aware of the existing circumstances and take timely action.

Rule 18, entitled "Responsibility Between Vessels" specifies which vessels must "keep out of the way" or give room to what other type of vessels. The specifics must be learned and obeyed. For example, a power driven vessel must keep out of the way of a vessel not under command, a sailing vessel, one engaged in fishing and one restricted in the ability to maneuver. Other subsections specify additional situations.

The next Rule 19, entitled "Conduct of Vessels in Restricted Visibility" specifies what ships may or shall do in fog, mist, heavy rain or other conditions restricting visibility. Well until after World War II the Rule was that a ship must reduce speed and may only proceed at such speed that it can stop in one half of the distance of visibility. Although strictly enforced in casualty situations, in practice this was ignored in most situations. And, if not completely ignored, it was only partially observed. In certain areas of the world the existence of fog was quite frequent and if the old Rule had been fully complied with commerce would have suffered quite a bit. Particularly, when crossing the ocean, in certain areas of the ocean there were frequent fog situations in certain times of the year. Yes, the sounding of fog signals was usually complied with, but also not always.

The invention and introduction of radar changed things drastically. In the beginning, however, there were quite a few "radar assisted collisions" because there were a number of years when first, the officers did not understand radar and there were a good number of experienced ship captains who did not fully understand relative motion.[19]

---

[19] Personally sailing in the early 1960's I sailed with two very experienced captains who had problems with relative motion used in radar navigation. One recognized his shortcomings and in fog situations put the young mates on the radar, but the other thought he knew it and wound up in some close calls. This changed as the years progressed and the study of radar became required and then the radar improved and today exists ARPA which does the radar calculations for the navigator.

Today there is ARPA that should serve to avoid all dangerous close quarters situations and avoid collisions. But that is not how this world works. There will always be someone who does not pay sufficient attention to the existing situations and collisions will ensue. And there are other situations that enter the picture, such as Part C of the Rules dealing with the lights and shapes vessels must carry to show what type of a vessel they are and what they are engaged in.

Lights and Shapes – Rules 20 – 31. These are signals or indications that show the other ship what type of a vessel one is and the general area in which it is traveling at any particular time. The details are set forth in the Appendix. Here the discussion cannot deal with particular rules as full courses are necessary to deal with all situations. What is important to know is that the Rules are strictly enforced because they are all part of avoiding dangerous situations and collisions. Just as one example, Rule 21 specifies the side lights (red on port and green on starboard) but then in Annex I (5) it adds the requirement for the screens for the sidelights so that they do not show across the bows. In practice this is very important in that when one sees ahead the red and green sidelights of the other ship one knows that she is heading right at you. Those who have sailed will also know that seeing such lights most likely shortly later will show a change and that the other vessel will then show only the red light indication the passage will be port to port. This is just a short example of how knowledge of all the lights is absolutely necessary for one to safely navigate. As noted before, the navigator in charge of the watch must be intimately familiar with all these Rules.

The next section Rules 32 – 36 describe the sound and light signals vessels must exchange to show to each other what they are doing and what are their intentions, AND Rule 37 describes the various distress signals. Again it is an area requiring specific study which is needed to safely operate a vessel.

And there are Annexes that amplify a number of specifics. The short answer is that the navigator in charge of a vessel under way must know them all. And, one should, and really must, review them from time to time to keep them currently in mind. Having handled several collision cases and having looked at the ANDREA DORIA – STOCKHOLM collision in some detail, the only conclusion that I can make is that every collision came about because one (or most likely both ships) violated more than one of the foregoing collision prevention rules.

Limitation of liability

In the first four chapters we dealt with the special attributes of admiralty and, among others, mentioned limitation of liability. The idea was, and still is, to encourage investment in shipping. It came in the middle of the 19th century and first became law in the U.S. in 1851. One must keep in mind that in the 1800's when a sailing ship left the home port it often did not come back for a year or more. Particularly, ships setting out from New England on the way to the Pacific did not come back until years later. Even ones going to Europe would not come back for months. There were no radios, cell phones, telephones or other ways of communication between the home office and the ship at sea. The master, in charge of the vessel, and his officers held in their hands the entire investment of the owner in the vessel. And, as we have seen, the ship still could incur *in rem* liabilities that sometimes could come back and haunt the owner with *in personam* claims. Thus, to encourage investment in shipping the limiting of the owner's liability was considered and statutes were enacted limiting the owner's liability to the value of his investment should things go sour. Basically the statutes provide that if the owner did not participate in the wrong causing damage his liability would be limited to his investment – the ship itself. With modern times and occurrences and the increasing concern for personal safety and compensation for injuries the amounts have changed. But, basically, they still remain.

You should note, however, that although the "old" limitation of liability statutes contained in 46 U.S.C. 181 - 189 still remain (as shown in the appendix) and the "new" sections 46 U.S.C. 30501 - 30512 although very similar they do have several significant changes.

The "new" sections of 46 U.S. Code sections 30501 – 30512 provide:

Sec. 30501. Definition

In this chapter, the term "owner" includes a charterer that mans, supplies, and navigates a vessel at the charterer's own expense or by the charterer's own procurement.

> This means that only a bareboat charterer can petition for limitation of liability. It is not available to time or voyage charterer. But keep in mind that in time and voyage charters the owner's master and crew run the vessel.

Sec. 30502. Application

Except as otherwise provided, this chapter (except section 30503) applies to seagoing vessels and vessels used on lakes or rivers or in inland navigation, including canal boats, barges, and lighters.

> Here you must note that the new statute creates several exceptions. The case of *Foremost Insurance Co. v. Richardson,* 457 U.S. 558 (1982) is no longer good law as small fishing boats are now excluded from the limitation provisions.

Sec. 30503. Declaration of nature and value of goods

(a) In General. - If a shipper of an item named in subsection (b), contained in a parcel, package, or trunk, loads the item as freight or baggage on a vessel, without at the time of loading giving to the person receiving the item a written notice of the true character and value of the item and having that information entered on the bill of lading, the owner and master of the vessel are not liable as carriers. The owner and master are not liable beyond the value entered on the bill of lading.

(b) Items. - The items referred to in subsection (a) are precious metals, gold or silver plated articles, precious stones, jewelry, trinkets, watches, clocks, glass, china, coins, bills, securities, printings, engravings, pictures, stamps, maps, papers, silks, furs, lace, and similar items of high value and small size.

> This is a change in the law. The old section provided, in essence, that if the shipper had not declared the value of the cargo on the bill of lading, the amount recoverable for loss of the goods was limited to $500 per package or commercial unit. That provision is now no longer part of the law.

Sec. 30504. Loss by fire

The owner of a vessel is not liable for loss or damage to merchandise on the vessel caused by a fire on the vessel unless the fire resulted from the design or neglect of the owner.

Sec. 30505. General limit of liability

(a) In General. - Except as provided in section 30506 of this title, the liability of the owner of a vessel for any claim, debt, or liability described in subsection (b) shall not exceed the value of the vessel and pending freight. If the vessel has more than one owner, the proportionate share of the liability of any one owner shall not exceed that owner's proportionate interest in the vessel and pending freight.

(b) Claims Subject to Limitation. - Unless otherwise excluded by law, claims, debts, and liabilities subject to limitation under subsection (a) are those arising from any embezzlement, loss, or destruction of any property, goods, or merchandise shipped or put on board the vessel, any loss, damage, or injury by collision, or any act, matter, or thing, loss, damage, or forfeiture, done, occasioned, or incurred, without the privity or knowledge of the owner.

(c) Wages. - Subsection (a) does not apply to a claim for wages.

Sec. 30506. Limit of liability for personal injury or death

(a) Application. - This section applies only to seagoing vessels, but does not apply to pleasure yachts, tugs, towboats, towing vessels, tank vessels, fishing vessels, fish tender vessels, canal boats, scows, car floats, barges, lighters, or nondescript vessels.

(b) Minimum Liability. - If the amount of the vessel owner's liability determined under section 30505 of this title is insufficient to pay all losses in full, and the portion available to pay claims for personal injury or death is less than $420 times the tonnage of the vessel, that portion shall be increased to $420 times the tonnage of the vessel. That portion may be used only to pay claims for personal injury or death.

(c) Calculation of Tonnage. - Under subsection (b), the tonnage of a self-propelled vessel is the gross tonnage without deduction for engine room, and the tonnage of a sailing vessel is the tonnage for documentation. However, space for the use of seamen is excluded.

(d) Claims Arising on Distinct Occasions. - Separate limits of liability apply to claims for personal injury or death arising on distinct occasions.

(e) Privity or Knowledge. - In a claim for personal injury or death, the privity or knowledge of the master or the owner's superintendent or managing agent, at or before the beginning of each voyage, is imputed to the owner.

Sec. 30507. Apportionment of losses

If the amounts determined under sections 30505 and 30506 of this title are insufficient to pay all claims -

(1) all claimants shall be paid in proportion to their respective losses out of the amount determined under section 30505 of this title; and

(2) personal injury and death claimants, if any, shall be paid an additional amount in proportion to their respective losses out of the additional amount determined under section 30506(b) of this title.

Sec. 30508. Provisions requiring notice of claim or limiting time for bringing action

(a) Application. - This section applies only to seagoing vessels, but does not apply to pleasure yachts, tugs, towboats, towing vessels, tank vessels, fishing vessels, fish tender vessels, canal boats, scows, car floats, barges, lighters, or nondescript vessels.

(b) Minimum Time Limits. - The owner, master, manager, or agent of a vessel transporting passengers or property between ports in the United States, or between a port in the United States and a port in a foreign country, may not limit by regulation, contract, or otherwise the period for

(1) giving notice of, or filing a claim for, personal injury or death to less than 6 months after the date of the injury or death; or

(2) bringing a civil action for personal injury or death to less than one year after the date of the injury or death.

(c) Effect of Failure To Give Notice. - When notice of a claim for personal injury or death is required by a contract, the failure to give the notice is not a bar to recovery if -

(1) the court finds that the owner, master, or agent of the vessel had knowledge of the injury or death and the owner has not been prejudiced by the failure;

(2) the court finds there was a satisfactory reason why the notice could not have been given; or

(3) the owner of the vessel fails to object to the failure to give the notice.

(d) Tolling of Period To Give Notice. - If a claimant is a minor or mental incompetent, or if a claim is for wrongful death, any period provided by a contract for giving notice of the claim is tolled until the earlier of -

(1) the date a legal representative is appointed for the minor, incompetent, or decedent's estate; or

(2) 3 years after the injury or death.

Sec. 30509. Provisions limiting liability for personal injury or death

(a) Prohibition. -

(1) In general. - The owner, master, manager, or agent of a vessel transporting passengers between ports in the United States, or between a port in the United States and a port in a foreign country, may not include in a regulation or contract a provision limiting -

(A) the liability of the owner, master, or agent for personal injury or death caused by the negligence or fault of the owner or the owner's employees or agents; or

(B) the right of a claimant for personal injury or death to a trial by court of competent jurisdiction.

(2) Voidness. - A provision described in paragraph (1) is void.

(b) Emotional Distress, Mental Suffering, and Psychological Injury. -
(1) In general. - Subsection (a) does not prohibit a provision in a contract or in ticket conditions of carriage with a passenger that relieves an owner, master, manager, agent, operator, or crewmember of a vessel from liability for infliction of emotional distress, mental suffering, or psychological injury so long as the provision does not limit such liability when the emotional distress, mental suffering, or psychological injury is -

(A) the result of physical injury to the claimant caused by the negligence or fault of a crewmember or the owner, master, manager, agent, or operator;

(B) the result of the claimant having been at actual risk of physical injury, and the risk was caused by the negligence or fault of a crewmember or the owner, master, manager, agent, or operator; or

(C) intentionally inflicted by a crewmember or the owner, master, manager, agent, or operator.

(2) Sexual offenses. - This subsection does not limit the liability of a crewmember or the owner, master, manager, agent, or operator of a vessel in a case involving sexual harassment, sexual assault, or rape.

Sec. 30510. Vicarious liability for medical malpractice with regard to crew

In a civil action by any person in which the owner or operator of a vessel or employer of a crewmember is claimed to have vicarious liability for medical malpractice with regard to a crewmember occurring at a shoreside facility, and to the extent the damages resulted from the conduct of any shoreside doctor, hospital, medical facility, or other health care provider, the owner, operator, or employer is entitled to rely on any statutory limitations of liability applicable to the doctor, hospital, medical facility, or other health care provider in the State of the United States in which the shoreside medical care was provided.

Sec. 30511. Action by owner for limitation

(a) In General. - The owner of a vessel may bring a civil action in a district court of the United States for limitation of liability under this chapter. The action must be brought within 6 months after a claimant gives the owner written notice of a claim.

(b) Creation of Fund. - When the action is brought, the owner (at the owner's option) shall -

(1) deposit with the court, for the benefit of claimants -

(A) an amount equal to the value of the owner's interest in the vessel and pending freight, or approved security; and

(B) an amount, or approved security, that the court may fix from time to time as necessary to carry out this chapter; or

(2) transfer to a trustee appointed by the court, for the benefit of claimants -

(A) the owner's interest in the vessel and pending freight; and

(B) an amount, or approved security, that the court may fix from time to time as necessary to carry out this chapter.

(c)   Cessation of Other Actions. - When an action has been brought
       under this section and the owner has complied with subsection (b),
       all claims and proceedings against the owner related to the matter
       in question shall cease.

Sec. 30512. Liability as master, officer, or seaman not affected

This chapter does not affect the liability of an individual as a master,
officer, or seaman, even though the individual is also an owner of
the vessel.

In addition, one has to understand the meaning of the owner's "privity."
This is a term that appears in several areas of our maritime law. While
there are many facets to it, it comes down to whether the owner, or
his shoreside supervisory personnel were in any way involved, had
knowledge of, or should have had knowledge of and should have done
something. Here the case of *Tug Ocean Prince, Inc. v. United States*, 584
F.2d 1151 (2d Cir. 1978) is a good illustration. Due to the tug boat strike
in New York Harbor tug pilots from southern states were brought to
New York and one such tug pilot was hired on board the tug OCEAN
PRINCE going up the Hudson in February when there was ice on the
river. The other local man did not talk to him much and at one point
he did not pay attention to the chart and ran his tow on the reef causing
substantial pollution. In denying limitation the appeals court noted that
the shoreside supervisor should have inquired further into the man's
knowledge of the Hudson. That is a good illustration of the "owner's
privity." He should have inquired. Just saying "I did not know," when
he had an opportunity to find out is not enough.

Starting with the old standby, the case of *The Linseed King (Spencer
Kellogg & Sons v. Hicks)*, 285 U.S. 502 (1932) dealt with a ferry between
Manhattan and New Jersey sinking because it was holed by the ice in
the Hudson River. Limitation of liability was denied on the grounds

that the owner knew, should have known, that there was ice in the river and that the ferry's hull could be punctured by the ice.

Similarly, insufficient manning is unseaworthiness, *Horn v. C/A Navegacion Fruco,* 404 F.2d 422 (5ᵗʰ Cir. 1968) cert. denied 394 U.S. 943 (1969). Also see *Getty Oil Co. v. Ponce De Leon,* 409 F. Supp. 909 (SDNY 1976) aff'd 555 F.2d 328 (2d Cir. 1977).

And more recently, *In re Dieber,*793 F. Supp. 2d 632 (S.D.N.Y. 2011) where the father, the owner of the motor boat was denied limitation when his son, known to often speed and use alcohol on the boat ran into another boat causing serious injuries.

The bottom line is that the owner may not close his eyes to what he should know and should take care of.

The reading of the foregoing sections is quite tedious. And it requires several readings before the meaning sinks in. Thus, the following discussion should be of some help (after you re-read the sections).

Having reviewed the sections, your attention is drawn to the case of *Grubart v. Great Lakes Dredge & Dock Co.,* 513 U.S. 527 (1995) discussed at the end of Lecture 1, where the owner of the barge and the pile driver wanted to limit his liability to the value of the two rather insignificant vessels when the pile driving caused the tunnel to collapse and flood downtown Chicago resulting in billions worth of damages.

The crux of limitation is the concept that the casualty was caused "without the privity or knowledge of such owner or owners." Thus, in limitation of liability situations, the same as cargo damage cases caused by a collision due to the master's error in navigation, the shipowner is protected if he did not have knowledge and did not participate. But, that does not mean that the shipowner can turn a blind eye to obvious facts.

Similarly, a British case, decided during times when in fog vessels were required to proceed at such speed that the vessel could be stopped in half the distance of available visibility (meaning a crawling speed in dense fog) held the owner liable when the ferry between England and France collided in the English Channel during fog. The owner claimed that it was the Master's "error in navigation" in speeding through fog without the owner's oversight. The facts, however, showed that the ferry had been keeping its schedule for months when everyone knew that fog in the English Channel was frequently there – if the ferry had obeyed the fog rules it could not possibly have kept the schedule, which it did keep. The court held that the owners "obviously know" that the Master is frequently speeding in fog. Thus the collision was within "privity" of the owner.

The next thing is the amount of the owner's liability. As sections 30505 and 30506 state, for physical damage, such as the damage to the vessel, its loss of use during repairs, damage to cargo and any other physical damage the owner's liability "shall not exceed the value of the vessel and pending freight." Pending freight here means the unpaid or due amounts for the carriage of cargo or passengers on that voyage. Thus, for the TITANIC the physical damage claims (assuming everyone had paid for their ticket) was ZERO as the vessel ended up on the bottom of the ocean.

For personal injuries and death, under §30506 today the amount is $420 per gross ton of the vessel. In the days of the TITANIC, until 1984, it was $60 per gross ton. So, today a large passenger ship of 50,000 gross tons for personal injury and death claims would be liable up to $21 million. [Where prior to 1984 it would have been $3 million.]

The other aspects of significance are the time limits set forth in section 30508 above. As a practical matter in case of a real major casualty (usually a collision) the real thing is a "race to the court" not awaiting the passage of the six months. The reason for such a race to court is that in some countries the limitation funds are smaller. Thus, under the old sections I was involved with several cases where the real question was whether the limitation of liability was to be tried in a United States Court on the West Coast, or the East Coast (in NY) or in Korea. As between federal courts on the East or West coast the amounts would not differ, although the dockets of the courts might have significant differences. But in the mentioned case the amounts per Korean limitation statutes were different and the difference was worth several million dollars.

Upon compliance with the requirements of sections 30508 and 30509 all claims and proceedings against the owner with respect to the matter in question shall cease.

Note that this amount may be in millions of dollars, depending on (a) whether the vessel is still around and **regardless of whether the vessel still exists** an amount of the gross tonnage times $420 for death and injury claims. If he complies the last sentence of the section comes into play and

> Upon compliance with the requirements of these section all claims and proceedings against the owner with respect to the matter in question shall cease.

What this means is that the owner gets the benefit of "concursus" a very valuable tool, in that all claims will be tried in that one court per section 30511. Thus, the owner only once has to prove that he is entitled to limit liability, and all claimants have to stop their other actions in all other courts and bring their claims in that one court. This is a very powerful and beneficial tool. There are two exceptions to this:

1   The monition issued by the court to stay all other proceedings does not have "extraterritorial effect." This means that it does not reach

into a foreign country. Therefore, if a shipowner also has assets in say England or Germany, an American court's monition against other lawsuits is of no effect in England or Germany, assuming the claimant does not have "contacts" in U.S.A. where an American court could hold him in contempt for violating the monition by the American judge issued upon the filing of security.

2   The second exception deals with the "saving to suitors" clause and discussed earlier with seamens' Jones Act right to sue in state courts and have a jury. This, latter situation, however is only a partial impediment. First of all, it is still the federal court that will try and decide whether the shipowner is entitled to limit his liability. It is only if either (a) limitation is denied, or (b) the individual seaman's claim is less than the limitation amount. In such a case the federal court will send the seaman's case back to the state court with the understanding that there is the cap on the case as set forth in the federal case. This can be quite tedious. This was the effect of the prior sections. No case is known under the new statute, but it is presumed the effect will be the same.

XV

Pollution of navigable waterways and pollution abatement

Years ago people used to think that the ocean can take care of everything, and when oil was spilled, either as a result of a collision, accidental dumping or just plainly washing the tanker's tanks it was not a "big deal" unless it somehow soiled someone else's property. It took the efforts of Jacques Cousteau to convince the world that oil damaged coral and other marine organisms and that the ocean can not continue taking the pollution, that fish, shrimp, and other marine organisms were being killed by oil. So, in the United States we first had several statutes up to the Federal Water Pollution and Control Act in the 1970's and now we have the Oil Pollution Act of 1990 and many other statutes aimed at protecting the environment. The OPA 90 statute is contained in 33 U.S.C. §§ 2701 – 2761. Where years ago many things were dumped overboard, now there have to be holding tanks, treatment mechanisms and records must be kept. For example, bilge water can not be discharged overboard as it used to be done without it first being treated. Same goes for discharges from heads. Also, every time a discharge is made there must be a log entry of how the material first was treated and how many parts per million of the substance is being discharged, etc., etc. And, if there is a casualty and oil is being discharged (which happens in almost all collisions) there must be cooperation with the authorities, as otherwise there may be jail sentences to the involved officers or crew members.

The one thing that must be kept in mind is that as far as the United States Coast Guard is concerned, if oil is being discharged the ship's officers must cooperate in minimizing and stopping the discharge right away, but talking about how it happened can be delayed until there is a formal investigation. Also, the strictness of the pollution laws is such that whenever there is a casualty that results in or permits the discharge of fuel criminal attorneys need to be called in right away.

Under OPA 90 there are only 3 defenses to the discharge of oil from your ship: (1) act of God, (2) act of war, and (3) act of a "third party." And a "third party" is not an employee nor an "independent contractor" working for you. To have a "third party" defense it must be truly someone else who did it. Also, the discharging party has to prove that it exercised due care to prevent the discharge and that it had taken precautions against a third party causing the discharge. See §2703. Also, the defense of "Act of God" in the "old days" could be used for hurricanes that appeared suddenly. That no longer is the case today. Today, the weather and approaching storms are advertised more than once every day. The bottom line is that this defense most likely will not be provable as the injured party or the authorities can point to the time period when you knew, or should have known, that the heavy storm was approaching and you had time to get out of the way.

Also, there are limits to the liability for accidental discharge, but they are not small. For a vessel of 3000 gross tons or less (really a small vessel today) it is the greater of $1,200 per gross ton or $2 million (the greater being $3.6 million for a 3000 ton vessel); or $10 million for vessels greater than 3000 gross tons, and this does not include the removal costs (removal costs being the cost in picking up the oil). See §2704. Another part of this liability is the environmental damage assessment the government can make against the spiller. See §§2702 and 2706. Those costs are usually very heavy. And, one more thing needs to be noted. Prior to OPA 90 the federal statute (FWPCA) preempted any

State statutes. OPA 90 specifically permits a state to make a claim for damage to its environment in addition to such a federal claim. Thus, for example, if one spills oil in Upper Bay New York Harbor there are three entities that will come after you and levy fines or seek criminal penalties: The Federal EPA, the New York State's EPA and New Jersey's EPA.

The bottom line with oil pollution is that it becomes very expensive for the one whose ship spilled the oil.

The Oil Pollution Act of 1990, or commonly called "OPA 90" consists of many rules and is contained in 33 U.S.C. §§ 2701 – 2761. There are too many sections to be reviewed here. The full wording of the statute can be obtained on the internet and in case a need arises it can be obtained free of charge (as can be with all other U.S. Government statutes and published federal court opinions). Here we mention only a few to give you an idea of the provisions against oil pollution.

§ 2701 contains more than 40 definitions such as a "barrel" means 42 U.S. gallons at 60 ° fahrenheit; a "discharge" meaning "any emission" etc., etc.

§ 2702 sets forth the elements of liability for the individual (including companies and corporations) responsible for the discharge, whether intentional or accidental. It includes, among other things the costs in removing the oil as well as the damage it has done to other persons or property. You should take a look at this section as it is very inclusive.

§ 2703 mentions the three defenses noted before act of God, war and a third party other than an employee.

§ 2704 entitled "limits of liability" shows, among other things that the limits are large. For example a single-hull vessel is liable for $3,000 per gross ton. This means a 100,000 ton vessel can be liable for $300 million. For some others there are smaller amounts, but they all are in the millions of dollars.

Also, under the criminal sections there are provisions that can send the one in charge of the navigation at the time of the accident that resulted in the pollution to jail. Staying with the civil part there are two cases recommended for your reading that deal with many of the issues and arguments that arise from this statute. They are, *In re Oil Spill by the Oil Rig Deep Horizon,* 808 Fed. Supp. 2d 943 (E. D. La. 2011) and *Exxon Shipping Co. v. Baker*, 554 U.S. 471 (2008). The main issue in the latter was the question of punitive damages in oil spill cases. There was no 5 justice majority as the Chief Justice did not participate having worked on the case before joining the bench and the others could not agree to a 5 justice majority. However, in discussing the issues by the various justices who wrote separate opinions it was clear that they had considered the approach to punitive damages in all 50 states and saw that there were many different ways of dealing with the punitive damages amounts. The only thing that comes out of this opinion, although not as a specific ruling, is that punitive damages can and most likely will be awarded in maritime pollution situations.

XVI

Salvage

This is another area in maritime law that has a long history. One who helps another to extricate himself from a marine peril is entitled to receive a salvage award. That is not so on land. As an example, consider yourself walking down 52nd street in Manhattan on the east side and you see a house on fire, people excited and you run in and see a valuable Rubens painting on the wall about to be consumed by the flames. You grab the painting and bring it out to the street. After the firemen put out the fire the owner of the painting thanks you profusely for saving the painting. Do you have to give it back? – Yes. Are you entitled to a reward? – No. Now consider the same situation on Mr. Rockefeller's yacht in the 72nd street marina. Again, the yacht is on fire and you jump on board and save the painting. After the fire is put out Mr. Rockefeller wants the painting back, but you say: "I am entitled to salvage." Are you right? – Yes, you are entitled to salvage remuneration.

The "reward" idea is to encourage seamen to go to aid the ones in peril at sea. Over the years salvage developed into a business. Up until the end of World War II and some 20 years thereafter there were a number of large salvage companies on the East Coast, the most famous being Merrit, Chapman & Scott. Things have changed and now there are very few such companies in the United States. In New York Harbor there is one – Don John, but salvage is not its only business. Worldwide there used to be salvage ships on station in areas of the world where casualties were frequent, but even that practice has been minimized. There are three large salvage companies, two in Holland and one in Germany, Wijsmuller, Smit and Bugsier, respectively. Today, however they keep most of their equipment in warehouses with airplanes (some seaplanes) ready to travel on moments' notice.

How do we determine how much remuneration you are entitled to? The leading case for that goes back to 1870, *The Blackwall*, 77 U.S. 1 (1869), where the court stated that Courts of admiralty usually consider the following circumstances as the main ingredients in determining the amount of the reward to be decreed for a salvage service: (1) The labor expended by the salvors in rendering the salvage service. (2) The promptitude, skill, and energy displayed in rendering the service and saving the property. (3) The value of the property employed by the salvors in rendering the service, and the danger to which such property was exposed. (4) The risk incurred by the salvors in securing the property from the impending peril. (5) The value of the property saved. (6) The degree of danger from which the property was rescued.

Compensation as salvage is not viewed by the admiralty courts merely as pay, on the principle of a *quantum meruit*, or as a remuneration PRO OPERE ET LABORE, but as a reward given for perilous services, voluntarily rendered, and as an inducement to seamen and others to embark in such undertakings to save life and property. Also, over the years a standard form of salvage agreement has been worked out and is almost always used. That is the standard Lloyds Standard form of Salvage agreement. Up until 1990's the usual form was almost exclusively, no cure – no pay with a provision that the amount of the award would be arbitrated in London by the professional salvage arbitrators there. That pretty much still is the practice, with two exceptions. Firstly, there was a salvage convention that has been entered into by most countries in 1989, and secondly the recognition of the harm being done to the marine environment by oil pollution has had an impact on salvage agreements.

More particularly the now are the "Scopic" provisions that deal with payment to the salvor, even if the entire attempt is not successful, for his success in minimizing pollution. The Appendix has the current Lloyds Standard Form Salvage Agreement.

One other thing needs to be kept in mind. While the Lloyd's agreement is well known it provides for the resolution of the matter or any dispute in England. There the rules provide that the loser has to pay the winner's attorney fees. In the United States in most situations each side pays for its own attorney and only in special situations the court will award the other side's attorney fees as a penalty. In England it is not that easy to determine who is the "winner" and who the "loser" in salvage situations. The fact that this is an issue must be kept in mind.

XVII

General Average

This is an ancient concept and, as some contend, it is the forerunner of marine insurance. Again we go back to the idea that maritime law has been applied for many centuries, really thousands of years, as long as people have traded. Most of our knowledge deals with the beginning of trade in the Mediterranean. So, let us begin with a voyage by a vessel from the Greek island Rhodes to Carthage, Hanibals's home, on the shores of North Africa some centuries before year 1 A.D. And let us imagine that Owner and Master of the vessel Dimitri had a ship and he made regular voyages between Rhodes and Carthage and that the value of his vessel was 100 Drahmes. On one such voyage he carried 9 merchants each bringing along his cargo worth 100 Drahmes, so that at the beginning of the voyage the total value was 1,000 Drahmes. The voyage proceeds nicely until a heavy storm kicks up and pushes the vessel onto a sand bar. Waves crash over the ship and threaten the breaking up of the vessel. In order to get off the sand bar Dimitri orders that the cargo of merchant 1 and merchant 2 be thrown overboard to lighten the ship. This is done and the ship floats over the sand bar and after the storm reaches Carthage. There merchants 3 – 9 all sell their cargo but merchants 1 and 2, of course, are out of luck. But, if the cargo of merchants 1 and 2 had not been sacrificed the entire voyage would have ended in disaster. Thus the other interests, Dimitri and merchants 3 – 9 have to "contribute" towards the general sacrifice, or "general average" (the word "average" here meaning loss). As the "general" loss was 200 Drahmes and there were ten interests, each has to pay 20 Drahmes. So Dimitri and merchants 3 – 9 each pays 20 Drahmes to merchants 1 and 2 so that each participant bears a 20 Drahme loss.

Today the principal is the same. The necessary elements for a General Average incident are: (1) The voyage must be in peril; (2) There must be a voluntary sacrifice (or expenditure) in order to save the venture; and (3) There must be success as a result of the sacrifice, you must reach port.

Thus, if Dimitri's ship had sunk anyway before it reached Carthage there would be no general average despite the initial sacrifice and its success of getting off the strand.

The shipowner's ability to collect from cargo G/A contributions is one reason why cargo owners should have cargo insurance, as cargo underwriters will regularly give the shipowner guarantees for payment of G/A contributions. If there is no such guarantee then the shipowner has a right not to release the cargo until he gets such a guarantee.

Earlier in the discussion in the Time Charter party you came across the "New Jason Clause." That is a clause that almost invariably is part of all bills of lading. It is a contractual provision that obligates cargo to contribute in General Average even if the ship is at fault for the events leading to the need for the general sacrifice. The Jason Clause in contracts of carriage (bills of lading and charters) came about as a result of a case called the *Irrawady (Flint v. Christall),*171 U.S. 187 (1898) which held that "a ship at fault" can not recover general average contributions from cargo. So shipowners came up with a clause in the contract of carriage stating that even if the ship is at fault, the shipowner can recover G/A contributions. In a case called *The Jason*, 225 U.S. 32 (1912) the validity of such a clause was upheld. As the rules changed over the years and the so called Hague Rules dealing with average adjustments came about the wording of the Jason clause was amended and now we have the "New Jason Clause" fully quoted on Bills of Lading and in the Time and Voyage Charter Parties.

This also brings up the subject of "non separation agreements." These are situations where a ship has met with a casualty and has to spend time repairing the ship before it can proceed. In such cases the question comes up whether the cargo should be stored while the ship is repairing or whether it should be sent forward on another ship. The decision is one of economics.

If the ship was seriously damaged and requires drydocking the cargo has to be unloaded and stored while the ship is repaired as a ship with heavy cargo can not be drydocked. The unloading, reloading and storage charges very likely would be valid general average expenses. Thus the question comes up whether it would be less expensive and better for both the shipowner and the various cargo owners to forward the cargo on another ship. The practical problem is the expense and the arrangements for it. If it is sent forward the ship loses its custodial right for the cargo's general average proportion. The way that often is dealt with, is that the cargo's underwriter (or the owner) gives the shipowner a so called "non separation agreement" – a guarantee to pay the cargo's appropriate general average contributions when the casualty's general average settlement is made.

XVIII

Marine Insurance

Marine Insurance is a subject usually covered by a separate course at the Maritime College. Here we look at the four policies that usually are part of almost all ocean shipments. Yes, there are others, but these are the four basic marine insurance policies.

One is for the cargo that is shipped and the other three deal with the type of ship operation that exists at that particular situation.

Practical maritime law really does not exist without reference to marine insurance. In fact, marine business cannot exist without marine insurance. In carrying out marine business will there be claims against marine policies? – Yes, invariably YES!!!

That is so because marine business has many dangerous aspects some of which almost always cause or result in damage to some property. Such property damage usually is quite expensive.

Marine insurance is different from land insurance in that dealing with your homeowner's insurance you do not expect your house to burn down, you do not expect to have a serious automobile casualty. But, as a shipowner will you have maritime claims? – Yes. The ocean is very unforgiving, ships do not drive like automobiles or bicycles. Thus, marine insurance is based on the party's existing or anticipated "loss record" initially based on the type of business or policy (freighter, tanker, tugboat, passenger ship etc.) and the company's actual loss record. Marine policies are usually written for a one year period, so the loss record is always reviewed at the end of the year.

Although there are a number of other insurances one can buy, such as charterer's liability, loss of profits, etc., the three basic marine policies for the shipowner (as distinguished from the cargo policy taken out by the cargo owner) are: 1 – Hull insurance; 2 – Protection & Indemnity insurance (commonly referred to as "P & I"); and 3 – War risk insurance. The names are self explanatory, except for a few brief comments.

The hull insurance is a valued policy and actually is four (4) policies in one in that the underwriter can wind up paying out four times the face value of the policy. The four parts are: (a) Physical damage to your ship – paying for the costs repairing your ship.

(b) Collision liability – liability the shipowner has to the other ship if his ship winds up in a collision. (c) The ship's proportion of General Average and Salvage expenses. (d) - Sue and labor expenses – the cost of the shipowner traveling in the preservation of the ship after a casualty, including the hiring of attorneys to litigate the liabilities arising after a casualty. Hull insurance can pay up to the face value of the policy for each of the four subjects noted. Up to what amount? Depends on the agreement between the shipowner and his underwriter. Here is how it works.

The Hull policy is a "Valued" policy. This means that at the beginning of the insurance year the shipowner and his underwriter agree that the ship is worth say $20 million, a fair market value for that ship. Premiums are based on the type of ship it is, its age and the reputation and experience of the operator. The next thing after agreeing on the value is the amount insured. It can be 100% or a lesser percentage. If the percentage is less, say 80% then the premium will be less but for every loss the underwriter will only pay 80% and the shipowner remains as co-insurer. And, the shipowner must make the repairs and pay his 20% to keep the ship operating. Also, there can be either a "franchise" or a "deductible" for every incident (here really voyages).

A deductible works the same as automobile deductibles. If there is a $5,000 deductible the shipowner bears the first $5,000 of every loss, the underwriter paying amounts above that up to the limit of the policy.

A "franchise" on the other hand works differently. A $5,000 franchise means that for the first $5,000 the underwriter pays nothing. But if the loss is $5000. 01 the underwriter pays the entire loss.

P & I insurance insures the shipowner's liabilities to other parties. It pays for crew member and visitor injuries, seamen repatriation, maintenance and cure payments to injured crew members, damage to cargo, wash damage to marinas if the vessel goes up river too fast and causes damage on shore, fines to governments, wreck removal, pollution liabilities, generally liabilities to third parties. Prior to Oil Pollution Act of 1990 those amounts did not have limits, now they do for pollution liabilities, the basic usually being $3 million with ability to buy up to $30 million.

The third is war risk insurance. This covers the usual exclusions from the hull policy for war-like acts, strikes, riots, civil commotions, capture by pirates or other unfriendly governments. Nuclear disasters in most cases are excluded, although some unwarlike incidents are covered.

XIX

Criminal Issues for the Mariner and Maritime Executives

Unfortunately, today both shoreside and shipboard maritime professionals and particularly ships' officers - masters, mates and engineers must be vigilant in not breaking any criminal laws. In any marine pollution incident or mass casualty, there are many law enforcement agencies and prosecutors who are ever vigilant to prosecute individuals and corporations.

In the United States, mariners have been prosecuted for maritime manslaughter in the Staten Island Ferry allision in 2003, the magic pipe cases involving engineers by passing the Oily Water Separator and making false log entries re discharges of fluids and in oil pollution cases for violating the Migratory Bird Acts and other environmental crimes. Criminal law has gone to sea!

In the United States we have both federal and state prosecutors. In the federal system, we have the U.S. Attorney's Office for the various federal districts in the 50 states and territories and Commonwealth of Puerto Rico. In addition, there are state and county prosecutors in the 50 states who have jurisdiction to prosecute violations of state law. In a grounding in the Kill van Kull the waterway which separates Staten Island, New York from Bayonne, New Jersey, there were representatives from approximately 20 different federal, state, county and city environmental and law enforcement agencies and prosecutors.

In the United States, the U.S. Coast Guard is the chief maritime law enforcement agency. Their marine investigators have federal law enforcement status and can arrest. In the case of U.S. mariners, the Coast Guard is the licensing and regulatory agency and has the investigatory role and can recommend suspension and revocation of licenses and prosecution by the U.S. Attorney's office.

In any maritime casualty, the Coast Guard is normally the first responder and they have a primary role of rescue and recovery. Then they have an investigatory role and can subpoena witnesses to attend informal and formal proceedings.

A mariner who is involved in a casualty must cooperate with the Coast Guard in curtailing the on going emergency and prevent further damage, pollution and save lives and property. The issue of 5th Amendment and potential criminal liability may arise in the initial response. Ships' officers and crew should never lie to government investigators. Lying to a federal official may and often does constitute Obstruction of Justice under 18 U.S.C. 1001.

Fifth Amendment Considerations and Miranda Warnings

Most times, the Coast Guard investigating officers feel that they need not give Miranda warnings to mariners because they have not arrested a person nor have they been taken into custody. However, mariners, after assisting in preventive measures should decline to speak to investigators, Coast Guard and/or law enforcement officers regarding the potential causes and their involvement until they have had an opportunity to talk to THEIR attorney. Now more so than ever, it is important for the mariner and maritime executive to know that the attorney that they are talking to does not have a conflict with the company and other employees. If necessary, a witness should invoke their rights under the Fifth Amendment of the U.S. Constitution.

When and How to Invoke the Fifth Amendment Privilege Against Self-Incrimination

The Fifth Amendment of the U.S. Constitution states in part:

> "No person shall be held to answer for a capital, or otherwise infamous crime, unless on presentment or indictment of a Grand Jury, except in cases arising in the land or naval forces, or in the Militia, when in actual service in time of War or public danger . . . nor shall be compelled in any criminal case to be a witness against himself . . ."

A. Informal or Investigatory Procedures

The invocation of a party's fifth amendment privilege against self-incrimination is consistent with innocence in a criminal investigation. *Grunewald v. United States*, 353 U.S. 391 (1956). "The privilege serves to protect the innocent who otherwise might be ensnared by ambiguous circumstances." *Slochower v. Board of Higher Educ.*, 350 U.S. 551, 557-58 (1956).

In *Grunewald*, supra, a grand jury subpoenaed a witness to testify before it regarding corruption at the Bureau of Internal Revenue. The witness declined to answer certain questions on grounds that the answers might incriminate him. At his trial, the witness answered the same questions posed by the grand jury before, consistent with his innocence. On cross examination, the government used his previous assertion of the privilege to impeach his credibility. The witness/defendant objected and on appeal, the Court did not consider this type of cross-examination permissible because invoking the fifth amendment is not tantamount to an admission of culpability. Id. At 421.

A witness who desires the privilege against self-incrimination must claim the privilege or he will not be considered to have been "compelled within the meaning of the Amendment." *United States v. Monia*, 317 U.S. 424, 427 (1943). The privilege is "deemed waived unless invoked." *United States v. Murdock*, 284 U.S. 141, 148 (1931). Further, the Court has made it clear that an individual may lose the benefit of the privilege against self-incrimination without making a knowing and intelligent waiver of the privilege. *Garner v. United States*, 424 U.S. 648, 653, 654 n. 9 (1976); see also *Schneckloth v. Bustamonte*, 412 U.S. 218, 227, 235-40 (1973). Thus, the absence of counsel may result in waiver by ignorance.

It is well settled that disclosure of a fact by a witness waives the privilege as to details about that fact. *Rogers v. United States*, 340 U.S. 367, 372-73 (1951); see also *Brown v. Walker*, 161 U.S. 591, 597 (1896). In *Rogers v. United States*, 340 U.S. 367 (1951) the witness before a grand jury freely admitted being a member of the Communist Party. The witness refused to identify to whom she turned over certain documents on the grounds of not subjecting that party to "the same thing I was going through." Id. At 368. She was held in contempt of court. In affirming the contempt charge on appeal, the Supreme Court reasoned where incriminating facts have been voluntarily revealed, the privilege cannot be invoked to avoid disclosure of the details. Id. At 373.

The question then is when should a witness invoke his or her fifth amendment privilege? The simple answer is, the first time an incriminating question is asked, because failure to do so means the privilege is waived. See *McCormack on Evidence*, §§ 130, 132 (3d ed. 1984).

Mariners, including pilots, are required by statute or regulation to report marine casualties and provide a description of what occurred to the authorities, whether it is the Coast Guard or Pilot Board. See, e.g., 33 U.S.C. §§ 1321(b)(5)(1988). A master, mate or pilot accurately completing the report might provide incriminating evidence and should be very careful on how to comply with the requirements and regulations. Thus, they should seek legal advice before completing "Report of Maritime Casualty."

In a Florida State Court decision, *McDonald v. Dep't of Professional Regulation, Bd. of Pilot Comm'rs*, 582 So.2d 660 (Fla.Dist.Ct.App. 1991) one of the issues raised by the appellant pilot was that Section 310.111 Fla.Stat.Ann. §§ 310.111 (West 1991) of the Florida Statues required a pilot to report a casualty to the Board of Commissioners within 48 hours and Section 310.101(1)(g), Fla.Stat.Ann. § 310.101 (West 1991) provided that failing to file the report or making a false report were grounds for disciplinary action. The court held that there was no violation of the pilot's fifth amendment privilege because he could have filed the report and asserted therein his privilege at whatever time he believed a truthful statement would be self-incriminating. *McDonald*, 582 So.2d at 662-63. The court stated, "As this avenue was available to him, his fifth amendment right was not self-executing." Id. At 663; see also *Minnesota v. Murphy*, 465 U.S. 420, 434-39 (1984). Thus, the court held that the pilot forfeited his fifth amendment privilege because he failed to timely assert it in the original report to the Board. 582 So.2d at 663.

Witnesses should be aware of their rights - Attorneys representing witnesses should counsel their clients before they give evidence at a Coast Guard or NTSB proceeding. Counsel must explain to them their fifth amendment privilege against self-incrimination and give clear advice on their recommendation. Coast Guard investigating officers may at the conclusion of the investigation recommend further legal action against the witness. 46 U.S.C. § 6301 (1988). Such actions may include providing federal and/or state prosecutors with copies of the Coast Guard report, if the investigating officer finds evidence of possible criminal violations. 46 C.F.R. § 4.32-1 (1990). The possibility that the investigating officer may feel obliged to turn over the results of his/her investigation to prosecutors is enough to make any attorney representing an individual in a marine casualty investigation think very carefully of advising his clients early on concerning fifth amendment rights and the consequence of giving self-incriminating evidence to the Coast Guard, even at an informal casualty investigation.

B. Formal Proceedings.

Similar considerations arise during formal hearings before the U.S. Coast Guard and the NTSB. Again, maritime attorneys should carefully explain to the witness his or her rights and point out that the fifth amendment privilege must be invoked early to preclude waiver. Some attorneys recommend that clients invoke their fifth amendment privilege after answering the so-called pedigree questions as to name, address, place and date of birth. This is not meant to be disruptive to the conduct of the proceedings, but only to safeguard the rights of the witnesses before that particular tribunal and any later criminal proceeding.

The Coast Guard investigating officer or marine board may issue a subpoena requiring a person to appear and bring certain documents or other evidence requested by the subpoena. The Coast Guard does not have the power to enforce its subpoenas and must look to the federal courts for enforcement. A witness may challenge a subpoena in court on any appropriate ground. *Reisman v. Caplin*, 375 U.S. 440, 449 (1964); see also *United States v. Henry*, 491 F.2d 702, 705 (6th Cir. 1974). This includes the defense that the material sought is for the improper purpose of obtaining evidence for use in criminal prosecutions. *Reisman*, 375 U.S. 440 at 449. Furthermore, if individual witnesses move to quash the subpoena and thereafter appear at the Coast Guard hearing, they still may invoke the fifth amendment privilege at any time during the hearing. *Ionian Shipping Co. v. British Law Ins. Co.*, 314 F.Supp. 1121, 1124 (S.D.N.Y. 1970).

Foreign seamen are also entitled to the protection of the fifth amendment when called to testify in proceedings before the Coast Guard, NTSB or other agencies, including federal and state grand juries. The court in *Mishima v. United States*, 507 F.Supp. 131 (D. Alaska 1981) held that Japanese seamen could invoke fifth amendment rights in a U.S. Coast Guard hearing on the ground that incriminating statements made therein could be used against them in Japan. Id. At 135.

C. Types of Immunity

Witnesses called to testify before the U.S. Coast Guard, the NTSB or other federal agencies may be granted testimonial immunity, also called use immunity. 18 U.S.C. §§ 6001, 6002, 6004 (1988). The procedure is as follows: the witness should attend at the time and place designated in the subpoena and upon being questioned, refuse to answer on the basis of his or her fifth amendment privilege against self-incrimination. The person presiding over the proceeding must dispense with either the questioning and/or recess and seek to obtain an order of immunity from the Attorney General or his/her authorized Deputy Attorney General, and then communicate the order of immunity to the person appearing before the agency. 46 U.S.C. § 6304 (1988); 46 C.F.R. § 4.07 (1990). U.S. attorneys may also grant use immunity with the approval of the Attorney General or his/her authorized Deputy. 18 U.S.C. § 6003(b) (1988). It should be noted that federal use immunity, if the order so provides, may also shield the witness from state prosecution as well.

There are two separate types of immunity, use (or testimonial) immunity and transactional immunity. Immunity granted under 18 U.S.C. §§ 6001-6005 is use immunity as distinguished from transactional immunity. See *Tierney v. United States*, 409 U.S. 1232 (1972)(Douglas, Cir.J.). Use immunity protects a witness from prosecution based upon any statements and evidence that is derived from immunized testimony that is presented to a grand jury or other investigating body. Transactional immunity, on the other hand, is much broader than use immunity and protects the witness from any and all prosecution arising out of the same set of facts. In any subsequent criminal case, determining what evidence is derived from use-immunized testimony can be a problem. The problem was highlighted in the case of Lieutenant Colonel Oliver North ("North"). Prior to his criminal trial, North was required to testify before a congressional committee where he was given use immunity for his testimony before the committee. When he was later tried by the Special Prosecutor, the issue successfully taken on appeal was whether or not the Special Prosecutor used any evidence obtained by or derived from the congressional committee hearing at which North testified pursuant to use immunity. *United States v. North*, 910 F.2d 843 (D.C.Cir.1990), en banc, modified, reh'g denied, in part, 920 F.2d 940 (D.C.Cir. 1990). Sorting evidence given under use immunity from evidence obtained by other sources - Although the government may not use use-immunized testimony, nor any fruits thereof, as evidence in a later criminal proceeding, it may use any evidence for which it can show an independent source. Such "independent source" evidence must be derived from a legitimate source wholly independent of the immunized testimony. *Kastigar v. United States*, 406 U.S. 441, 460 (1972) - is a procedural nightmare. One should walk very carefully in this area and seek the advice of competent criminal defense counsel before venturing too far into this mine field.

Procedures for obtaining immunity from state grand juries vary from state to state. In New York, a witness called to testify before a grand jury has use immunity for anything on which he or she testifies. N.Y.Crim. Proc.Law § 190.40 (McKinney 1982). A different approach is taken in New Jersey, where a witness called before a grand jury does not automatically have use immunity and must exercise his or her fifth amendment privilege; upon doing so, the witness is taken before a special grand jury judge who, after hearing from the state why the witness should be required to testify, issues an order of immunity to the witness. N.J.Stat.Ann. § 2A:81-17.3 (West 1976). As these procedures vary from state to state, maritime attorneys should work closely with criminal defense counsel to safeguard the rights of maritime professionals called to testify in grand jury proceedings, as well as any state administrative hearing.

In addition to being granted at a federal or state proceeding, immunity may also be provided by statute. One major federal statute providing use immunity is included in the Federal Water Pollution Control Act (FWCPA). 33 U.S.C. § 1321(b)(5)(1988). FWCPA requires that any person in charge of a vessel or facility that discharges oil must immediately notify the government of the discharge, and that in any later criminal proceeding, neither the statement of notification nor any information obtained in exploitation of the notification may be used as evidence in a criminal trial against the notifier. Id.

Immunity granted under FWPCA provided the grounds for a successful appeal of criminal charges in the case of Joseph Hazelwood, Master of the EXXON VALDEZ. Captain Hazelwood's state conviction for negligent discharge of oil was reversed because the evidence used to convict was based on the fruits of the immunized report under FWPCA, and the state did not meet its burden of showing an "independent source" for the evidence. *Hazelwood v. State*, 836 P.2d 943, 954, 1992 AMC 2423 (Alaska Ct.App. 1992).

The protections of legislatively granted immunity have also been extended to corporations in some instances, even though as a rule corporations are not entitled to the protections of the privilege against self-incrimination. In *United States v. Mobil Oil Corp.*, 464 F.2d 1124 (5th Cir. 1972), an employee of Mobil reported, pursuant to FWPCA, a discharge into a navigable creek. Mobil was subsequently convicted of violating the Rivers and Harbors Act 33 U.S.C. § 407, 411, based solely on the employee's report and the fruits thereof. On appeal, the conviction was reversed because the court held that use immunity granted under FWPCA extended to corporations as well as individuals reasoning that to rule otherwise would frustrate the purpose of granting use immunity, which is to obtain quick reports of discharges to facilitate measure to minimize or abate environmental damage. *United States v. Mobil Oil Corp.*, 464 F.2d at 1127.

Maritime Manslaughter

In October 2003 the Staten Island Ferry, ANDREW BARBERI, struck the ferry terminal killing 11 passengers and injuring 76 passengers. The Master, Captain Smith, and the Marine Superintendent, Patrick Ryan, both plead guilty to maritime manslaughter and making false statements to the Coast Guard and were sentenced to imprisonment.

In the COSTA CONCORDIA grounding off the Italian Coast, the Master was tried and convicted of manslaughter and sentenced to prison.

In Korea, the master of the ferry boat involved in a sinking was convicted of manslaughter/murder and sentenced to prison.

Thus, Masters and Watch-Standers must be cognizant of their rights.

The Dangers of Concurrent Civil and Criminal Proceedings

The next major issue which a witness must face is the danger of concurrent civil and criminal proceedings. The fifth amendment provides that a witness shall not be compelled in any criminal case to be a witness against himself. U.S.Const. Amend V. But in a civil proceeding, the witness's testimony may incriminate the speaker or expand discovery beyond Federal Rules of Criminal Procedure 16(b), Fed.R.Crim.Pro. 16(b) which would allow the evidence into the criminal proceeding. See *Securities and Exchange Comm'n v. Dresser*, 628 F.2d 1368, 1375 (D.C.1980) (en banc), cert. Denied, 449 U.S. 993 (1980).

It is common for a civil action to be commenced immediately following a maritime casualty. In the absence of substantial prejudice to the rights of the parties involved, such parallel proceedings are objectionable. *Dresser*, 628 F.2d at 1374. In many cases, vessel owners will file an action seeking Exoneration from or Limitation of Liability. 46 U.S.C.App. § 181 (1988). Any witness with relevant information to the limitation case may also be the target or subject of a pending state and/or federal grand jury. Furthermore, the target or subject of the grand jury may become a party defendant in the civil case. If one of the claimants or parties to the civil action subpoenas the witness or party who is a target of the grand jury, the party subpoenaed should promptly move for a protective order under Federal Rules of Civil Procedure 30(b) Fed.R.Civ.P. 30(b) postponing the deposition until termination of the criminal action. See. *United States v. Kordal*, 397 U.S. 19 (1970) (quoting Paul Haragan & Sons v. Enterprise Animal Oil Co., 14 F.R.D. 333 (E.D.PA. 1953)).

In practice, a civil case will rarely be tried before the criminal case because the criminal proceeding will usually be adjudicated prior to the trial of the civil action. However, the party subject to a grand jury investigation who is also a party defendant in a civil case should not be pressured into giving testimony in the civil action. Such testimony would probably be deemed a waiver of the fifth amendment privilege in the criminal proceeding. The appropriate remedy would be for a protective order under Rule 30(b) Fed.R.Civ.P. 30(b). 5 U.S.F. Mar. L.J. 357 postponing civil discovery until termination of the criminal action.

Conclusion

This chapter has touched on those issues that may face the maritime professional as soon as a pollution incident or casualty occurs. In light of the Oil Pollution Act of 1990, witnesses must consider more than mere civil liability. He or she must be aware of criminal implications, most notably the fifth amendment privilege against self-incrimination during investigations and formal proceedings. Additionally, potential conflict of interest issues may arise and need to be anticipated along with the criminal possibilities. The need for witnesses to contact competent criminal defense attorneys is apparent.

Today, owners, P & I Clubs, and maritime attorneys have to work with criminal defense lawyers to protect the rights of both shoreside and shipboard personnel. In today's environment, mariners on the navigable waters of the United States involved in a spill or casualty can be charged with negligent discharge or other serious crimes even where personnel are not under the influence of drugs or alcohol or acting recklessly. The federal government and/or the state government can charge that individual with illegal discharge of petroleum products with the possibility of imprisonment or heavy fines. Mariners and other maritime professionals must be vigilant to obey all laws and when and if involved in a marine incident, must promptly seek competent advice.

Table of cases cited

Appendix

The federal courts and reported case system

The court system in the U.S.A. The Federal Circuits, District Courts the Supreme Court and the 50 States and the District of Columbia.

For a very mundane technical discussion of where one can find our federal maritime cases. This is a country where decisions by the courts are open to the public. While there are some areas, such as child molestation or especially intimate situations where the court can seal the record, the opinions of the judges are open to the public. Except for minor procedural rulings, the opinions of the courts are printed and published. There are reporter systems for all the state court systems, but these are not discussed here. Their workings are similar to the federal system. Here we briefly look at the federal and the Maritime reporters.

Within the last few years, because of the extended use of the internet, most federal opinions can be found on the internet by going into the particular court's website and obtaining the text of the opinion. Also, most maritime colleges subscribe to the published versions of the cases. For most the "West" system is the accepted method and is described here. Also, there are the American Maritime Cases reports that can be found in the libraries of maritime colleges.

Here follows the West system for the federal cases. Keep in mind that ALL opinions of the United States Supreme Court and the eleven Circuit Courts of Appeals are transcribed and published. For the federal district courts most substantive opinions are published.

The official reporter systems are:

For the Supreme Court: Case Name, Volume, U.S., Page (year), thus: City of Milwaukee v. Cement Div. National Gypsum, 515 U.S. 189 (1995)

For the eleven federal Circuit Courts of Appeals:
Name,Volume Fed. [or F.2d, or F.3rd] page (Circuit, year), thus:
Tagarapulos, S.A. v. S.S. Santa Paula, 502 F.2d 1171 (9th Cir. 1974)

For the various district Courts: Name, F. Supp. [or F. Supp. 2d] (Court year), thus:
Atlantic Ship Supply Inc. v. M/V Lucy, 392 F. Supp. 179 (M.D. Fla. 1975)

There also is a set of volumes entitled 'Federal Rules Decisions' that deal with opinions deciding procedural questions. While procedural issues and decisions are very important and can determine which way a case goes, that is not treated here as doing so would require extensive review of rules of procedure.

More importantly, there are the volumes published by the American Maritime Cases, which volumes are in the library at the Maritime College. The system started in 1923 and still is active. It publishes most maritime related opinions. The format is:

Case name, Year, A.M.C., Page (Court, year), thus:
Reliable Transfer Co., Inc. v. United States, 1975 A.M.C. 541 (1975) on remand 975 A.M.C. 1508 (2d Cir. 1975).

The A.M.C. cases almost exclusively deal with admiralty matters, but also include major rulings on evidence or apportionment of fault that may apply to admiralty. The use of the "West" system is more for the use by attorneys and the courts. For all popular Supreme Court decisions one can go to the Supreme Court website and get the opinion's full text. Similarly, the federal Circuit Courts of Appeals and many District Courts now have their opinions on the internet. This applies to all kinds of cases, civil and criminal.

Federal Employees Liability Act 45 U.S.C. §§ 51-56

— **Initially created for railroad workers – now also applicable to seamen**

§ 51 Every common carrier by railroad . . . shall be liable in damages to any person suffering injury while he is employed by such carrier in such commerce, or, in case of the death of such employee, to his or her personal representative, for the benefit of the surviving widow or husband and children of such employee; and, if none, then of such employee's parents; and, if none, then of the next of kin dependent upon such employee, for such injury or death resulting in whole or in part from the negligence of any of the officers, agents, or employees of such carrier, or by reason of any defect or insufficiency, due to its negligence, in its cars, engines, appliances, machinery, track, roadbed, works, boats, wharves, or other equipment * * *.

§ 52 Every common carrier by railroad . . . shall be liable in damages to any person suffering injury while he is employed by such carrier in any of said jurisdictions, or, **in case of the death of such employee, to his or her personal representative, for the benefit of the surviving widow or husband and children of such employee; and, if none, then of such employee's parents; and, if none, then of the next of kin dependent upon such employee,** for such injury or death resulting in whole or in part from the negligence of any of the officers, agents, or employees of such carrier, or by reason of any defect or insufficiency, due to its negligence, in its cars, engines, appliances, machinery, track, roadbed, works, boats, wharves, or other equipment. (Emphasis supplied.)

§ 53 In all actions . . . the fact that the employee may have been guilty of **contributory negligence shall not bar a recovery**, but the damages shall be diminished by the jury in proportion to the amount of negligence attributable to such employee: *Provided,* That no such employee who may be injured or killed shall be held to have been guilty of contributory negligence in any case where the violation by such common carrier of any statute enacted for the safety of employees contributed to the injury or death of such employee. (Emphasis supplied.)

§ 54 In any action brought against any common carrier under or by virtue of any of the provisions of this chapter to recover damages for injuries to, or the death of, any of its employees, **such employee shall not be held to have assumed the risks of his employment** . . . and no employee shall be held to have assumed the risks of his employment in any case where the violation by such common carrier of any statute enacted for the safety of employees contributed to the injury or death of such employee. (Emphasis supplied.)

§ 55 **Any contract, rule, regulation, or device** whatsoever, the purpose or intent of which shall be **to enable any common carrier to exempt itself from any liability** created by this chapter, **shall to that extent be void** * * * (Emphasis supplied.)

§ 56 No action shall be maintained under this chapter unless commenced within three years from the day the cause of action accrued.

c

Liability of Water Carriers to Cargo the Vessel carries

The relationship between the vessel's owner and the owner of the cargo.

Originally enacted as the Carriage of Goods by Sea Act in 1936, to supplement the Harter Act of 1893, in 2006 when Chapter 46 of the U.S. Code was revamped and the water carrier liabilities were set forth in the "new" Harter Act the same text and provisions were included in the "new" 46 U.S.C. § 30701. Only now the same wording is all in § 30701 with new subsections. The relevant parts of the new section are quoted here.

TITLE I

Section 1. When used in this Act -

(a) The term 'carrier' includes the owner or the charterer who enters into a contract of carriage with a shipper.
(b) The term 'contract of carriage' applies only to contracts of carriage covered by a bill of lading or any similar document of title, insofar as such document relates to the carriage of goods by sea, including any bill of lading or any similar document as aforesaid issued under or pursuant to a charter party from the moment at which such

bill of lading or similar document of title regulates the relations between a carrier and a holder of the same.

(c) The term 'goods' includes goods, wares, merchandise, and articles of every kind whatsoever, except live animals and cargo which by the contract of carriage is stated as being carried on deck and is so carried.

(d) The term 'ship' means any vessel used for the carriage of goods by sea.

(e) The term 'carriage of goods' covers the period from the time when the goods are loaded on to the time when they are discharged from the ship.

* * *

Sec. 3. Responsibilities and liabilities

(1) The carrier shall be bound, before and at the beginning of the voyage, to exercise due diligence to--
   (a) Make the ship seaworthy;
   (b) Properly man, equip, and supply the ship;
   (c) Make the holds, refrigerating and cooling chambers, and all other parts of the ship in which goods are carried, fit and safe for their reception, carriage, and preservation.

(2) The carrier shall properly and carefully load, handle, stow, carry, keep, care for, and discharge the goods carried.

(3) After receiving the goods into his charge the carrier, or the master or agent of the carrier, shall, on demand of the shipper, issue to the shipper a bill of lading showing among other things-
   (a) The leading marks necessary for identification of the goods as the same are furnished in writing by the shipper before the loading of such goods starts, provided such marks are stamped or otherwise shown clearly upon the goods if uncovered, or

on the cases or coverings in which such goods are contained, in such a manner as should ordinarily remain legible until the end of the voyage.

(b) Either the number of packages or pieces, or the quantity or weight, as the case may be, as furnished in writing by the shipper.

(c) The apparent order and condition of the goods: *Provided*, That no carrier, master, or agent of the carrier, shall be bound to state or show in the bill of lading any marks, number, quantity, or weight which he has reasonable ground for suspecting not accurately to represent the goods actually received, or which he has had no reasonable means of checking.

(4) Such a bill of lading shall be prima facie evidence of the receipt by the carrier of the goods as therein described in accordance with paragraphs (3)(a), (b), and (c), of this section: Provided, That nothing in this Act shall be construed as repealing or limiting the application of any part of the Act, as amended, entitled 'An Act relating to bills of lading in interstate and foreign commerce', approved August 29, 1916 (U.S.C., title 49, secs. 81-124), commonly known as the 'Pomerene Bill of Lading Act' [now chapter 801 of Title 49, Transportation].

(5) The shipper shall be deemed to have guaranteed to the carrier the accuracy at the time of shipment of the marks, number, quantity, and weight, as furnished by him; and the shipper shall indemnify the carrier against all loss, damages, and expenses arising or resulting from inaccuracies in such particulars. The right of the carrier to such indemnity shall in no way limit his responsibility and liability under the contract of carriage to any person other than the shipper.

(6) Unless notice of loss or damage and the general nature of such loss or damage be given in writing to the carrier or his agent at the port of discharge before or at the time of the removal of the

goods into the custody of the person entitled to delivery thereof under the contract of carriage, such removal shall be prima facie evidence of the delivery by the carrier of the goods as described in the bill of lading. If the loss or damage is not apparent, the notice must be given within three days of the delivery. Said notice of loss or damage may be endorsed upon the receipt for the goods given by the person taking delivery thereof. The notice in writing need not be given if the state of the goods has at the time of their receipt been the subject of joint survey or inspection. In any event the carrier and the ship shall be discharged from all liability in respect of loss or damage unless suit is brought within one year after delivery of the goods or the date when the goods should have been delivered: *Provided*, That if a notice of loss or damage, either apparent or concealed, is not given as provided for in this section, that fact shall not affect or prejudice the right of the shipper to bring suit within one year after the delivery of the goods or the date when the goods should have been delivered. In the case of any actual or apprehended loss or damage the carrier and the receiver shall give all reasonable facilities to each other for inspecting and tallying the goods.

(7) After the goods are loaded the bill of lading to be issued by the carrier, master, or agent of the carrier to the shipper shall, if the shipper so demands, be a "shipped" bill of lading: *Provided*, That if the shipper shall have previously taken up any document of title to such goods, he shall surrender the same as against the issue of the "shipped" bill of lading, but at the option of the carrier such document of title may be noted at the port of shipment by the carrier, master, or agent with the name or names of the ship or ships upon which the goods have been shipped and the date or dates of shipment, and when so noted the same shall for the purpose of this section be deemed to constitute a "shipped" bill of lading.

(8) Any clause, covenant, or agreement in a contract of carriage relieving the carrier or the ship from liability for loss or damage

to or in connection with the goods, arising from negligence, fault, or failure in the duties and obligations provided in this section, or lessening such liability otherwise than as provided in this chapter, shall be null and void and of no effect. A benefit of insurance in favor of the carrier, or similar clause, shall be deemed to be a clause relieving the carrier from liability.

Sec. 4. Rights and immunities

(1) Neither the carrier nor the ship shall be liable for loss or damage arising or resulting from unseaworthiness unless caused by want of due diligence on the part of the carrier to make the ship seaworthy, and to secure that the ship is properly manned, equipped, and supplied, and to make the holds, refrigerating and cool chambers, and all other parts of the ship in which goods are carried fit and safe for their reception, carriage, and preservation in accordance with the provisions of paragraph (1) of section 3. Whenever loss or damage has resulted from unseaworthiness, the burden of proving the exercise of due diligence shall be on the carrier or other persons claiming exemption under this section.

(2) Neither the carrier nor the ship shall be responsible for loss or damage arising or resulting from--

    (a) Act, neglect, or default of the master, mariner, pilot, or the servants of the carrier in the navigation or in the management of the ship;

    (b) Fire, unless caused by the actual fault or privity of the carrier;

    (c) Perils, dangers, and accidents of the sea or other navigable waters;

    (d) Act of God;

    (e) Act of war;

    (f) Act of public enemies;

    (g) Arrest or restraint of princes, rulers, or people, or seizure under legal process;

(h) Quarantine restrictions;

(i) Act or omission of the shipper or owner of the goods, his agent or representative;

(j) Strikes or lockouts or stoppage or restraint of labor from whatever cause, whether partial or general: Provided, That nothing herein contained shall be construed to relieve a carrier from responsibility for the carrier's own acts;

(k) Riots and civil commotions;

(l) Saving or attempting to save life or property at sea;

(m) Wastage in bulk or weight or any other loss or damage arising from inherent defect, quality, or vice of the goods;

(n) Insufficiency of packing;

(o) Insufficiency or inadequacy of marks;

(p) Latent defects not discoverable by due diligence; and

(q) Any other cause arising without the actual fault and privity of the carrier and without the fault or neglect of the agents or servants of the carrier, but the burden of proof shall be on the person claiming the benefit of this exception to show that neither the actual fault or privity of the carrier nor the fault or neglect of the agents or servants of the carrier contributed to the loss or damage.

(3) The shipper shall not be responsible for loss or damage sustained by the carrier or the ship arising or resulting from any cause without the act, fault, or neglect of the shipper, his agents, or his servants.

(4) Any deviation in saving or attempting to save life or property at sea, or any reasonable deviation shall not be deemed to be an infringement or breach of this chapter or of the contract of carriage, and the carrier shall not be liable for any loss or damage resulting therefrom: *Provided, however,* That if the deviation is for the purpose of loading or unloading cargo or passengers it shall, prima facie, be regarded as unreasonable.

(5) Neither the carrier nor the ship shall in any event be or become liable for any loss or damage to or in connection with the transportation of goods in an amount exceeding $500 per package lawful money of the United States, or in case of goods not shipped in packages, per customary freight unit, or the equivalent of that sum in other currency, unless the nature and value of such goods have been declared by the shipper before shipment and inserted in the bill of lading. This declaration, if embodied in the bill of lading, shall be prima facie evidence, but shall not be conclusive on the carrier.

By agreement between the carrier, master, or agent of the carrier, and the shipper another maximum amount than that mentioned in this paragraph may be fixed: *Provided*, That such maximum shall not be less than the figure above named. In no event shall the carrier be liable for more than the amount of damage actually sustained. Neither the carrier nor the ship shall be responsible in any event for loss or damage to or in connection with the transportation of the goods if the nature or value thereof has been knowingly and fraudulently misstated by the shipper in the bill of lading.

(6) Goods of an inflammable, explosive, or dangerous nature to the shipment whereof the carrier, master or agent of the carrier, has not consented with knowledge of their nature and character, may at any time before discharge be landed at any place or destroyed or rendered innocuous by the carrier without compensation, and the shipper of such goods shall be liable for all damages and expenses directly or indirectly arising out of or resulting from such shipment. If any such goods shipped with such knowledge and consent shall become a danger to the ship or cargo, they may in like manner be landed at any place, or destroyed or rendered innocuous by the carrier without liability on the part of the carrier except to general average, if any.

Extracts from Longshore and Harbor Workers' Compensation Act as amended in 1972

33 U.S.C.A. § 901

This chapter may be cited as "Longshore and Harbor Workers' Compensation Act."

33 U.S.C.A. § 902 * * *

(1) The term "person" means individual, partnership, corporation, or association.

(2) The term "injury" means accidental injury or death arising out of and in the course of employment, and such occupational disease or infection as arises naturally out of such employment or as naturally or unavoidably results from such accidental injury, and includes an injury caused by the willful act of a third person directed against an employee because of his employment.

(3) The term "employee" means any person engaged in maritime employment, including any longshoreman or other person engaged in longshoring operations, and any harbor-worker including a ship repairman, shipbuilder, and ship-breaker, but such term does not include--

(A) individuals employed exclusively to perform office clerical, secretarial, security, or data processing work;

(B) individuals employed by a club, camp, recreational operation, restaurant, museum, or retail outlet;

[This exception did not appear in the original 1972 enactment and caused an uproar in yacht club and summer camp industries as they could not afford the necessary costs to have the summer help covered.]

(C) individuals employed by a marina and who are not engaged in construction, replacement, or expansion of such marina (except for routine maintenance);
[Same for this exception]
* * *

(G) **a master or member of a crew of any vessel;**
[This is a very important exception as it tells clearly that sailors and ship's officers are not covered by this act.]

(H) any person engaged by a master to load or unload or repair any small vessel under eighteen tons net;
* * *

(4) The term "employer" means an employer any of whose employees are employed in maritime employment, in whole or in part, upon the navigable waters of the United States (including any adjoining pier, wharf, dry dock, terminal, building way, marine railway, or other adjoining area customarily used by an employer in loading, unloading, repairing, or building a vessel).
* * *

(10) "Disability" means incapacity because of injury to earn the wages which the employee was receiving at the time of injury in the same

or any other employment; but such term shall mean permanent impairment, determined (to the extent covered thereby) under the guides to the evaluation of permanent impairment promulgated and modified from time to time by the American Medical Association * * *

(11) "Death" as a basis for a right to compensation means only death resulting from an injury.

(12) **"Compensation" means the money allowance payable to an employee or to his dependents as provided for in this chapter, and includes funeral benefits provided therein.**

(13) The term "wages" means the money rate at which the service rendered by an employee is compensated by an employer under the contract of hiring in force at the time of the injury, including the reasonable value of any advantage which is received from the employer and included for purposes of any withholding of tax under subtitle C of title 26 (relating to employment taxes). **The term wages does not include fringe benefits,** including (but not limited to) employer payments for or contributions to a retirement, pension, health and welfare, life insurance, training, social security or other employee or dependent benefit plan for the employee's or dependent's benefit, or any other employee's dependent entitlement.

> [The benefit exclusion is important as it is not excluded from seamen injury claims, as "benefits" make up part of the damages items.]
> * * *

(16) The terms "widow or widower" includes only the decedent's wife or husband living with or dependent for support upon him or her at the time of his or her death; or living apart for justifiable cause or by reason of his or her desertion at such time.
> * * *

(19) The term "national average weekly wage" means the national average weekly earnings of production or nonsupervisory workers on private nonagricultural payrolls.

> [Now it is tied to the national weekly wage which includes changes due to inflation.]

(20) The term "Board" shall mean the Benefits Review Board.

(21) Unless the context requires otherwise, the term "vessel" means any vessel upon which or in connection with which any person entitled to benefits under this chapter suffers injury or death arising out of or in the course of his employment, and said vessel's owner, owner pro hac vice, agent, operator, charter or bare boat charterer, master, officer, or crew member.

(22) The singular includes the plural and the masculine includes the feminine and neuter.

33 U.S.C.A. § 903 Coverage

(a) Disability or death; injuries occurring upon navigable waters of United States

Except as otherwise provided in this section, compensation shall be payable under this chapter in respect of disability or death of an employee, but only if the disability or death results from an injury occurring upon the navigable waters of the United States (including any adjoining pier, wharf, dry dock, terminal, building way, marine railway, or other adjoining area customarily used by an employer in loading, unloading, repairing, dismantling, or building a vessel).

(b) Governmental officers and employees

No compensation shall be payable in respect of the disability or death of an officer or employee of the United States, or any agency thereof, or of any State or foreign government, or any subdivision thereof.

[This is again important because the federal and most state governments have their own worker compensation statutes]

(c)   Intoxication; willful intention to kill
No compensation shall be payable if the injury was occasioned **solely** by the intoxication of the employee or by the willful intention of the employee to injure or kill himself or another. [Note the "solely"]

(d)   Small vessels
    (1) No compensation shall be payable to an employee employed at a facility of an employer if, as certified by the Secretary, the facility is engaged in the business of building, repairing, or dismantling exclusively small vessels (as defined in paragraph (3) of this subsection), unless the injury occurs while upon the navigable waters of the United States or while upon any adjoining pier, wharf, dock, facility over land for launching vessels, or facility over land for hauling, lifting, or drydocking vessels.

        * * *

33 U.S.C.A. § 904

(a)   Every employer shall be liable for and shall secure the payment to his employees of the compensation payable under sections 907, 908 and 909. In the case of an employer who is a subcontractor, only if such subcontractor fails to secure the payment of compensation shall the contractor be liable for and be required to secure the payment of compensation. A subcontractor shall not be deemed to have failed to secure the payment of compensation if the contractor has provided insurance for such compensation for the benefit of the subcontractor.

(b) **Compensation shall be payable irrespective of fault as a cause for the injury.**

> [Note that here payments are "irrespective of fault, similar to a seaman being entitled to repatriation, maintenance and cure and wages to end of voyage irrespective of fault.]

33 U.S.C.A. § 905 Exclusiveness of liability **[This is the crux of the 1972 amendments]**

(a) Employer liability; failure of employer to secure payment of compensation

The liability of an employer prescribed in section 904 of this title **shall be exclusive** and in place of all other liability of such employer to the employee, his legal representative, husband or wife, parents, dependents, next of kin, and anyone otherwise entitled to recover damages from such employer at law or in admiralty on account of such injury or death, except that if an employer fails to secure payment of compensation as required by this chapter, an injured employee, or his legal representative in case death results from the injury, may elect to claim compensation under the chapter, or to maintain an action at law or in admiralty for damages on account of such injury or death. In such action the defendant may not plead as a defense that the injury was caused by the negligence of a fellow servant, or that the employee assumed the risk of his employment, or that the injury was due to the contributory negligence of the employee. For purposes of this subsection, a contractor shall be deemed the employer of a subcontractor's employees only if the subcontractor fails to secure the payment of compensation as required by section 904 of this title.

(b)   Negligence of vessel

In the event of injury to a person covered under this chapter **caused by the negligence of a vessel**, then such person, or anyone otherwise entitled to recover damages by reason thereof, **may bring an action against such vessel as a third party in accordance with the provisions of section 933 of this title, and the employer shall not be liable to the vessel for such damages directly or indirectly and any agreements or warranties to the contrary shall be void.** If such person was employed by the vessel to provide stevedoring services, no such action shall be permitted if the injury was caused by the negligence of persons engaged in providing stevedoring services to the vessel. If such person was employed to provide shipbuilding, repairing, or breaking services and such person's employer was the owner, owner pro hac vice, agent, operator, or charterer of the vessel, no such action shall be permitted, in whole or in part or directly or indirectly, against the injured person's employer (in any capacity, including as the vessel's owner, owner pro hac vice, agent, operator, or charterer) or against the employees of the employer. **The liability of the vessel under this subsection shall not be based upon the warranty of seaworthiness or a breach thereof at the time the injury occurred. The remedy provided in this subsection shall be exclusive of all other remedies against the vessel except remedies available under this chapter.**

(c)   Outer Continental Shelf

In the event that the negligence of a vessel causes injury to a person entitled to receive benefits under this Act by virtue of section 1333 of Title 43, then such person, or anyone otherwise entitled to recover damages by reason thereof, may bring an action against such vessel in accordance with the provisions of subsection (b) of this section. Nothing contained in subsection (b) of this section shall preclude the enforcement according to its terms of any reciprocal indemnity provision whereby the employer of a person entitled to receive benefits under this chapter by virtue of section 1333 or Title 43 and the vessel agree to defend and indemnify the other for cost of defense and loss or liability for damages arising out of or resulting from death or bodily injury to their employees.

33 U.S.C.A. § 906 Compensation

(a)   Time for commencement

No compensation shall be allowed for the first three days of the disability, except the benefits provided for in section 907 of this title: *Provided, however,* That in case the injury results in disability of more than fourteen days the compensation shall be allowed from the date of the disability.

(b)   Maximum rate of compensation

(1) Compensation for disability or death (other than compensation for death required by this chapter to be paid in a lump sum) shall not exceed an amount equal to 200 per centum of the applicable national average weekly wage, as determined by the Secretary under paragraph (3).

(2) Compensation for total disability shall not be less than 50 per centum of the applicable national average weekly wage determined by the Secretary under paragraph (3), except that if the employee's average weekly wages as computed under section 910 of this title are less than 50 per centum of such national average weekly wage, he shall receive his average weekly wages as compensation for total disability.

(3) As soon as practicable after June 30 of each year, and in any event prior to October 1 of such year, the Secretary shall determine the national average weekly wage for the three consecutive calendar quarters ending June 30. Such determination shall be the applicable national average weekly wage for the period beginning with October 1 of that year and ending with September 30 of the next year. The initial determination under this paragraph shall be made as soon as practicable after October 27, 1972.

[Note that now there has to be an annual determination what the average weekly wage is – no longer left to some nebulous determination.]

(c)   Applicability of determinations

Determinations under subsection (b)(3) of this section with respect to a period shall apply to employees or survivors currently receiving compensation for permanent total disability or death benefits during such period, as well as those newly awarded compensation during such period.

33 U.S.C.A. § 907 Medical services and supplies

(a)   General requirement

The employer shall furnish such medical, surgical, and other attendance or treatment, nurse and hospital service, medicine, crutches, and apparatus, for such period as the nature of the injury or the process of recovery may require.

(b)   Physician selection; administrative supervision; change of physicians and hospitals

The employee shall have the right to choose an attending physician authorized by the Secretary to provide medical care under this chapter as hereinafter provided. If, due to the nature of the injury, the employee is unable to select his physician and the nature of the injury requires immediate medical treatment and care, the employer shall select a physician for him. The Secretary shall actively supervise the medical care rendered to injured employees, shall require periodic reports as to the medical care being rendered to injured employees, shall have authority to determine the necessity, character, and sufficiency of any medical aid furnished or to be furnished, and may, on his own initiative or at the request of the employer, order a change of physicians or hospitals when in his judgment such change is desirable or necessary in the interest of the employee or where the charges exceed those prevailing within the community for the same or similar services or exceed the provider's customary charges. Change of physicians at the request of employees shall be permitted in accordance with regulations of the Secretary.

(c)   Physicians and health care providers not authorized to render medical care or provide medical services

(1) (A) The Secretary shall annually prepare a list of physicians and health care providers in each compensation district who are not authorized to render medical care or provide medical services under this chapter. The names of physicians and health care providers contained on the list required under this subparagraph shall be made available to employees and employers in each compensation district through posting and in such other forms as the Secretary may prescribe.

[This is probably due to the fact that at certain times in the litigation there "were medical experts" well known to be either defense or plaintiff oriented, one such having a comical reputation of saying there is nothing wrong with the person if he can crawl into his office for an examination.]

(2) Whenever the employer or carrier acquires knowledge of the employee's injury, through written notice or otherwise as prescribed by the chapter, **the employer or carrier shall forthwith authorize medical treatment and care from a physician selected by an employee pursuant to subsection (b) of this section.** * * *

[Many other provisions dealing with the providing of medical services, the injured employees rights, refusal of treatment on religious or other grounds, etc,]

33 U.S.C.A. § 908 Compensation for disability

[Just a few as examples for the general idea.]

Compensation for disability shall be paid to the employee as follows:

(a) Permanent total disability: In case of total disability adjudged to be permanent 66 2/3 per centum of the average weekly wages shall be paid to the employee during the continuance of such total disability. Loss of both hands, or both arms, or both feet, or both legs, or both eyes, or of any two thereof shall, in the absence of conclusive proof to the contrary, constitute permanent total disability. In all other cases permanent total disability shall be determined in accordance with the facts.

(b) Temporary total disability: In case of disability total in character but temporary in quality 66 2/3 per centum of the average weekly wages shall be paid to the employee during the continuance thereof.

(c) Permanent partial disability: In case of disability partial in character but permanent in quality the compensation shall be 66 2/3 per centum of the average weekly wages, which shall be in addition to compensation for temporary total disability or temporary partial disability paid in accordance with subsection (b) or subsection (e) of this section, respectively, and shall be paid to the employee, as follows:

(1) Arm lost, three hundred and twelve weeks' compensation.
(2) Leg lost, two hundred and eighty-eight weeks' compensation.
(3) Hand lost, two hundred and forty-four weeks' compensation.
(4) Foot lost, two hundred and five weeks' compensation.
(5) Eye lost, one hundred and sixty weeks' compensation.
(6) Thumb lost, seventy-five weeks' compensation.
(7) First finger lost, forty-six weeks' compensation.
　　　* * *

(A) Compensation for loss of hearing in one ear, fifty-two weeks.
　　　* * *

(E) Determinations of loss of hearing shall be made in accordance with the guides for the evaluation of permanent impairment as promulgated and modified from time to time by the American Medical Association.
　　　* * *

Etc., many other provisions

33 U.S.C.A. § 909 Compensation for death

If the injury causes death, the compensation therefore shall be known as a death benefit and shall be payable in the amount and to or for the benefit of the persons following:

(a) Reasonable funeral expenses not exceeding $3,000.

(b) If there be a widow or widower and no child of the deceased, to such widow or widower 50 per centum of the average wages of the deceased, during widowhood, or dependent widowerhood, with two years' compensation in one sum upon remarriage; and if there be a surviving child or children of the deceased, the additional amount of 16 2/3 per centum of such wages for each such child; in case of the death or remarriage of such widow or widower, if there be one surviving child of the deceased employee, such child shall have his compensation increased to 50 per centum of such wages, and if there be more than one surviving child of the deceased employee, to such children, in equal parts, etc., etc.

1972 COLREGS as amended

Part A General

Rule 1 Application

(a)   These Rules shall apply to all vessels upon the high seas and in all waters connected therewith navigable by seagoing vessels.

(b)   Nothing in these Rules shall interfere with the operation of special rules made by an appropriate authority for roadsteads, harbors, rivers, lakes, or inland waterways connected with the high seas and navigable by seagoing vessels. Such special rules shall conform as closely as possible to these Rules.

(c)   Nothing in these Rules shall interfere with the operation of any special rules made by the Government of any State with respect to additional station or signal lights, shaper or whistle signals for ships of war and vessels proceeding under convoy, or with respect to additional station or signal lights or shapes for fishing vessels engaged in fishing as a fleet. These additional station or signal lights, shapes or whistle signals shall, so far as possible, be such that they cannot be mistaken for any light, shape, or signal authorized elsewhere under these Rules.[1]

(d)   Traffic separation schemes may be adopted by the Organization for the purpose of these Rules.

(e)   Whenever the Government concerned shall have determined that a vessel of special construction or purpose cannot comply fully with the provisions of any of these Rules with respect to number, position, range or arc of visibility of lights or shapes, as well as to the disposition and characteristics of sound-signaling appliances, such vessel shall comply with such other provisions in regard to number, position, range or arc of visibility of lights or shapes, as well as to the disposition and characteristics of sound-signaling appliances, as her Government shall have determined to be the closest possible compliance with these Rules in respect to that vessel.

[1]Submarines may display, as a distinctive means of identification, an intermittent flashing amber (yellow) beacon with a sequence of operation of one flash per second for three (3) seconds followed by a three (3) second off-period. Other special rules made by the Secretary of the Navy with respect to additional station and signal lights are found in Part 706 of Title 32, Code of Federal Regulations (32 CFR 706).

Rule 2 Responsibility

(a)   Nothing in these Rules shall exonerate any vessel, or the owner, master, or crew thereof, from the consequences of any neglect to comply with these Rules or of the neglect of any precaution which may be required by the ordinary practice of seamen, or by the special circumstances of the case.

(b)   In construing and complying with these Rules due regard shall be had to all dangers of navigation and collision and to any special circumstances, including the limitations of the vessels involved, which may make a departure from these Rules necessary to avoid immediate danger.

Rule 3 General Definitions

For the purpose of these Rules *and this Chapter* [Inld], except where the context otherwise requires:

(a) The word "vessel" includes every description of watercraft, including non-displacement craft, <u>*WIG craft*</u>, and seaplanes, used or capable of being used as a means of transportation on water.

(b) The term "power-driven vessel" means any vessel propelled by machinery.

(c) The term "sailing vessel" means any vessel under sail provided that propelling machinery, if fitted, is not being used.

(d) The term "vessel engaged in fishing" means any vessel fishing with nets, lines, trawls, or other fishing apparatus which restrict maneuverability, but does not include a vessel fishing with trolling lines or other fishing apparatus which do not restrict maneuverability.

(e) The term "seaplane" includes any aircraft designed to maneuver on the water.

(f) The term "vessel not under command" means a vessel which through some exceptional circumstance is unable to maneuver as required by these Rules and is therefore unable to keep out of the way of another vessel.

(g) The term "vessel restricted in her ability to maneuver" means a vessel which from the nature of her work is restricted in her ability to maneuver as required by these Rules and is therefore unable to keep out of the way of another vessel. *The term* [Int] "vessels restricted in their ability to maneuver" *shall* [Int] include but not be limited to:
A vessel engaged in laying, servicing, or picking up a navigational mark, submarine cable or pipeline;
A vessel engaged in dredging, surveying or underwater operations;

A vessel engaged in replenishment or transferring persons, provisions or cargo while underway;

A vessel engaged in the launching or recovery of aircraft;

A vessel engaged in mine clearance operations;

A vessel engaged in a towing operation such as severely restricts the towing vessel and her tow in their ability to deviate from their course.

(h) *The term "vessel constrained by her draft" means a power-driven vessel which because of her draft in relation to the available depth and width of navigable water is severely restricted in her ability to deviate from the course she is following.* [Int]

(i/h) The word "underway" means that a vessel is not at anchor, or made fast to the shore, or aground.

(j/i) The words "length" and "breadth" of a vessel mean her length overall and greatest breadth.

(k/j) Vessels shall be deemed to be in sight of one another only when one can be observed visually from the other.

(l/k) The term "restricted visibility" means any condition in which visibility is restricted by fog, mist, falling snow, heavy rainstorms, sandstorms or any other similar causes.

(l) *"Western Rivers" means the Mississippi River, its tributaries, South Pass, and Southwest Pass, to the navigational demarcation lines dividing the high seas from harbors, rivers and other inland waters of the United States, and the Port Allen-Morgan City Alternate Route, and that part of the Atchafalaya River above its junction with the Port Allen-Morgan City Alternate Route including the Old River and the Red River;* [Inld]

(m) *The term "Wing-In-Ground (WIG) craft" means a multimodal craft which, in its main operational mode, flies in close proximity to the surface by utilizing surface-effect action.* [Intl]]

(m) *"Great Lakes" means the Great Lakes and their connecting tributary waters including the Calumet River as far as the Thomas J. O'Brien*

Lock and Controlling Waters (between mile 326 and 327), the Chicago River as far as the east side of the Ashland Avenue Bridge (between mile 321 and 322), and the Saint Lawrence River as far east as the lower exit of Saint Lambert Lock; [Inld]

(n)   *"Secretary" means the Secretary of the department in which the Coast Guard is operating;* [Inld]

(o)   *"Inland Waters" means the navigable waters of the United States shoreward of the navigational demarcation lines dividing the high seas from harbors, rivers and other inland waters of the United States and the waters of the Great Lakes on the United States side of the International Boundary;* [Inld]

(p)   *"Inland Rules" or "Rules" mean the Inland Navigational Rules and the annexes thereto, which govern the conduct of vessels and specify the lights, shapes, and sound signals that apply on inland waters; and* [Inld]

(q)   *"International Regulations" means the International Regulations for Preventing Collisions as Sea, 1972, including annexes currently in force for the United States.* [Inld]

Part B Steering and sailing Rules

Subpart 1 – Conduct of vessels in any condition of visibility

Rule 4 Application

Rules in this section apply to any condition of visibility.

Rule 5 Safe speed

Every vessel shall at all times maintain a proper look-out by sight and hearing as well as by all available means appropriate in the prevailing circumstances and conditions so as to make a full appraisal of the situation and of the risk of collision.

Rule 6 Safe speed

Every vessel shall at all times proceed at a safe speed so that she can take proper and effective action to avoid collision and be stopped within a distance appropriate to the prevailing circumstances and conditions.

In determining a safe speed the following factors shall be among those taken into account:

(a) By all vessels:
     The state of visibility;
     The traffic density including concentrations of fishing vessels or any other vessels;
     The manageability of the vessel with special reference to stopping distance and turning ability in the prevailing conditions;
     At night, the presence of background light such as from shore lights or from back scatter from her own lights;
     The state of wind, sea and current, and the proximity of navigational hazards;
     The draft in relation to the available depth of water.

(b) Additionally, by vessels with operational radar:
     The characteristics, efficiency and limitations of the radar equipment;
     Any constraints imposed by the radar range scale in use;
     The effect on radar detection of the sea state, weather and other sources of interference;
     The possibility that small vessels, ice and other floating objects may not be detected by radar at an adequate range;
     The number, location and movement of vessels detected by radar;
     The more exact assessment of the visibility that may be possible when radar is used to determine the range of vessels or other objects in the vicinity.

Rule 7 Risk of Collision

(a) Every vessel shall use all available means appropriate to the prevailing circumstances and conditions to determine if risk of collision exists. If there is any doubt such risk shall be deemed to exist.

(b) Proper use shall be made of radar equipment if fitted and operational, including long-range scanning to obtain early warning of risk of collision and radar plotting or equivalent systematic observation of detected objects.

(c) Assumptions shall not be made on the basis of scanty information, especially scanty radar information.

(d) In determining if risk of collision exists the following considerations shall be among those taken into account:
    Such risk shall be deemed to exist if the compass bearing of an approaching vessel does not appreciably change;
    Such risk may sometimes exist even when an appreciable bearing change is evident, particularly when approaching a very large vessel or a tow or when approaching a vessel at close range.

Rule 8 Action to Avoid Collision

(a) Any action taken to avoid collision shall *be taken in accordance with the Rules of this Part and* [Intl] shall, if the circumstances of the case admit, be positive, made in ample time and with due regard to the observance of good seamanship.

(b) Any alteration of course and/or speed to avoid collision shall, if the circumstances of the case admit, be large enough to be readily apparent to another vessel observing visually or by radar; a succession of small alterations of course and/or speed should be avoided.

(c) If there is sufficient sea room, alteration of course alone may be the most effective action to avoid a close-quarters situation provided that it is made in good time, is substantial and does not result in another close-quarters situation.

(d) Action taken to avoid collision with another vessel shall be such as to result in passing at a safe distance. The effectiveness of the action shall be carefully checked until the other vessel is finally past and clear.

(e) If necessary to avoid collision or allow more time to assess the situation, a vessel may slacken her speed or take all way off by stopping or reversing her means of propulsion.

(f) A vessel which, by any of these rules, is required not to impede the passage or safe passage of another vessel shall, when required by the circumstances of the case, take early action to allow sufficient sea room for the safe passage of the other vessel.

A vessel required not to impede the passage or safe passage of another vessel is not relieved of this obligation if approaching the other vessel so as to involve risk of collision and shall, when taking action, have full regard to the action which may be required by the rules of this part.

A vessel, the passage of which is not to be impeded remains fully obliged to comply with the rules of this part when the two vessels are approaching one another so as to involve risk of collision.

Rule 9 Narrow Channel

(a) *(i)* [Inld] A vessel proceeding along the course of a narrow channel or fairway shall keep as near to the outer limit of the channel or fairway which lies on her starboard side as is safe and practicable.

(ii) Notwithstanding paragraph (a)(i) and Rule 14(a), a power-driven vessel operating in narrow channels or fairways on the Great Lakes, Western Rivers, or <u>waters specified by the Secretary</u>, and proceeding downbound with a following current shall have the <u>right-of-way</u> over an upbound vessel, shall propose the manner and place of

passage, and shall initiate the maneuvering signals prescribed by Rule 34(a)(i), as appropriate. The vessel proceeding upbound against the current shall hold as necessary to permit safe passing. [Inld]

(b) A vessel of less than 20 meters in length or a sailing vessel shall not impede the passage of a vessel which can safely navigate only within a narrow channel or fairway.

(c) A vessel engaged in fishing shall not impede the passage of any other vessel navigating within a narrow channel or fairway.

(d) A vessel shall not cross a narrow passage or fairway if such crossing impedes the passage of a vessel which can safely navigate only within such channel or fairway. The latter vessel may use the sound signal prescribed in Rule 34(d) if in doubt as to the intention of the crossing vessel.

(i) In a narrow channel or fairway when overtaking can take place only if the vessel to be overtaken has to take action to permit safe passing, the vessel intending to overtake shall indicate her intention by sounding the appropriate signal prescribed in Rule 34(c)(i). The vessel to be overtaken shall, if in agreement, sound the appropriate signal prescribed in Rule 34(c)(ii) and take steps to permit safe passing. If in doubt she may sound the signals prescribed in Rule 34(d).	(i) In a narrow channel or fairway when overtaking, the power-driven vessel intending to overtake another power-driven vessel shall indicate her intention by sounding the appropriate signal prescribed in Rule 34(c) and take steps to permit safe passing. The power-driven vessel being overtaken, if in agreement, shall sound the same signal and may, if specifically agreed to take steps to permit safe passing. If in doubt, she shall sound the danger signal prescribed in Rule 34(d).

(ii) This rule does not relieve the overtaking vessel of her obligation under Rule 13.

(f)   A vessel nearing a bend or an area of a narrow channel or fairway where other vessels may be obscured by an intervening obstruction shall navigate with particular alertness and caution and shall sound the appropriate signal prescribed in Rule 34(e).

(g)   Any vessel shall, if the circumstances of the case admit, avoid anchoring in a narrow channel.

Rule 10 Traffic Separation Schemes / Vessel Traffic Service

(a)   This Rule applies to traffic separation schemes *adopted by the Organization* [Intl] and does not relieve any vessel of her obligation under any other rule.

(b)   A vessel using a traffic separation scheme shall:
Proceed in the appropriate traffic lane in the general direction of traffic flow for that lane.
So far as is practicable keep clear of a traffic separation line or separation zone.
Normally join or leave a traffic lane at the termination of the lane, but when joining or leaving from either side shall do so at as small an angle to the general direction of traffic flow as practicable.

(c)   A vessel, shall so far as practicable, avoid crossing traffic lanes but if obliged to do so shall cross on a heading as nearly as practicable at right angles to the general direction of traffic flow.

(d)   A vessel shall not use an inshore traffic zone when she can safely use the appropriate traffic lane within the adjacent traffic separation scheme. However, vessels of less than 20 meters in length, sailing vessels and vessels engaged in fishing may use the inshore traffic zone.

Notwithstanding subparagraph (d)(i), a vessel may use an inshore traffic zone when en route to or from a port, offshore installation or structure, pilot station or any other place situated within the inshore traffic zone, or to avoid immediate danger.

(e) A vessel, other than a crossing vessel or a vessel joining or leaving a lane shall not normally enter a separation zone or cross a separation line except:
in cases of emergency to avoid immediate danger;
to engage in fishing within a separation zone.

(f) A vessel navigating in areas near the terminations of traffic separation schemes shall do so with particular caution.

(g) A vessel shall so far as practicable avoid anchoring in a traffic separation scheme or in areas near its terminations.

(h) A vessel not using a traffic separating scheme shall avoid it by as wide a margin as is practicable.

(i) A vessel engaged in fishing shall not impede the passage of any vessel following a traffic lane.

(j) A vessel of less than 20 meters in length or a sailing vessel shall not impede the safe passage of a power-driven vessel following a traffic lane.

(k) A vessel restricted in her ability to maneuver when engaged in an operation for the maintenance of safety of navigation in a traffic separation scheme is exempted from complying with this Rule to the extent necessary to carry out the operation.

(l) A vessel restricted in her ability to maneuver when engaged in an operation for the laying, servicing or picking up of a submarine cable, within a traffic separation scheme, is exempted from complying with this Rule to the extent necessary to carry out the operation.

Subpart II Conduct of Vessels In Sight of One Another

Rule 11 Application

Rules in this section apply to vessels in sight of one another.

Rule 12 Sailing Vessels

(a)   When two sailing vessels are approaching one another, so as to involve risk of collision, one of them shall keep out of the way of the other as follows:
when each has the wind on a different side, the vessel which has the wind on the port side shall keep out of the way of the other; when both have the wind on the same side, the vessel which is to windward shall keep out of the way of the vessel which is to leeward; if a vessel with the wind on the port side sees a vessel to windward and cannot determine with certainty whether the other vessel has the wind on the port or on the starboard side, she shall keep out of the way of the other.

(b)   For the purposes of this Rule the windward side shall be deemed to be the side opposite that on which the mainsail is carried or, in the case of a square-rigged vessel, the side opposite to that on which the largest fore-and-aft sail is carried.

Rule 13 Overtaking

(a)   Notwithstanding anything contained in the Rules [of Part B, Sections I and II / 4 through 18], any vessel overtaking any other shall keep out of the way of the vessel being overtaken.

(b)   A vessel shall be deemed to be overtaking when coming up with another vessel from a direction more than 22.5 degrees abaft her beam, that is, in such a position with reference to the vessel

she is overtaking, that at night she would be able to see only the
sternlight of that vessel but neither of her sidelights.

(c)   When a vessel is in any doubt as to whether she is overtaking
another, she shall assume that this is the case and act accordingly.

(d)   Any subsequent alteration of the bearing between the two vessels
shall not make the overtaking vessel a crossing vessel within the
meaning of these Rules or relieve her of the duty of keeping clear
of the overtaken vessel until she is finally past and clear.

Rule 14 Head on Situation

(a)   *Unless otherwise agreed* [Inld] When two power-driven vessels are
meeting on reciprocal or nearly reciprocal courses so as to involve
risk of collision each shall alter her course to starboard so that each
shall pass on the port side of the other.

(b)   Such a situation shall be deemed to exist when a vessel sees the other
ahead or nearly ahead and by night she could see the masthead
lights of the other in a line or nearly in a line and/ [Intl] or both
sidelights and by day she observes the corresponding aspect of the
other vessel.

(c)   When a vessel is in any doubt as to whether such a situation exists
she shall assume that it does exist and act accordingly.

(d)   *Notwithstanding paragraph (a) of this Rule, a power-driven vessel
operating on the Great Lakes, Western Rivers, or waters specified by
the Secretary, and proceeding downbound with a following current
shall have the right-of-way over an upbound vessel, shall propose
the manner of passage, and shall initiate the maneuvering signals
prescribed by Rule 34(a)(i), as appropriate.* [Inld]

Rule 15 Crossing Situation

When two power-driven vessels are crossing so as to involve risk of
collision, the vessel which has the other on her own starboard side shall

keep out of the way and shall, if the circumstances of the case admit, avoid crossing ahead of the other vessel.

(b) Notwithstanding paragraph (a), on the Great Lakes, Western Rivers, or <u>water specified by the Secretary,</u> a power-driven vessel crossing a river shall keep out of the way of a power-driven vessel ascending or descending the river. [Inld]

Rule 16 Action by Give-way Vessel;

Every vessel which is directed to keep out of the way of another vessel shall, so far as possible, take early and substantial action to keep well clear.

Rule 17 Action by Stand-on Vessel

(a) Where one of two vessels is to keep out of the way, the other shall keep her course and speed. The latter vessel may however take action to avoid collision by her maneuver alone, as soon as it becomes apparent to her that the vessel required to keep out of the way is not taking appropriate action in compliance with these Rules.

(b) When, from any cause, the vessel required to keep her course and speed finds herself so close that collision cannot be avoided by the action of the give-way vessel alone, she shall take such action as will best aid to avoid collision.

(c) A power-driven vessel which takes action in a crossing situation in accordance with subparagraph (a)(ii) of this Rule to avoid collision with another power-driven vessel shall, if the circumstances of the case admit, not alter course to port for a vessel on her own port side.

(d) This Rule does not relieve the give-way vessel of her obligation to keep out of the way.

Rule 18 Responsibility between vessels

Except where Rules 9, 10, and 13 otherwise require:

(a)   A power-driven vessel underway shall keep out of the way of:
a vessel not under command;
a vessel restricted in her ability to maneuver;
a vessel engaged in fishing;
a sailing vessel.

(b)   A sailing vessel underway shall keep out of the way of:
a vessel not under command;
a vessel restricted in her ability to maneuver;
a vessel engaged in fishing.

(c)   A vessel engaged in fishing when underway shall, so far as possible, keep out of the way of:
a vessel not under command;
a vessel restricted in her ability to maneuver.

(d)   *Any vessel other than a vessel not under command or a vessel restricted in her ability to* maneuver shall, if the circumstances of the case admit, avoid impeding the safe passage of a vessel constrained by her draft, exhibiting the signals in Rule 28. A vessel constrained by her draft shall navigate with particular caution having full regard to her special condition. [Intl]

(e/d) A seaplane on the water shall, in general, keep well clear of all vessels and avoid impeding their navigation. In circumstances, however, where risk of collision exists, she shall comply with the Rules of this Part.

(i) *A __WIG craft__ shall, when taking off, landing and in flight near the surface, keep well clear of all other vessels and avoid impeding their navigation;*

(ii) a <u>WIG craft</u> operating on the water surface shall comply with the Rules of this Part as a power-driven vessel. [Intl]

Subpart III Conduct of Vessels in Restricted Visibility

Rule 19 Conduct of Vessels in Restricted Visibility

(a)   This Rule applies to vessels not in sight of one another when navigating in or near an area of restricted visibility.
(b)   Every vessel shall proceed at a safe speed adapted to the prevailing circumstances and conditions of restricted visibility. A power-driven vessel shall have her engines ready for immediate maneuver.
(c)   Every vessel shall have due regard to the prevailing circumstances and conditions of restricted visibility when complying with the Rules [of Section I of this Part / 4 through 10].
(d)   A vessel which detects by radar alone the presence of another vessel shall determine if a close-quarters situation is developing *and/* [Intl] or risk of collision exists. If so, she shall take avoiding action in ample time, provided that when such action consists of an alteration in course, so far as possible the following shall be avoided:
    (i)   An alteration of course to port for a vessel forward of the beam, other than for a vessel being overtaken;
    (ii)   An alteration of course toward a vessel abeam or abaft the beam.

(e)   Except where it has been determined that a risk of collision does not exist, every vessel which hears apparently forward of her beam the fog signal of another vessel, or which cannot avoid a close-quarters situation with another vessel forward of her beam, shall reduce her speed to be the minimum at which she can be kept on her course. She shall if necessary take all her way off and in any event navigate with extreme caution until danger of collision is over.

Part C – Lights and Shapes

Rule 20 Application

(a)   Rules in this part shall be complied with in all weathers.

(b)   The Rules concerning lights shall be complied with from sunset to sunrise, and during such times no other lights shall be exhibited, except such lights which cannot be mistaken for the lights specified in these Rules or do not impair their visibility or distinctive character, or interfere with the keeping of a proper look-out.

(c)   The lights prescribed by these Rules shall, if carried, also be exhibited from sunrise to sunset in restricted visibility and may be exhibited in all other circumstances when it is deemed necessary.

(d)   The Rules concerning shapes shall be complied with by day.

(e)   The lights and shapes specified in these Rules shall comply with the provisions of Annex I [to these Regulations / of these Rules].

Rule 21 Definitions

(a)   "Masthead light" means a white light placed over the fore and aft centerline of the vessel showing an unbroken light over an arc of the horizon of 225 degrees and so fixed as to show the light from right ahead to 22.5 degrees abaft the beam on either side of the vessel, *except that on a vessel of less than 12 meters in length the masthead light shall be placed as nearly as practicable to the fore and aft centerline of the vessel.* [Inld]

(b)   "Sidelights" means a green light on the starboard side and a red light on the port side each showing an unbroken light over an arc of the horizon of 112.5 degrees and so fixed as to show the light from right ahead to 22.5 degrees abaft the beam on its respective side. In a vessel of less than 20 meters in length the sidelights may be combined in one lantern carried on the fore and aft centerline of the vessel, except that on a vessel of less than 12 meters in length the sidelights when combined in one lantern shall be placed as nearly as practicable to the fore and aft centerline of the vessel. [Inld]

(c) "Sternlight" means a white light placed as nearly as practicable at the stern showing an unbroken light over an arc of the horizon of 135 degrees and so fixed as to show the light 67.5 degrees from right aft on each side of the vessel.

(d) "Towing light" means a yellow light having the same characteristics as the "sternlight" defined in paragraph (c) of this Rule.

(e) "All-round light" means a light showing an unbroken light over an arc of the horizon of 360 degrees.

(f) "Flashing light" means a light flashing at regular intervals at a frequency of 120 flashes or more per minute.

(g) *"Special flashing light" means a yellow light flashing at regular intervals at a frequency of 50 to 70 flashes per minute, placed as far forward and as nearly as practicable on the fore and aft centerline of the tow and showing an unbroken light over an arc of the horizon of not less than 180 degrees nor more than 225 degrees and so fixed as to show the light from right ahead to abeam and no more than 22.5 degrees abaft the beam on either side of the vessel.* [Inld]

Rule 22 Visibility of Lights

The lights prescribed in these Rules shall have an intensity as specified in *Section 8* [Intl] of Annex I to these [Regulations / Rules] so as to be visible at the following minimum ranges:

(a) In vessels of 50 meters or more in length:
a masthead light, 6 miles;
a sidelight, 3 miles;
a towing light, 3 miles;
a white red, green or yellow all-round light, 3 miles.
a special flashing light, 2 miles. [Inld]

(b)   In vessels of 12 meters or more in length but less than 50 meters in length;
a masthead light, 5 miles; except that where the length of the vessel is less than 20 meters, 3 miles;
a sidelight, 2 miles;
a sternlight, 2 miles;
a towing light, 2 miles;
a white, red, green or yellow all-round light, 2 miles.
a special flashing light, 2 miles. [Inld]

(c)   In vessels of less than 12 meters in length:
a masthead light, 2 miles;
a sidelight, 1 mile;
a towing light, 2 miles;
a white red, green or yellow all-round light, 2 miles.
a special flashing light, 2 miles. [Inld]

(d)   In inconspicuous, partly submerged vessels or objects being towed;
a white all-round light; 3 miles.

Rule 23 Power Driven Vessels Underway

(a)   A power-driven vessel underway shall exhibit (picture):
a masthead light forward;
a second masthead light abaft of and higher than the forward one; except that a vessel of less than 50 meters in length shall not be obliged to exhibit such a light but may do so;
sidelights: and
a sternlight.

(b)   An air-cushion vessel when operating in nondisplacement mode shall, in addition to the lights prescribed in paragraph (a) of this Rule, exhibit an all-round flashing yellow light, *where it can best be seen.* [Inld]

(c) *A WIG craft only when taking off, landing and in flight near the surface shall, in addition to the lights prescribed in paragraph (a) of this Rule, exhibit a high intensity all-round flashing red light. [Intl]*

(c/d)

A power-driven vessel of less than 12 meters in length may in lieu of the lights prescribed in paragraph (a) of this Rule exhibit an all-round white light and sidelights.

a power-driven vessel of less than 7 meters in length whose maximum speed does not exceed 7 knots may in lieu of the lights prescribed in paragraph (a) of this Rule exhibit an all-round white light and shall, if practicable, also exhibit sidelights. [Intl]

the masthead light or all-round white light on a power-driven vessel of less than 12 meters in length may be displaced from the fore and aft centerline of the vessel if centerline fitting is not practicable, provided the sidelights are combined in one lantern which shall be carried on the fore and aft centerline of the vessel or located as nearly as practicable in the same fore and aft line as the masthead light or the all-round white light. [Intl]

(d) *A power-driven vessel when operating on the Great Lakes may carry an all-round white light in lieu of the second masthead light and sternlight prescribed in paragraph (a) of this Rule. The light shall be carried in the position of the second masthead light and be visible at the same minimum range. [Inld]*

Rule 24 Towing and Pushing

(a) A power-driven vessel when towing *astern* [Inld] shall exhibit:
Instead of the light prescribed in Rule 23(a)(i) or 23(a)(ii), two masthead lights in a vertical line. When the length of the tow,

measuring from the stern of the towing vessel to the after end of the tow exceeds 200 meters, three such lights in a vertical line; sidelights;

a sternlight;

a towing light in a vertical line above the sternlight; and

when the length of the tow exceeds 200 meters, a diamond shape where it can best be seen.

(b) When a pushing vessel and a vessel being pushed ahead are rigidly connected in a composite unit they shall be regarded as a power-driven vessel and exhibit the lights prescribed in Rule 23. (*pictures of a unit over 50m / unit less than 50m*)

(c) A power-driven vessel when pushing ahead or towing alongside, except [in the case of a composite unit / as required by paragraphs (b) and (i) of this Rule], shall exhibit:

instead of the light prescribed in Rule 23(a)(i) or 23(a)(ii), two masthead lights in a vertical line;

sidelights; and

[a sternlight / two towing lights in a vertical line]

(d) A power-driven vessel to which paragraph (a) or (c) of this Rule apply shall also comply with rule *23(a)(i)* [Inld] and 23(a)(ii). (*picture of vessel with tow 200m or less AND less than 50m in length / 50m or more in length*)

(e) A vessel or object being towed, other than those mentioned in paragraph (g) of this Rule, shall exhibit:

sidelights;

a sternlight;

when the length of the tow exceeds 200 meters, a diamond shape where it can best be seen.

(f) Provided that any number of vessels being towed alongside or pushed in a group shall be lighted as one vessel, *except as provided in paragraph (iii)* [Inld] (*pictures of International and Inland configurations*)

a vessel being pushed ahead, not being part of a composite unit, shall exhibit at the forward end, sidelights, *and a special flashing light* [Inld];

a vessel being towed alongside shall exhibit a sternlight and at the forward end, sidelights, *and a special flashing light* [Inld];

when vessels are towed alongside on both sides of the towing vessels a sternlight shall be exhibited on the stern of the outboard vessel on each side of the towing vessel, and a single set of sidelights as far forward an as far outboard as is practicable, and a single special flashing light

(g) An inconspicuous, partly submerged vessel or object, or *combination of such vessels or objects being towed,* [Intl] shall exhibit:

International	Inland
(i) if it is less than 25 meters in breadth, one all-round white light at or near the forward end and one at or near the after end except that dracones need not exhibit a light at or near the forward end.	(i) if it is less than 25 meters in breadth, one all-round white light at or near each end.
(ii) if it is 25 meters or more in breadth, two or more additional all-round white lights at or near the extremities of its breadth;	(ii) if it is 25 meters or more in breadth, four all-round white lights to mark its length and breadth;

if it exceeds 100 meters in length, additional all-round white lights between the lights prescribed in subparagraphs (i) and (ii) so that the distance between the lights shall not exceed 100 meters. *Provided, that any vessels or objects being towed alongside each other shall be lighted as one vessel or object* [Inld];

a diamond shape at or near the aftermost extremity of the last vessel or object being towed and *if the length of the tow exceeds 200 meters an additional diamond shape where it can best be seen and located as far forward as is practicable.* [Intl]

the towing vessel may direct a searchlight in the direction of the tow to indicate its presence to an approaching vessel. [Inld]

(h)   When from any sufficient cause it is impracticable for a vessel or object being towed to exhibit the lights *or shapes* [Intl] prescribed in paragraph (e) or (g) of this Rule, all possible measures shall be taken to light the vessel or object being towed or at least indicate the presence of [such / unlighted] vessel or object.

(i)   *Notwithstanding paragraph (c), on the Western Rivers (except below the Huey P. Long Bridge on the Mississippi River) and on* <u>*waters specified by the Secretary,*</u> *a power-driven vessel when pushing ahead or towing alongside, except as paragraph (b) applies, shall exhibit:* [Inld] *sidelights; and* [Inld]
two towing lights in a vertical line. [Inld]

(j/j)   Where from any sufficient cause it is impracticable for a vessel not normally engaged in towing operations to display the lights prescribed in paragraph (a), (c) *or (i)* [Inld] of this Rule, such vessel shall not be required to exhibit those lights when engaged in towing another vessel in distress or otherwise in need of assistance. All possible measures shall be taken to indicate the nature of the relationship between the towing vessel and the vessel being towed as authorized by Rule 36, in particular by illuminating the [towline / tow].

Rule 25 Sailing Vessels Underway and Vessels Under Oars

(a)   A sailing vessel underway shall exhibit:
sidelights;
a sternlight.

(b)   In a sailing vessel of less than 20 meters in length the lights prescribed in paragraph (a) of this Rule may be combined in one lantern carried at or near the top of the mast where it can best be seen.

(c)   A sailing vessel underway may, in addition to the lights prescribed in paragraph (a) of this Rule, exhibit at or near the top of the mast, where they can best be seen, two all-round lights in a vertical line, the upper being red and the lower Green, but these lights shall not be exhibited in conjunction with the combined lantern permitted by paragraph (b) of this Rule.
A sailing vessel of less than 7 meters in length shall, if practicable, exhibit the lights prescribed in paragraph (a) or (b) of this Rule, but if she does not, she shall have ready at hand an electric torch or lighted lantern showing a white light which shall be exhibited in sufficient time to prevent collision.
A vessel under oars may exhibit the lights prescribed in this rule for sailing vessels, but if she does not, she shall have ready at hand an electric torch or lighted lantern showing a white light which shall be exhibited in sufficient time to prevent collision.

(d)   A vessel proceeding under sail when also being propelled by machinery shall exhibit forward where it can best be seen a conical shape, apex downwards. *A vessel of less than 12 meters in length is not required to exhibit this shape, but may do so.* [Inld]

Rule 26 Fishing Vessels

(a)   A vessel engaged in fishing, whether underway or at anchor, shall exhibit only the lights and shapes prescribed in this Rule.

(b)   A vessel when engaged in trawling, by which is meant the dragging through the water of a dredge net or other apparatus used as a fishing appliance, shall exhibit:
two all-round lights in a vertical line, the upper being green and the lower white, or a shape consisting of two cones with their apexes together in a vertical line one above the other;
a masthead light abaft of and higher than the all-round green light; a vessel of less than 50 meters in length shall not be obliged to exhibit such a light but may do so;
when making way through the water, in addition to the lights prescribed in this paragraph, sidelights and a sternlight.

(c)   A vessel engaged in fishing, other than trawling, shall exhibit:
two all-round lights in a vertical line, the upper being red and the lower white, or a shape consisting of two cones with their apexes together in a vertical line one above the other;
when there is outlying gear extending more than 150 meters horizontally from the vessel, an all-round white light or a cone apex upwards in the direction of the gear.
when making way through the water, in addition to the lights prescribed in this paragraph, sidelights and a sternlight.

(d)   The additional signals described in Annex II to these Rules apply to a vessel engaged in fishing in close proximity to other vessels engaged in fishing.

(e)   A vessel when not engaged in fishing shall not exhibit the lights or shapes prescribed in this Rule, but only those prescribed for a vessel of her length.

Rule 27 Vessels Not Under Command or Restricted in Their Ability to Maneuver

(a) A vessel not under command shall exhibit:
two all-round red lights in a vertical line where they can best be seen;
two balls or similar shapes in a vertical line where they can best be seen;
when making way through the water, in addition to the lights prescribed in this paragraph, sidelights and a sternlight.

(b) A vessel restricted in her ability to maneuver, except a vessel engaged in mine clearance operations, shall exhibit:
three all-round lights in a vertical line where they can best be seen. The highest and lowest of these lights shall be red and the middle light shall be white;
three shapes in a vertical line where they can best be seen. The highest and lowest of these shapes shall be balls and the middle one a diamond.
when making way through the water, [a masthead light or lights/ masthead lights], sidelights and a sternlight in addition to the lights prescribed in subparagraph (b)(i);
when at anchor, in addition to the lights or shapes prescribed in subparagraphs (b)(i) and (b) (ii), the light, lights, or shapes prescribed in Rule 30.

(c) A power-driven vessel engaged in a towing operation such as severely restricts the towing vessel and her tow in their ability to deviate from their course shall, in addition to the lights or shapes prescribed in [Rule 24(a) / subparagraph (b)(i) and (ii) of this Rule], exhibit the lights or shape prescribed in [subparagraph (b) (i) and (ii) of this Rule / Rule 24].

(d)   (d) A vessel engaged in dredging or underwater operations, when restricted in her ability to maneuver, shall exhibit the lights and shapes prescribed in subparagraphs (b)(i),(ii) and (iii) of this Rule and shall in addition when an obstruction exists, exhibit:
two all-round red lights or two balls in a vertical line to indicate the side on which the obstruction exists;
two all-round green lights or two diamonds in a vertical line to indicate the side on which another vessel may pass;
when at anchor, the lights or shapes prescribed in this paragraph instead of the lights or shapes prescribed in Rule 30, *for anchored vessels.* [Inld]

(e)   Whenever the size of a vessel engaged in diving operations makes it impracticable to exhibit all lights and shapes prescribed in paragraph (d) of this Rule, the following shall be exhibited:
Three all-round lights in a vertical line where they can best be seen. The highest and lowest of these lights shall be red and the middle light shall be white;
a rigid replica of the International Code flag "A" not less than 1 meter in height. Measures shall be taken to ensure its all-round visibility.

(f)   A vessel engaged in mine clearance operations shall, in addition to the lights prescribed for a power-driven vessel in Rule 23 or to the lights or shape prescribed for a vessel at anchor in Rule 30 as appropriate, exhibit three all-round green lights or three balls. One of these lights or shapes shall be exhibited near the foremast head and one at each end of the fore yard. These lights or shapes indicate that it is dangerous for another vessel to approach within 1000 meters of the mine clearance vessel.

(g)   Vessels of less than 12 meters in length, except those engaged in diving operations, shall not be required to exhibit the lights prescribed in this Rule.

(h)   The signals prescribed in this Rule are not signals of vessels in distress and requiring assistance. Such signals are contained in Annex IV to these [Regulations / Rules].

Rule 28 Vessels Constrained by Their Draft

INTERNATIONAL ONLY

A vessel <u>constrained by her draft</u> may, in addition to the lights prescribed for power-driven vessels in Rule 23, exhibit where they can best be seen three <u>all-round</u> red lights in a vertical line, or a cylinder.

Rule 29 Pilot Vessels

(a)   A vessel engaged on pilotage duty shall exhibit:
    (i)   at or near the masthead, two all-round lights in a vertical line, the upper being white and the lower red;
    (ii) when underway, in addition, sidelights and a sternlight;
    (iii) when at anchor, in addition to the lights prescribed in subparagraph (i), the light, lights, or shape prescribed in Rule 30 for [vessels at anchor / anchored vessels].

(b)   A pilot vessel when not engaged on pilotage duty shall exhibit the lights or shapes prescribed for a similar vessel of her length.

Rule 30 Anchored Vessels and Vessels Aground

(a)   A vessel at anchor shall exhibit where it can best be seen:
    in the fore part, an all-round white light or one ball;
    at or near the stern and at a lower level than the light prescribed in subparagraph (i), an all-round white light.

(b) A vessel of less than 50 meters in length may exhibit an all-round white light where it can best be seen instead of the lights prescribed in paragraph (a) of this Rule.

(c) A vessel at anchor may, and a vessel of 100 meters and more in length shall, also use the available working or equivalent lights to illuminate her decks.

(d) A vessel aground shall exhibit the lights prescribed in paragraph (a) or (b) of this Rule and in addition, *if practicable,* [Inld] where they can best be seen;

two all-round red lights in a vertical line;

three balls in a vertical line.

(e) A vessel of less than 7 meters in length, when at anchor not in or near a narrow channel, fairway or where other vessels normally navigate, shall not be required to exhibit the shape prescribed in paragraphs (a) and (b) of this Rule.

(f) A vessel of less than 12 meters in length, when aground, shall not be required to exhibit the lights or shapes prescribed in subparagraphs (d)(i) and (ii) of this Rule.

(g) *A vessel of less than 20 meters in length, when at anchor in a special anchorage area designated by the Secretary, shall not be required to exhibit the anchor lights and shapes required by this Rule.* [Inld]

Rule 31 Seaplanes

Where it is impracticable for a seaplane *or a WIG craft* [Intl] to exhibit lights or shapes of the characteristics or in the positions prescribed in the Rules of this Part she shall exhibit lights and shapes as closely similar in characteristics and position as is possible.

Part D Sound and Light Signals

Rule 32 Definitions

(a) The word "whistle" means any sound signaling appliance capable of producing the prescribed blasts and which complies with the specifications in Annex III to these [Regulations / Rules].

(b) The term "short blast" means a blast of about one second's duration.

(c) The term "prolonged blast" means a blast of from four to six seconds' duration.

Rule 33 Equipment for Sound Signals

(a) A vessel of 12 meters or more in length shall be provided with a whistle and a bell [Intd], *a vessel of 20 meters or more in length shall be provided with a bell in addition to a whistle* [Intl], and a vessel of 100 meters or more in length shall, in addition be provided with a gong, the tone and sound of which cannot be confused with that of the bell. The whistle, bell and gong shall comply with the specifications in Annex III to these Regulations. The bell or gong or both may be replaced by other equipment having the same respective sound characteristics, provided that manual sounding of the prescribed signals shall always be possible.

(b) (b) A vessel of less than 12 meters in length shall not be obliged to carry the sound signaling appliances prescribed in paragraph (a) of this Rule but if she does not, she shall be provided with some other means of making an efficient signal.

Rule 34 Maneuvering and Warning Signals

International	Inland
(a) When vessels are in sight of one another, a power-driven vessel underway, when maneuvering as authorized or required by these Rules, shall indicate that maneuver by the following signals on her whistle: • one short blast to mean "I am altering my course to starboard"; • two short blasts to mean "I am altering my course to port"; • three short blasts to mean "I am operating astern propulsion".	(a) When power-driven vessels are in sight of one another and meeting or crossing at a distance within half a mile of each other, each vessel underway, when maneuvering as authorized or required by these Rules: (i) shall indicate that maneuver by the following signals on her whistle: • one short blast to mean "I intend to leave you on my port side"; • two short blasts to mean "I intend to leave you on my starboard side"; • three short blasts to mean "I am operating astern propulsion". (ii) upon hearing the one or two blast signal of the other shall, if in agreement, sound the same whistle signal and take the steps necessary to effect a safe passing. If, however, from any cause, the vessel doubts the safety of the proposed maneuver, she shall sound

	the danger signal specified in paragraph (d) of this Rule and each vessel shall take appropriate precautionary action until a safe passing agreement is made.
(b) Any vessel may supplement the whistle signals prescribed in paragraph (a) of this Rule by light signals, repeated as appropriate, while the maneuver is being carried out: (i) these signals shall have the following significance: one flash to mean "I am altering my course to starboard"; two flashes to mean "I am altering my course to port"; three flashes to mean "I am operating astern propulsion". (ii) the duration of each flash shall be about one second, the interval between flashes shall be about one second, and the interval between successive signals shall not be less than ten seconds. (iii) the light used for this signal shall, if fitted, be an all-round white light, visible at a minimum range of 5 miles, and shall comply with the provisions of Annex I to these Regulations.	(b) Any vessel may supplement the whistle signals prescribed in paragraph (a) of this Rule by light signals: (i) these signals shall have the following significance: one flash to mean "I intend to leave you on my port side"; two flashes to mean "I intend to leave you on my starboard side"; three flashes to mean "I am operating astern propulsion". (ii) the duration of each flash shall be about one second; (iii) the light used for this signal shall, if fitted, be an all-round white or yellow light, visible at a minimum range of 2 miles, synchronized with the whistle, and shall comply with the provisions of Annex I to these Rules.

(c) When in sight of one another in a narrow channel or fairway:

(i) a vessel intending to overtake another shall in compliance with Rule 9 (e) (i) indicate her intention by the following signals on her whistle:

two prolonged blasts followed by one short blast to mean "I intend to overtake you on your starboard side"

two prolonged blasts followed by two short blasts to mean "I intend to overtake you on your port side"

(ii) the vessel about to be overtaken when acting in accordance with 9(e)(i) shall indicate her agreement by the following signal on her whistle:

- one prolonged, one short, one prolonged and one short blast, in that order.

(c) When in sight of one another:

(i) a power-driven vessel intending to overtake another power-driven vessel shall indicate her intention by the following signals on her whistle:

one short blast to mean "I intend to overtake you on your starboard side"

two short blasts to mean "I intend to overtake you on your port side".

(ii) the power-driven vessel about to be overtaken shall, if in agreement, sound a similar signal. If in doubt she shall sound the danger signal prescribed in paragraph (d).

(d) When vessels in sight of one another are approaching each other and from any cause either vessel fails to understand the intentions or actions of the other, or is in doubt whether sufficient action is being taken by the other to avoid collision, the vessel in doubt shall immediately indicate such doubt by giving at least five short and rapid blasts on the whistle. [Such / This] signal may be supplemented by at least five short and rapid flashes.

(e) A vessel nearing a bend or an area of a channel or fairway where other vessels may be obscured by an intervening obstruction shall sound one prolonged blast. Such signal shall be answered with a prolonged blast by any approaching vessel that may be within hearing around the bend or behind the intervening obstruction.

(f) If whistles are fitted on a vessel at a distance apart of more than 100 meters, one whistle only shall be used for giving maneuvering and warning signals.

(g) When a power-driven vessel is *leaving a dock or berth, she shall sound one prolonged blast.* [Inld]

(h) *A vessel that reaches agreement with another vessel in a head-on, crossing, or overtaking situation, as for example, by using the radiotelephone as prescribed by the* <u>*Vessel Bridge-to-Bridge Radiotelephone Act*</u> *(85 Stat. 164; 33 U.S.C. 1201 et seq.), is not obliged to sound the whistle signals prescribed by this Rule, but may do so. If agreement is not reached, then whistle signals shall be exchanged in a timely manner and shall prevail.* [Inld]

Rule 35 Sound Signals in Restricted Visibility

In or near an area of restricted visibility, whether by day or night the signals prescribed in this Rule shall be used as follows:

(a) A power-driven vessel making way through the water shall sound at intervals of not more than 2 minutes one prolonged blast.

(b) A power-driven vessel underway but stopped and making no way through the water shall sound at intervals of no more than 2 minutes two prolonged blasts in succession with an interval of about 2 seconds between them.

(c)　A vessel not under command, a vessel restricted in her ability to maneuver whether underway or at anchor [Inld], a vessel constrained by her draft [Intl], a sailing vessel, a vessel engaged in fishing whether underway or at anchor [Inld] and a vessel engaged in towing or pushing another vessel shall, instead of the signals prescribed in paragraph (a) or (b) of this Rule, sound at intervals of not more than 2 minutes three blasts in succession, namely one prolonged followed by two short blasts.

(d)　A vessel engaged in fishing, when at anchor, and a vessel restricted in her ability to maneuver when carrying out her work at anchor, shall instead of the signals prescribed in paragraph (g) of this Rule sound the signal prescribed in paragraph (c) of this Rule. [Intl]

(e/d) A vessel towed or if more than one vessel is towed the last vessel of the tow, if manned, shall at intervals of not more than 2 minutes sound four blasts in succession, namely one prolonged followed by three short blasts. When practicable, this signal shall be made immediately after the signal made by the towing vessel.

(f/e)　When a pushing vessel and a vessel being pushed ahead are rigidly connected in a composite unit they shall be regarded as a power-driven vessel and shall give the signals prescribed in paragraphs (a) or (b) of this Rule.

(g/f) A vessel at anchor shall at intervals of not more than 1 minute ring the bell rapidly for about 5 seconds. In a vessel 100 meters or more in length the bell shall be sounded in the forepart of the vessel and immediately after the ringing of the bell the gong shall be sounded rapidly for about 5 seconds in the after part of the vessel. A vessel at anchor may in addition sound three blasts in succession, namely one short, one long and one short blast, to give warning of her position and of the possibility of collision to an approaching vessel.

(h/g) A vessel aground shall give the bell signal and if required the gong signal prescribed in paragraph [(g) / (f)] of this Rule and shall, in addition, give three separate and distinct strokes on the bell immediately before and after the rapid ringing of the bell. A vessel aground may in addition sound an appropriate whistle signal.

(i/h) A vessel of less than 12 meters in length shall not be obliged to give the above mentioned signals but, if she does not, shall make some other efficient sound signal at intervals of not more than 2 minutes.

(i) A vessel of 12 meters or more but less than 20 meters in length shall not be obliged io give the bell signals prescribed in paragraphs (g) and (h) of this Rule. However, if she does not, she shall make some other efficient sound signal at intervals of not more than 2 minutes. [Intl]

(j/h) A vessel of less than 12 meters in length shall not be obliged to give the above mentioned signals but, if she does not, shall make some other efficient sound signal at intervals of not more than 2 minutes.

(k/i) A pilotage vessel when engaged on pilotage duty may in addition to the signals prescribed in paragraph (a), (b) or [(g) / (f)] of this Rule sound an identity signal consisting of four short blasts.

(k) *The following vessels shall not be required to sound signals as prescribed in paragraph (f) of this Rule when anchored in a special anchorage area designated by the Secretary:*
   (ii) *a vessel of less than 20 meters in length; and*
   (iii) *a barge canal boat, scow, or other nondescript craft.* [Inld]

Rule 36 Signals to Attract Attention

If necessary to attract the attention of another vessel, any vessel may make light or sound signals that cannot be mistaken for any signal authorized elsewhere in these Rules, or may direct the beam of her searchlight in the direction of the danger, in such a way as not to embarrass any vessel. *Any light to attract the attention of another vessel shall be such that it cannot be mistaken for any aid to navigation. For the purpose of this Rule the use of high intensity intermittent or revolving lights, such as strobe lights, shall be avoided.* [Intl]

Rule 37 Distress Signals

When a vessel is in distress and requires assistance she shall use or exhibit the signals described in Annex IV to these Regulations.

Rule 37
Distress Signals 72 COLREGS

The distress signals for inland waters are the same as those displayed in the table above with the following additional signal:

Rule 37 - Inland only A high intensity white light flashing at regular intervals from 50 to 70 times per minute.

Part E Exemptions

Rule 38 Exemptions

Any vessel (or class of vessel) provided that she complies with the requirements of the International Regulations for the Preventing of Collisions at Sea, 1960, the keel of which is laid or is at a corresponding stage of construction before the entry into force of these Regulations may be exempted from compliance therewith as follows:

(a) The installation of lights with ranges prescribed in Rule 22, until 4 years after the date of entry into force of these regulations.

(b) The installation of lights with color specifications as prescribed in Section 7 of Annex I to these Regulations, until 4 years after the entry into force of these Regulations.

(c) The repositioning of lights as a result of conversion from Imperial to metric units and rounding off measurement figures, permanent exemption.

(d) The repositioning of masthead lights on vessels of less than 150 meters in length, resulting from the prescriptions of Section 3 (a) of Annex I to these regulations, permanent exemption. The repositioning of masthead lights on vessels of 150 meters or more in length, resulting from the prescriptions of Section 3 (a) of Annex I to these regulations, until 9 years after the date of entry into force of these Regulations.

(e)   The repositioning of masthead lights resulting from the prescriptions of Section 2(b) of Annex I to these Regulations, until 9 years after the date of entry into force of these Regulations.

(f)   The repositioning of sidelights resulting from the prescriptions of Section 2(g) and 3(b) of Annex I to these Regulations, until 9 years after the date of entry into force of these Regulations.

(g)   The requirements for sound signal appliances prescribed in Annex II to these Regulations, until 9 years after the date of entry into force of these Regulations.

(h)   The repositioning of all-round lights resulting from the prescription of Section 9(b) of Annex I to these Regulations, permanent exemption.

Vessel Arrest and Sale expenses

Although there is no statute setting the priorities, case law indicates the following in the order discussed.

1   The *custodia legis* expenses – the costs payable to the Marshal discussed above.
2   Maritime tort claims. These include such things as collision claims, seamen injury claims, wash damage caused by a vessel proceeding up river too fast, negligent towage (although there is authority to the contrary saying it is a contract claim), and some minimal authority that cargo damage might rise to a level of a tort although generally not.
3   Destruction of the *res*. While a seaman injured on or by a vessel has a tort claim that rises to a level of a maritime lien (disregarding the *in personam* claim against the shipowner) the *in rem* claim disappears if the vessel is destroyed. Thus, while the injured seaman may have a claim against the shipowner, he can not assert an *in rem* claim against the owner's other ships. His maritime lien is only against that one ship.

G

Death on the High Seas Act as first enacted in 1920 and contained in 46 U.S. C. §§ 761 – 767 provided

§ 761 **Right of action; where and by whom brought**

(a)   Subject to subsection (b), whenever the death of a person shall be caused by wrongful act, neglect, or default occurring on the high seas **beyond a marine league from the shore** of any State, or the District of Columbia, or the Territories or dependencies of the United States, **the personal representative of the decedent may maintain a suit for damages in the district courts of the United States, in admiralty, for the exclusive benefit of the decedent's wife, husband, parent, child, or dependent relative against the vessel, person, or corporation which would have been liable if death had not ensued.**

(b)   In the case of a commercial aviation accident, whenever the death of a person shall be caused by wrongful act, neglect, or default occurring on the high seas 12 nautical miles or closer to the shore of any State, or the District of Columbia, or the Territories or dependencies of the United States, this chapter shall not apply and the rules applicable under Federal, State, and other appropriate law shall apply.

[This aviation provision is an addition in the year 2000.]

§ 762 Amount and apportionment of recovery

(a)   The recovery in such suit shall be a fair and just compensation **for the pecuniary loss sustained by the persons for whose benefit the suit is brought** and shall be apportioned among them by the court in proportion to the loss they may severally have suffered by reason of the death of the person by whose representative the suit is brought.

(b)   (1) If the death resulted from a commercial aviation accident occurring on the high seas beyond 12 nautical miles from the shore of any State, or the District of Columbia, or the Territories or dependencies of the United States, additional compensation for nonpecuniary damages for wrongful death of a decedent is recoverable. Punitive damages are not recoverable.

> [This section also added in the year 2000 indicates that in aircraft crashes at sea "nonpecuniary" recovery would be available. This is contrary to *Miles v. Apex Marine Corp,* 498 U.S. 19 (1990) the case discussed above which denied nonpecuniary damages to all maritime workers. Ironically, it was the "pecuniary" limitation provision in subsection (a) in existence since 1920 that was one of the basis for Justice O'Connor's analyses in *Miles v. Apex* cutting out the nonpecuniary losses to maritime workers and their dependants when that opinion was decided in 1990.]

(2) In this subsection, the term "nonpecuniary damages" means damages for loss of care, comfort, and companionship.

§ 763a. Limitations

Unless otherwise specified by law, a suit for recovery of damages for personal injury or death, or both, arising out of a maritime tort, shall not be maintained unless commenced within three years from the date the cause of action accrued.

§ 764 Rights of action given by laws of foreign countries

Whenever a right of action is granted by the law of any foreign State on account of death by wrongful act, neglect, or default occurring upon the high seas, such right may be maintained in an appropriate action in admiralty in the courts of the United States without abatement in respect to the amount for which recovery is authorized, any statute of the United States to the contrary notwithstanding.

> [Under this section there are cases that permit foreign nonpecuniary recoveries]

§ 765 Death of plaintiff pending action

If a person dies as the result of such wrongful act, neglect, or default as is mentioned in Section 761 of this title during the pendency in a court of admiralty of the United States of a suit to recover damages for personal injuries in respect of such act, neglect, or default, the personal representative of the decedent may be substituted as a party and the suit may proceed as a suit under this chapter for the recovery of the compensation provided in section 762 of this title.

> [Just a practical notation that this may take place and provides for an easy solution.]

§ 766 **Contributory negligence (added in 2000)**

In suits under this chapter the fact that the decedent has been guilty of contributory negligence shall not bar recovery, but the court shall take into consideration the degree of negligence attributable to the decedent and reduce the recovery accordingly.

§ 767 Exceptions from operation of chapter (added in 2000)

The provisions of any State statute giving or regulating rights of action or remedies for death shall not be affected by this Act. Nor shall this Act apply to the Great Lakes or to any waters within the territorial limits of any State, or to any navigable waters in the Panama Canal Zone.

Rotterdam Rules

United Nations Convention on Contracts for the International Carriage of Goods Wholly or Partly by Sea *(Preliminary and introductory statements omitted.)*

Chapter 1 General provisions

Article 1 Definitions

For the purposes of this Convention:

1. "Contract of carriage" means a contract in which a carrier, against the payment of freight, undertakes to carry goods from one place to another. The contract shall provide for carriage by sea and may provide for carriage by other modes of transport in addition to the sea carriage.
2. "Volume contract" means a contract of carriage that provides for the carriage of a specified quantity of goods in a series of shipments during an agreed period of time. The specification of the quantity may include a minimum, a maximum or a certain range.
3. "Liner transportation" means a transportation service that is offered to the public through publication or similar means and includes transportation by ships operating on a regular schedule

between specified ports in accordance with publicly available timetables of sailing dates.

4. "Non-liner transportation" means any transportation that is not liner transportation.

5. "Carrier" means a person that enters into a contract of carriage with a shipper.

6. (*a*) "Performing party" means a person other than the carrier that performs or undertakes to perform any of the carrier's obligations under a contract of carriage with respect to the receipt, loading, handling, stowage, carriage, care, unloading or delivery of the goods, to the extent that such person acts, either directly or indirectly, at the carrier's request or under the carrier's supervision or control.

    (*b*) "Performing party" does not include any person that is retained, directly or indirectly, by a shipper, by a documentary shipper, by the controlling party or by the consignee instead of by the carrier.

7. "Maritime performing party" means a performing party to the extent that it performs or undertakes to perform any of the carrier's obligations during the period between the arrival of the goods at the port of loading of a ship and their departure from the port of discharge of a ship. An inland carrier is a maritime performing party only if it performs or undertakes to perform its services exclusively within a port area.

8. "Shipper" means a person that enters into a contract of carriage with a carrier.

9. "Documentary shipper" means a person, other than the shipper, that accepts to be named as "shipper" in the transport document or electronic transport record.

10. "Holder" means:

    (*a*) A person that is in possession of a negotiable transport document; and (i) if the document is an order document, is identified in it as the shipper or the consignee, or is the person to which the document is duly endorsed; or (ii) if the document is a blank endorsed order document or bearer document, is the bearer thereof; or

(b) The person to which a negotiable electronic transport record has been issued or transferred in accordance with the procedures referred to in article 9, paragraph 1.

11. "Consignee" means a person entitled to delivery of the goods under a contract of carriage or a transport document or electronic transport record.

12. "Right of control" of the goods means the right under the contract of carriage to give the carrier instructions in respect of the goods in accordance with chapter 10.

13. "Controlling party" means the person that pursuant to article 51 is entitled to exercise the right of control.

14. "Transport document" means a document issued under a contract of carriage by the carrier that:

(a) Evidences the carrier's or a performing party's receipt of goods under a contract of carriage; and

(b) Evidences or contains a contract of carriage.

15. "Negotiable transport document" means a transport document that indicates, by wording such as "to order" or "negotiable" or other appropriate wording recognized as having the same effect by the law applicable to the document, that the goods have been consigned to the order of the shipper, to the order of the consignee, or to bearer, and is not explicitly stated as being "non-negotiable" or "not negotiable".

16. "Non-negotiable transport document" means a transport document that is not a negotiable transport document.

17. "Electronic communication" means information generated, sent, received or stored by electronic, optical, digital or similar means

with the result that the information communicated is accessible so as to be usable for subsequent reference.

18. "Electronic transport record" means information in one or more messages issued by electronic communication under a contract of carriage by a carrier, including information logically associated with the electronic transport record by attachments or otherwise linked to the electronic transport record contemporaneously with or subsequent to its issue by the carrier, so as to become part of the electronic transport record, that:

    (a) Evidences the carrier's or a performing party's receipt of goods under a contract of carriage; and

    (b) Evidences or contains a contract of carriage.

19. "Negotiable electronic transport record" means an electronic transport record:

    (a) That indicates, by wording such as "to order", or "negotiable", or other appropriate wording recognized as having the same effect by the law applicable to the record, that the goods have been consigned to the order of the shipper or to the order of the consignee, and is not explicitly stated as being "non-negotiable" or "not negotiable"; and

    (b) The use of which meets the requirements of article 9, paragraph 1.

20. "Non-negotiable electronic transport record" means an electronic transport record that is not a negotiable electronic transport record.

21. The "issuance" of a negotiable electronic transport record means the issuance of the record in accordance with procedures that ensure that the record is subject to exclusive control from its creation until it ceases to have any effect or validity.

22. The "transfer" of a negotiable electronic transport record means the transfer of exclusive control over the record.

23. "Contract particulars" means any information relating to the contract of carriage or to the goods (including terms, notations, signatures and endorsements) that is in a transport document or an electronic transport record.

24. "Goods" means the wares, merchandise, and articles of every kind whatsoever that a carrier undertakes to carry under a contract of carriage and includes the packing and any equipment and container not supplied by or on behalf of the carrier.

25. "Ship" means any vessel used to carry goods by sea.

26. "Container" means any type of container, transportable tank or flat, swapbody, or any similar unit load used to consolidate goods, and any equipment ancillary to such unit load.

27. "Vehicle" means a road or railroad cargo vehicle.

28. "Freight" means the remuneration payable to the carrier for the carriage of goods under a contract of carriage.

29. "Domicile" means (a) a place where a company or other legal person or association of natural or legal persons has its (i) statutory seat or place of incorporation or central registered office, whichever is applicable, (ii) central administration or (iii) principal place of business, and (*b*) the habitual residence of a natural person.

30. "Competent court" means a court in a Contracting State that, according to the rules on the internal allocation of jurisdiction among the courts of that State, may exercise jurisdiction over the dispute.

Article 2 Interpretation of this Convention

In the interpretation of this Convention, regard is to be had to its international character and to the need to promote uniformity in its application and the observance of good faith in international trade.

Article 3 Form requirements

The notices, confirmation, consent, agreement, declaration and other communications referred to in articles 19, paragraph 2; 23, paragraphs 1 to 4; 36, subparagraphs 1 (*b*), (*c*) and (*d*); 40, subparagraph 4 (*b*); 44; 48, paragraph 3; 51, subparagraph 1 (*b*); 59, paragraph 1; 63; 66; 67, paragraph 2; 75, paragraph 4; and 80, paragraphs 2 and 5, shall be in writing. Electronic communications may be used for these purposes, provided that the use of such means is with the consent of the person by which it is communicated and of the person to which it is communicated.

Article 4 Applicability of defences and limits of liability

1. Any provision of this Convention that may provide a defence for, or limit the liability of, the carrier applies in any judicial or arbitral proceeding, whether founded in contract, in tort, or otherwise, that is instituted in respect of loss of, damage to, or delay in delivery of goods covered by a contract of carriage or for the breach of any other obligation under this Convention against:
    (*a*) The carrier or a maritime performing party;
    (*b*) The master, crew or any other person that performs services on board the ship; or
    (*c*) Employees of the carrier or a maritime performing party.

2. Any provision of this Convention that may provide a defence for the shipper or the documentary shipper applies in any judicial or arbitral proceeding, whether founded in contract, in tort, or otherwise, that is instituted against the shipper, the documentary shipper, or their subcontractors, agents or employees.

Chapter 2 Scope of application

Article 5 General scope of application

1. Subject to article 6, this Convention applies to contracts of carriage in which the place of receipt and the place of delivery are in different States, and the port of loading of a sea carriage and the port of discharge of the same sea carriage are in different States, if, according to the contract of carriage, any one of the following places is located in a Contracting State:
    (a) The place of receipt;
    (b) The port of loading;
    (c) The place of delivery; or
    (d) The port of discharge.

2. This Convention applies without regard to the nationality of the vessel, the carrier, the performing parties, the shipper, the consignee, or any other interested parties.

Article 6 Specific exclusions

1. This Convention does not apply to the following contracts in liner transportation:
    (a) Charter parties; and
    (b) Other contracts for the use of a ship or of any space thereon.

2. This Convention does not apply to contracts of carriage in non-liner transportation except when:
    (a) There is no charter party or other contract between the parties for the use of a ship or of any space thereon; and *(b)* A transport document or an electronic transport record is issued.

Article 7 Application to certain parties

Notwithstanding article 6, this Convention applies as between the carrier and the consignee, controlling party or holder that is not an original party to the charter party or other contract of carriage excluded from the application of this Convention. However, this Convention does not apply as between the original parties to a contract of carriage excluded pursuant to article 6.

Chapter 3 Electronic transport records

Article 8 Use and effect of electronic transport records

Subject to the requirements set out in this Convention:

(a) Anything that is to be in or on a transport document under this Convention may be recorded in an electronic transport record, provided the issuance and subsequent use of an electronic transport record is with the consent of the carrier and the shipper; and

(b) The issuance, exclusive control, or transfer of an electronic transport record has the same effect as the issuance, possession, or transfer of a transport document.

Article 9 Procedures for use of negotiable electronic transport records

1. The use of a negotiable electronic transport record shall be subject to procedures that provide for:
    (a) The method for the issuance and the transfer of that record to an intended holder;
    (b) An assurance that the negotiable electronic transport record retains its integrity;

(c) The manner in which the holder is able to demonstrate that it is the holder; and

(d) The manner of providing confirmation that delivery to the holder has been effected, or that, pursuant to articles 10, paragraph 2, or 47, subparagraphs 1 (*a*) (ii) and (*c*), the electronic transport record has ceased to have any effect or validity.

2. The procedures in paragraph 1 of this article shall be referred to in the contract particulars and be readily ascertainable.

Article 10 Replacement of negotiable transport document or negotiable electronic transport record

1. If a negotiable transport document has been issued and the carrier and the holder agree to replace that document by a negotiable electronic transport record:

(a) The holder shall surrender the negotiable transport document, or all of them if more than one has been issued, to the carrier;

(b) The carrier shall issue to the holder a negotiable electronic transport record that includes a statement that it replaces the negotiable transport document; and

(c) The negotiable transport document ceases thereafter to have any effect or validity.

2. If a negotiable electronic transport record has been issued and the carrier and the holder agree to replace that electronic transport record by a negotiable transport document:

(a) The carrier shall issue to the holder, in place of the electronic transport record, a negotiable transport document that includes a statement that it replaces the negotiable electronic transport record; and

(b) The electronic transport record ceases thereafter to have any effect or validity.

Chapter 4 Obligations of the carrier

Article 11 Carriage and delivery of the goods

The carrier shall, subject to this Convention and in accordance with the terms of the contract of carriage, carry the goods to the place of destination and deliver them to the consignee.

Article 12 Period of responsibility of the carrier

1. The period of responsibility of the carrier for the goods under this Convention begins when the carrier or a performing party receives the goods for carriage and ends when the goods are delivered.
2. (*a*) If the law or regulations of the place of receipt require the goods to be handed over to an authority or other third party from which the carrier may collect them, the period of responsibility of the carrier begins when the carrier collects the goods from the authority or other third party.

    (*b*) If the law or regulations of the place of delivery require the carrier to hand over the goods to an authority or other third party from which the consignee may collect them, the period of responsibility of the carrier ends when the carrier hands the goods over to the authority or other third party.

3. For the purpose of determining the carrier's period of responsibility, the parties may agree on the time and location of receipt and delivery of the goods, but a provision in a contract of carriage is void to the extent that it provides that:

    (*a*) The time of receipt of the goods is subsequent to the beginning of their initial loading under the contract of carriage; or

    (*b*) The time of delivery of the goods is prior to the completion of their final unloading under the contract of carriage.

Article 13 Specific obligations

1. The carrier shall during the period of its responsibility as defined in article 12, and subject to article 26, properly and carefully receive, load, handle, stow, carry, keep, care for, unload and deliver the goods.
2. Notwithstanding paragraph 1 of this article, and without prejudice to the other provisions in chapter 4 and to chapters 5 to 7, the carrier and the shipper may agree that the loading, handling, stowing or unloading of the goods is to be performed by the shipper, the documentary shipper or the consignee. Such an agreement shall be referred to in the contract particulars.

Article 14 Specific obligations applicable to the voyage by sea

The carrier is bound before, at the beginning of, and during the voyage by sea to exercise due diligence to:

(a) Make and keep the ship seaworthy;

(b) Properly crew, equip and supply the ship and keep the ship so crewed, equipped and supplied throughout the voyage; and

(c) Make and keep the holds and all other parts of the ship in which the goods are carried, and any containers supplied by the carrier in or upon which the goods are carried, fit and safe for their reception, carriage and preservation.

Article 15 Goods that may become a danger

Notwithstanding articles 11 and 13, the carrier or a performing party may decline to receive or to load, and may take such other measures as are reasonable, including unloading, destroying, or rendering goods harmless, if the goods are, or reasonably appear likely to become during the carrier's period of responsibility, an actual danger to persons, property or the environment.

Article 16 Sacrifice of the goods during the voyage by sea

Notwithstanding articles 11, 13, and 14, the carrier or a performing party may sacrifice goods at sea when the sacrifice is reasonably made for the common safety or for the purpose of preserving from peril human life or other property involved in the common adventure.

Chapter 5 Liability of the carrier for loss, damage or delay

Article 17 Basis of liability

1. The carrier is liable for loss of or damage to the goods, as well as for delay in delivery, if the claimant proves that the loss, damage, or delay, or the event or circumstance that caused or contributed to it took place during the period of the carrier's responsibility as defined in chapter 4.
2. The carrier is relieved of all or part of its liability pursuant to paragraph 1 of this article if it proves that the cause or one of the causes of the loss, damage, or delay is not attributable to its fault or to the fault of any person referred to in article 18.
3. The carrier is also relieved of all or part of its liability pursuant to paragraph 1 of this article if, alternatively to proving the absence of fault as provided in paragraph 2 of this article, it proves that one or more of the following events or circumstances caused or contributed to the loss, damage, or delay:
    (a) Act of God;
    (b) Perils, dangers, and accidents of the sea or other navigable waters;
    (c) War, hostilities, armed conflict, piracy, terrorism, riots, and civil commotions;

(d) Quarantine restrictions; interference by or impediments created by governments, public authorities, rulers, or people including detention, arrest, or seizure not attributable to the carrier or any person referred to in article 18;

(e) Strikes, lockouts, stoppages, or restraints of labour;

(f) Fire on the ship;

(g) Latent defects not discoverable by due diligence;

(h) Act or omission of the shipper, the documentary shipper, the controlling party, or any other person for whose acts the shipper or the documentary shipper is liable pursuant to article 33 or 34;

(i) Loading, handling, stowing, or unloading of the goods performed pursuant to an agreement in accordance with article 13, paragraph 2, unless the carrier or a performing party performs such activity on behalf of the shipper, the documentary shipper or the consignee;

(j) Wastage in bulk or weight or any other loss or damage arising from inherent defect, quality, or vice of the goods;

(k) Insufficiency or defective condition of packing or marking not performed by or on behalf of the carrier;

(l) Saving or attempting to save life at sea;

(m) Reasonable measures to save or attempt to save property at sea;

(n) Reasonable measures to avoid or attempt to avoid damage to the environment; or

(o) Acts of the carrier in pursuance of the powers conferred by articles 15 and 16.

4. Notwithstanding paragraph 3 of this article, the carrier is liable for all or part of the loss, damage, or delay:

(a) If the claimant proves that the fault of the carrier or of a person referred to in article 18 caused or contributed to the event or circumstance on which the carrier relies; or

(b) If the claimant proves that an event or circumstance not listed in paragraph 3 of this article contributed to the loss, damage, or delay, and the carrier cannot prove that this event or circumstance is not attributable to its fault or to the fault of any person referred to in article 18.

5. The carrier is also liable, notwithstanding paragraph 3 of this article, for all or part of the loss, damage, or delay if:

(a) The claimant proves that the loss, damage, or delay was or was probably caused by or contributed to by (i) the unseaworthiness of the ship; (ii) the improper crewing, equipping, and supplying of the ship; or (iii) the fact that the holds or other parts of the ship in which the goods are carried, or any containers supplied by the carrier in or upon which the goods are carried, were not fit and safe for reception, carriage, and preservation of the goods; and

(b) The carrier is unable to prove either that: (i) none of the events or circumstances referred to in subparagraph 5 (a) of this article caused the loss, damage, or delay; or (ii) it complied with its obligation to exercise due diligence pursuant to article 14.

6. When the carrier is relieved of part of its liability pursuant to this article, the carrier is liable only for that part of the loss, damage or delay that is attributable to the event or circumstance for which it is liable pursuant to this article.

Article 18 Liability of the carrier for other persons

The carrier is liable for the breach of its obligations under this Convention caused by the acts or omissions of:

(a) Any performing party;
(b) The master or crew of the ship;

(c) Employees of the carrier or a performing party; or

(d) Any other person that performs or undertakes to perform any of the carrier's obligations under the contract of carriage, to the extent that the person acts, either directly or indirectly, at the carrier's request or under the carrier's supervision or control.

Article 19 Liability of maritime performing parties

1. A maritime performing party is subject to the obligations and liabilities imposed on the carrier under this Convention and is entitled to the carrier's defences and limits of liability as provided for in this Convention if:

   (a) The maritime performing party received the goods for carriage in a Contracting State, or delivered them in a Contracting State, or performed its activities with respect to the goods in a port in a Contracting State; and

   (b) The occurrence that caused the loss, damage or delay took place: (i) during the period between the arrival of the goods at the port of loading of the ship and their departure from the port of discharge from the ship; (ii) while the maritime performing party had custody of the goods; or (iii) at any other time to the extent that it was participating in the performance of any of the activities contemplated by the contract of carriage.

2. If the carrier agrees to assume obligations other than those imposed on the carrier under this Convention, or agrees that the limits of its liability are higher than the limits specified under this Convention, a maritime performing party is not bound by this agreement unless it expressly agrees to accept such obligations or such higher limits.

3. A maritime performing party is liable for the breach of its obligations under this Convention caused by the acts or omissions of any person to which it has entrusted the performance of any of

the carrier's obligations under the contract of carriage under the conditions set out in paragraph 1 of this article.

4.   Nothing in this Convention imposes liability on the master or crew of the ship or on an employee of the carrier or of a maritime performing party.

Article 20 Joint and several liability

1.   If the carrier and one or more maritime performing parties are liable for the loss of, damage to, or delay in delivery of the goods, their liability is joint and several but only up to the limits provided for under this Convention.

2.   Without prejudice to article 61, the aggregate liability of all such persons shall not exceed the overall limits of liability under this Convention.

Article 21 Delay

Delay in delivery occurs when the goods are not delivered at the place of destination provided for in the contract of carriage within the time agreed.

Article 22 Calculation of compensation

1.   Subject to article 59, the compensation payable by the carrier for loss of or damage to the goods is calculated by reference to the value of such goods at the place and time of delivery established in accordance with article 43.

2.   The value of the goods is fixed according to the commodity exchange price or, if there is no such price, according to their market price or, if there is no commodity exchange price or market price, by reference to the normal value of the goods of the same kind and quality at the place of delivery.

3. In case of loss of or damage to the goods, the carrier is not liable for payment of any compensation beyond what is provided for in paragraphs 1 and 2 of this article except when the carrier and the shipper have agreed to calculate compensation in a different manner within the limits of chapter 16.

Article 23 Notice in case of loss, damage or delay

1. The carrier is presumed, in absence of proof to the contrary, to have delivered the goods according to their description in the contract particulars unless notice of loss of or damage to the goods, indicating the general nature of such loss or damage, was given to the carrier or the performing party that delivered the goods before or at the time of the delivery, or, if the loss or damage is not apparent, within seven working days at the place of delivery after the delivery of the goods.

2. Failure to provide the notice referred to in this article to the carrier or the performing party shall not affect the right to claim compensation for loss of or damage to the goods under this Convention, nor shall it affect the allocation of the burden of proof set out in article 17.

3. The notice referred to in this article is not required in respect of loss or damage that is ascertained in a joint inspection of the goods by the person to which they have been delivered and the carrier or the maritime performing party against which liability is being asserted.

4. No compensation in respect of delay is payable unless notice of loss due to delay was given to the carrier within twenty-one consecutive days of delivery of the goods.

5. When the notice referred to in this article is given to the performing party that delivered the goods, it has the same effect as if that notice was given to the carrier, and notice given to the carrier has the same effect as a notice given to a maritime performing party.

6.   In the case of any actual or apprehended loss or damage, the parties to the dispute shall give all reasonable facilities to each other for inspecting and tallying the goods and shall provide access to records and documents relevant to the carriage of the goods.

Chapter 6 Additional provisions relating to particular stages of carriage

Article 24 Deviation

When pursuant to applicable law a deviation constitutes a breach of the carrier's obligations, such deviation of itself shall not deprive the carrier or a maritime performing party of any defence or limitation of this Convention, except to the extent provided in article 61.

Article 25 Deck cargo on ships

1.   Goods may be carried on the deck of a ship only if:
      (a) Such carriage is required by law;
      (b) They are carried in or on containers or vehicles that are fit for deck carriage, and the decks are specially fitted to carry such containers or vehicles; or
      (c) The carriage on deck is in accordance with the contract of carriage, or the customs, usages or practices of the trade in question.

2.   The provisions of this Convention relating to the liability of the carrier apply to the loss of, damage to or delay in the delivery of goods carried on deck pursuant to paragraph 1 of this article, but the carrier is not liable for loss of or damage to such goods, or delay in their delivery, caused by the special risks involved in their carriage on deck when the goods are carried in accordance with subparagraphs 1 (a) or (c) of this article.

3.   If the goods have been carried on deck in cases other than those permitted pursuant to paragraph 1 of this article, the carrier is liable for loss of or damage to the goods or delay in their delivery that is exclusively caused by their carriage on deck, and is not entitled to the defences provided for in article 17.

4.   The carrier is not entitled to invoke subparagraph 1 (c) of this article against a third party that has acquired a negotiable transport document or a negotiable electronic transport record in good faith, unless the contract particulars state that the goods may be carried on deck.

5.   If the carrier and shipper expressly agreed that the goods would be carried under deck, the carrier is not entitled to the benefit of the limitation of liability for any loss of, damage to or delay in the delivery of the goods to the extent that such loss, damage, or delay resulted from their carriage on deck.

Article 26 Carriage preceding or subsequent to sea carriage

When loss of or damage to goods, or an event or circumstance causing a delay in their delivery, occurs during the carrier's period of responsibility but solely before their loading onto the ship or solely after their discharge from the ship, the provisions of this Convention do not prevail over those provisions of another international instrument that, at the time of such loss, damage or event or circumstance causing delay:

(a) Pursuant to the provisions of such international instrument would have applied to all or any of the carrier's activities if the shipper had made a separate and direct contract with the carrier in respect of the particular stage of carriage where the loss of, or damage to goods, or an event or circumstance causing delay in their delivery occurred;

(b) Specifically provide for the carrier's liability, limitation of liability, or time for suit; and *(c)* Cannot be departed from by contract either at all or to the detriment of the shipper under that instrument.

Chapter 7 Obligations of the shipper to the carrier

Article 27 Delivery for carriage

1. Unless otherwise agreed in the contract of carriage, the shipper shall deliver the goods ready for carriage. In any event, the shipper shall deliver the goods in such condition that they will withstand the intended carriage, including their loading, handling, stowing, lashing and securing, and unloading, and that they will not cause harm to persons or property.
2. The shipper shall properly and carefully perform any obligation assumed under an agreement made pursuant to article 13, paragraph 2.
3. When a container is packed or a vehicle is loaded by the shipper, the shipper shall properly and carefully stow, lash and secure the contents in or on the container or vehicle, and in such a way that they will not cause harm to persons or property.

Article 28 Cooperation of the shipper and the carrier in providing information and instructions

The carrier and the shipper shall respond to requests from each other to provide information and instructions required for the proper handling and carriage of the goods if the information is in the requested party's possession or the instructions are within the requested party's reasonable ability to provide and they are not otherwise reasonably available to the requesting party.

Article 29 Shipper's obligation to provide information, instructions and documents

1. The shipper shall provide to the carrier in a timely manner such information, instructions and documents relating to the goods that are not otherwise reasonably available to the carrier, and that are reasonably necessary:

    (a) For the proper handling and carriage of the goods, including precautions to be taken by the carrier or a performing party; and

    (b) For the carrier to comply with law, regulations or other requirements of public authorities in connection with the intended carriage, provided that the carrier notifies the shipper in a timely manner of the information, instructions and documents it requires.

2. Nothing in this article affects any specific obligation to provide certain information, instructions and documents related to the goods pursuant to law, regulations or other requirements of public authorities in connection with the intended carriage.

Article 30 Basis of shipper's liability to the carrier

1. The shipper is liable for loss or damage sustained by the carrier if the carrier proves that such loss or damage was caused by a breach of the shipper's obligations under this Convention.

2. Except in respect of loss or damage caused by a breach by the shipper of its obligations pursuant to articles 31, paragraph 2, and 32, the shipper is relieved of all or part of its liability if the cause or one of the causes of the loss or damage is not attributable to its fault or to the fault of any person referred to in article 34.

3. When the shipper is relieved of part of its liability pursuant to this article, the shipper is liable only for that part of the loss or damage

that is attributable to its fault or to the fault of any person referred to in article 34.

Article 31 Information for compilation of contract particulars

1. The shipper shall provide to the carrier, in a timely manner, accurate information required for the compilation of the contract particulars and the issuance of the transport documents or electronic transport records, including the particulars referred to in article 36, paragraph 1; the name of the party to be identified as the shipper in the contract particulars; the name of the consignee, if any; and the name of the person to whose order the transport document or electronic transport record is to be issued, if any.
2. The shipper is deemed to have guaranteed the accuracy at the time of receipt by the carrier of the information that is provided according to paragraph 1 of this article. The shipper shall indemnify the carrier against loss or damage resulting from the inaccuracy of such information.

Article 32 Special rules on dangerous goods

When goods by their nature or character are, or reasonably appear likely to become, a danger to persons, property or the environment:

(a) The shipper shall inform the carrier of the dangerous nature or character of the goods in a timely manner before they are delivered to the carrier or a performing party. If the shipper fails to do so and the carrier or performing party does not otherwise have knowledge of their dangerous nature or character, the shipper is liable to the carrier for loss or damage resulting from such failure to inform; and

(b) The shipper shall mark or label dangerous goods in accordance with any law, regulations or other requirements of public authorities that apply during any stage of the intended carriage of the goods. If the shipper fails to do so, it is liable to the carrier for loss or damage resulting from such failure.

Article 33 Assumption of shipper's rights and obligations by the documentary shipper

1. A documentary shipper is subject to the obligations and liabilities imposed on the shipper pursuant to this chapter and pursuant to article 55, and is entitled to the shipper's rights and defences provided by this chapter and by chapter 13.
2. Paragraph 1 of this article does not affect the obligations, liabilities, rights or defences of the shipper.

Article 34 Liability of the shipper for other persons

The shipper is liable for the breach of its obligations under this Convention caused by the acts or omissions of any person, including employees, agents and subcontractors, to which it has entrusted the performance of any of its obligations, but the shipper is not liable for acts or omissions of the carrier or a performing party acting on behalf of the carrier, to which the shipper has entrusted the performance of its obligations.

Chapter 8 Transport documents and electronic transport records

Article 35 Issuance of the transport document or the electronic transport record

Unless the shipper and the carrier have agreed not to use a transport document or an electronic transport record, or it is the custom, usage or practice of the trade not to use one, upon delivery of the goods for carriage to the carrier or performing party, the shipper or, if the shipper consents, the documentary shipper, is entitled to obtain from the carrier, at the shipper's option:

(a) A non-negotiable transport document or, subject to article 8, subparagraph (a), a non-negotiable electronic transport record; or

(b) An appropriate negotiable transport document or, subject to article 8, subparagraph (a), a negotiable electronic transport record, unless the shipper and the carrier have agreed not to use a negotiable transport document or negotiable electronic transport record, or it is the custom, usage or practice of the trade not to use one.

Article 36 Contract particulars

1. The contract particulars in the transport document or electronic transport record referred to in article 35 shall include the following information, as furnished by the shipper:
   (a) A description of the goods as appropriate for the transport;
   (b) The leading marks necessary for identification of the goods;
   (c) The number of packages or pieces, or the quantity of goods; and
   (d) The weight of the goods, if furnished by the shipper.

2. The contract particulars in the transport document or electronic transport record referred to in article 35 shall also include:
   (a) A statement of the apparent order and condition of the goods at the time the carrier or a performing party receives them for carriage;
   (b) The name and address of the carrier;
   (c) The date on which the carrier or a performing party received the goods, or on which the goods were loaded on board the ship, or on which the transport document or electronic transport record was issued; and

(*d*) If the transport document is negotiable, the number of originals of the negotiable transport document, when more than one original is issued.

3. The contract particulars in the transport document or electronic transport record referred to in article 35 shall further include:
    (*a*) The name and address of the consignee, if named by the shipper;
    (*b*) The name of a ship, if specified in the contract of carriage;
    (*c*) The place of receipt and, if known to the carrier, the place of delivery; and
    (*d*) The port of loading and the port of discharge, if specified in the contract of carriage.

4. For the purposes of this article, the phrase "apparent order and condition of the goods" in subparagraph 2 (*a*) of this article refers to the order and condition of the goods based on:
    (*a*) A reasonable external inspection of the goods as packaged at the time the shipper delivers them to the carrier or a performing party; and
    (*b*) Any additional inspection that the carrier or a performing party actually performs before issuing the transport document or electronic transport record.

Article 37 Identity of the carrier

1. If a carrier is identified by name in the contract particulars, any other information in the transport document or electronic transport record relating to the identity of the carrier shall have no effect to the extent that it is inconsistent with that identification.
2. If no person is identified in the contract particulars as the carrier as required pursuant to article 36, subparagraph 2 (*b*), but the contract particulars indicate that the goods have been loaded

on board a named ship, the registered owner of that ship is presumed to be the carrier, unless it proves that the ship was under a bareboat charter at the time of the carriage and it identifies this bareboat charterer and indicates its address, in which case this bareboat charterer is presumed to be the carrier. Alternatively, the registered owner may rebut the presumption of being the carrier by identifying the carrier and indicating its address. The bareboat charterer may rebut any presumption of being the carrier in the same manner.

3.   Nothing in this article prevents the claimant from proving that any person other than a person identified in the contract particulars or pursuant to paragraph 2 of this article is the carrier.

Article 38 Signature

1.   A transport document shall be signed by the carrier or a person acting on its behalf.

2.   An electronic transport record shall include the electronic signature of the carrier or a person acting on its behalf. Such electronic signature shall identify the signatory in relation to the electronic transport record and indicate the carrier's authorization of the electronic transport record.

Article 39 Deficiencies in the contract particulars

1.   The absence or inaccuracy of one or more of the contract particulars referred to in article 36, paragraphs 1, 2 or 3, does not of itself affect the legal character or validity of the transport document or of the electronic transport record.

2.   If the contract particulars include the date but fail to indicate its significance, the date is deemed to be:

   (a) The date on which all of the goods indicated in the transport document or electronic transport record were loaded on board

the ship, if the contract particulars indicate that the goods have been loaded on board a ship; or

(b) The date on which the carrier or a performing party received the goods, if the contract particulars do not indicate that the goods have been loaded on board a ship.

3. If the contract particulars fail to state the apparent order and condition of the goods at the time the carrier or a performing party receives them, the contract particulars are deemed to have stated that the goods were in apparent good order and condition at the time the carrier or a performing party received them.

Article 40 Qualifying the information relating to the goods in the contract particulars

1. The carrier shall qualify the information referred to in article 36, paragraph 1, to indicate that the carrier does not assume responsibility for the accuracy of the information furnished by the shipper if:

    (a) The carrier has actual knowledge that any material statement in the transport document or electronic transport record is false or misleading; or

    (b) The carrier has reasonable grounds to believe that a material statement in the transport document or electronic transport record is false or misleading.

2. Without prejudice to paragraph 1 of this article, the carrier may qualify the information referred to in article 36, paragraph 1, in the circumstances and in the manner set out in paragraphs 3 and 4 of this article to indicate that the carrier does not assume responsibility for the accuracy of the information furnished by the shipper.

3. When the goods are not delivered for carriage to the carrier or a performing party in a closed container or vehicle, or when they

are delivered in a closed container or vehicle and the carrier or a performing party actually inspects them, the carrier may qualify the information referred to in article 36, paragraph 1, if:

(a) The carrier had no physically practicable or commercially reasonable means of checking the information furnished by the shipper, in which case it may indicate which information it was unable to check; or

(b) The carrier has reasonable grounds to believe the information furnished by the shipper to be inaccurate, in which case it may include a clause providing what it reasonably considers accurate information.

4. When the goods are delivered for carriage to the carrier or a performing party in a closed container or vehicle, the carrier may qualify the information referred to in:

(a) Article 36, subparagraphs 1 (a), (b), or (c), if:

    (i)   The goods inside the container or vehicle have not actually been inspected by the carrier or a performing party; and

    (ii) Neither the carrier nor a performing party otherwise has actual knowledge of its contents before issuing the transport document or the electronic transport record; and

(b) Article 36, subparagraph 1 (d), if:

    (i)   Neither the carrier nor a performing party weighed the container or vehicle, and the shipper and the carrier had not agreed prior to the shipment that the container or vehicle would be weighed and the weight would be included in the contract particulars; or

    (ii) There was no physically practicable or commercially reasonable means of checking the weight of the container or vehicle.

Article 41 Evidentiary effect of the contract particulars

Except to the extent that the contract particulars have been qualified in the circumstances and in the manner set out in article 40:

(a) A transport document or an electronic transport record is prima facie evidence of the carrier's receipt of the goods as stated in the contract particulars;

(b) Proof to the contrary by the carrier in respect of any contract particulars shall not be admissible, when such contract particulars are included in:

  (i)   A negotiable transport document or a negotiable electronic transport record that is transferred to a third party acting in good faith; or

  (ii) A non-negotiable transport document that indicates that it must be surrendered in order to obtain delivery of the goods and is transferred to the consignee acting in good faith;

(c) Proof to the contrary by the carrier shall not be admissible against a consignee that in good faith has acted in reliance on any of the following contract particulars included in a non-negotiable transport document or a non-negotiable electronic transport record:

  (i)   The contract particulars referred to in article 36, paragraph 1, when such contract particulars are furnished by the carrier;

  (ii) The number, type and identifying numbers of the containers, but not the identifying numbers of the container seals; and

  (iii) The contract particulars referred to in article 36, paragraph 2.

Article 42 "Freight prepaid"

If the contract particulars contain the statement "freight prepaid" or a statement of a similar nature, the carrier cannot assert against the holder or the consignee the fact that the freight has not been paid. This article does not apply if the holder or the consignee is also the shipper.

Chapter 9 Delivery of the goods

Article 43 Obligation to accept delivery

When the goods have arrived at their destination, the consignee that demands delivery of the goods under the contract of carriage shall accept delivery of the goods at the time or within the time period and at the location agreed in the contract of carriage or, failing such agreement, at the time and location at which, having regard to the terms of the contract, the customs, usages or practices of the trade and the circumstances of the carriage, delivery could reasonably be expected.

Article 44 Obligation to acknowledge receipt

On request of the carrier or the performing party that delivers the goods, the consignee shall acknowledge receipt of the goods from the carrier or the performing party in the manner that is customary at the place of delivery. The carrier may refuse delivery if the consignee refuses to acknowledge such receipt.

Article 45 Delivery when no negotiable transport document or negotiable electronic transport record is issued

When neither a negotiable transport document nor a negotiable electronic transport record has been issued:

(a) The carrier shall deliver the goods to the consignee at the time and location referred to in article 43. The carrier may refuse delivery if the person claiming to be the consignee does not properly identify itself as the consignee on the request of the carrier;

(b) If the name and address of the consignee are not referred to in the contract particulars, the controlling party shall prior to or upon the arrival of the goods at the place of destination advise the carrier of such name and address;

(c) Without prejudice to article 48, paragraph 1, if the goods are not deliverable because (i) the consignee, after having received a notice of arrival, does not, at the time or within the time period referred to in article 43, claim delivery of the goods from the carrier after their arrival at the place of destination, (ii) the carrier refuses delivery because the person claiming to be the consignee does not properly identify itself as the consignee, or (iii) the carrier is, after reasonable effort, unable to locate the consignee in order to request delivery instructions, the carrier may so advise the controlling party and request instructions in respect of the delivery of the goods. If, after reasonable effort, the carrier is unable to locate the controlling party, the carrier may so advise the shipper and request instructions in respect of the delivery of the goods. If, after reasonable effort, the carrier is unable to locate the shipper, the carrier may so advise the documentary shipper and request instructions in respect of the delivery of the goods;

(d) The carrier that delivers the goods upon instruction of the controlling party, the shipper or the documentary shipper pursuant to subparagraph (c) of this article is discharged from its obligations to deliver the goods under the contract of carriage.

Article 46 Delivery when a non-negotiable transport document that requires surrender is issued

When a non-negotiable transport document has been issued that indicates that it shall be surrendered in order to obtain delivery of the goods:

(a) The carrier shall deliver the goods at the time and location referred to in article 43 to the consignee upon the consignee properly identifying itself on the request of the carrier and surrender of the non-negotiable document. The carrier may refuse delivery if the person claiming to be the consignee fails to properly identify itself on the request of the carrier, and shall refuse delivery if the non-negotiable document is not surrendered. If more than one original of the non-negotiable document has been issued, the surrender of one original will suffice and the other originals cease to have any effect or validity;

(b) Without prejudice to article 48, paragraph 1, if the goods are not deliverable because (i) the consignee, after having received a notice of arrival, does not, at the time or within the time period referred to in article 43, claim delivery of the goods from the carrier after their arrival at the place of destination, (ii) the carrier refuses delivery because the person claiming to be the consignee does not properly identify itself as the consignee or does not surrender the document, or (iii) the carrier is, after reasonable effort, unable to locate the consignee in order to request delivery instructions, the carrier may so

advise the shipper and request instructions in respect of the delivery of the goods. If, after reasonable effort, the carrier is unable to locate the shipper, the carrier may so advise the documentary shipper and request instructions in respect of the delivery of the goods;

(c) The carrier that delivers the goods upon instruction of the shipper or the documentary shipper pursuant to subparagraph (b) of this article is discharged from its obligation to deliver the goods under the contract of carriage, irrespective of whether the non-negotiable transport document has been surrendered to it.

Article 47 Delivery when a negotiable transport document or negotiable electronic transport record is issued

1. When a negotiable transport document or a negotiable electronic transport record has been issued:

   (a) The holder of the negotiable transport document or negotiable electronic transport record is entitled to claim delivery of the goods from the carrier after they have arrived at the place of destination, in which event the carrier shall deliver the goods at the time and location referred to in article 43 to the holder:

      (i) Upon surrender of the negotiable transport document and, if the holder is one of the persons referred to in article 1, subparagraph 10 (a) (i), upon the holder properly identifying itself; or

      (ii) Upon demonstration by the holder, in accordance with the procedures referred to in article 9, paragraph 1, that it is the holder of the negotiable electronic transport record;

   (b) The carrier shall refuse delivery if the requirements of subparagraph (a) (i) or (a) (ii) of this paragraph are not met;

   (c) If more than one original of the negotiable transport document has been issued, and the number of originals is stated in that document, the surrender of one original will suffice and the other originals cease to have any effect or validity. When a negotiable electronic transport record has been used, such electronic transport record ceases to have any effect or validity upon delivery to the holder in accordance with the procedures required by article 9, paragraph 1.

2. Without prejudice to article 48, paragraph 1, if the negotiable transport document or the negotiable electronic transport record expressly states that the goods may be delivered without the surrender of the transport document or the electronic transport record, the following rules apply:

(a) If the goods are not deliverable because (i) the holder, after having received a notice of arrival, does not, at the time or within the time period referred to in article 43, claim delivery of the goods from the carrier after their arrival at the place of destination, (ii) the carrier refuses delivery because the person claiming to be a holder does not properly identify itself as one of the persons referred to in article 1, subparagraph 10 (a) (i), or (iii) the carrier is, after reasonable effort, unable to locate the holder in order to request delivery instructions, the carrier may so advise the shipper and request instructions in respect of the delivery of the goods. If, after reasonable effort, the carrier is unable to locate the shipper, the carrier may so advise the documentary shipper and request instructions in respect of the delivery of the goods;

(b) The carrier that delivers the goods upon instruction of the shipper or the documentary shipper in accordance with subparagraph 2 (a) of this article is discharged from its obligation to deliver the goods under the contract of carriage to the holder, irrespective of whether the negotiable transport document has been surrendered to it, or the person claiming delivery under a negotiable electronic transport record has demonstrated, in accordance with the procedures referred to in article 9, paragraph 1, that it is the holder;

(c) The person giving instructions under subparagraph 2 (a) of this article shall indemnify the carrier against loss arising from its being held liable to the holder under subparagraph 2 (e) of this article. The carrier may refuse to follow those instructions if the person fails to provide adequate security as the carrier may reasonably request;

(d) A person that becomes a holder of the negotiable transport document or the negotiable electronic transport record after the carrier has delivered the goods pursuant to subparagraph 2 (b) of this article, but pursuant to contractual or other arrangements made before such delivery acquires rights against the carrier under the contract of carriage, other than the right to claim delivery of the goods;

(e) Notwithstanding subparagraphs 2 (b) and 2 (d) of this article, a holder that becomes a holder after such delivery, and that did not have and could not reasonably have had knowledge of such delivery at the time it became a holder, acquires the rights incorporated in the negotiable transport document or negotiable electronic transport record. When the contract particulars state the expected time of arrival of the goods, or indicate how to obtain information as to whether the goods have been delivered, it is presumed that the holder at the time that it became a holder had or could reasonably have had knowledge of the delivery of the goods.

Article 48 Goods remaining undelivered

1. For the purposes of this article, goods shall be deemed to have remained undelivered only if, after their arrival at the place of destination:

(a) The consignee does not accept delivery of the goods pursuant to this chapter at the time and location referred to in article 43;

(b) The controlling party, the holder, the shipper or the documentary shipper cannot be found or does not give the carrier adequate instructions pursuant to articles 45, 46 and 47;

(c) The carrier is entitled or required to refuse delivery pursuant to articles 44, 45, 46 and 47;

(d) The carrier is not allowed to deliver the goods to the consignee pursuant to the law or regulations of the place at which delivery is requested; or

(e) The goods are otherwise undeliverable by the carrier.

2.   Without prejudice to any other rights that the carrier may have against the shipper, controlling party or consignee, if the goods have remained undelivered, the carrier may, at the risk and expense of the person entitled to the goods, take such action in respect of the goods as circumstances may reasonably require, including:

(a) To store the goods at any suitable place;

(b) To unpack the goods if they are packed in containers or vehicles, or to act otherwise in respect of the goods, including by moving them; and

(c) To cause the goods to be sold or destroyed in accordance with the practices or pursuant to the law or regulations of the place where the goods are located at the time.

3.   The carrier may exercise the rights under paragraph 2 of this article only after it has given reasonable notice of the intended action under paragraph 2 of this article to the person stated in the contract particulars as the person, if any, to be notified of the arrival of the goods at the place of destination, and to one of the following persons in the order indicated, if known to the carrier: the consignee, the controlling party or the shipper.

4.   If the goods are sold pursuant to subparagraph 2 (c) of this article, the carrier shall hold the proceeds of the sale for the benefit of the person entitled to the goods, subject to the deduction of any costs incurred by the carrier and any other amounts that are due to the carrier in connection with the carriage of those goods.

5.   The carrier shall not be liable for loss of or damage to goods that occurs during the time that they remain undelivered pursuant to this article unless the claimant proves that such loss or damage resulted from the failure by the carrier to take steps that would have been reasonable in the circumstances to preserve the goods and that the carrier knew or ought to have known that the loss or damage to the goods would result from its failure to take such steps.

Article 49 Retention of goods

Nothing in this Convention affects a right of the carrier or a performing party that may exist pursuant to the contract of carriage or the applicable law to retain the goods to secure the payment of sums due.

Chapter 10 Rights of the controlling party

Article 50 Exercise and extent of right of control

1.   The right of control may be exercised only by the controlling party and is limited to:
      (a) The right to give or modify instructions in respect of the goods that do not constitute a variation of the contract of carriage;
      (b) The right to obtain delivery of the goods at a scheduled port of call or, in respect of inland carriage, any place en route; and
      (c) The right to replace the consignee by any other person including the controlling party.

2. The right of control exists during the entire period of responsibility of the carrier, as provided in article 12, and ceases when that period expires.

Article 51 Identity of the controlling party and transfer of the right of control

1. Except in the cases referred to in paragraphs 2, 3 and 4 of this article:

   (a) The shipper is the controlling party unless the shipper, when the contract of carriage is concluded, designates the consignee, the documentary shipper or another person as the controlling party;

   (b) The controlling party is entitled to transfer the right of control to another person. The transfer becomes effective with respect to the carrier upon its notification of the transfer by the transferor, and the transferee becomes the controlling party; and

   (c) The controlling party shall properly identify itself when it exercises the right of control.

2. When a non-negotiable transport document has been issued that indicates that it shall be surrendered in order to obtain delivery of the goods:

   (a) The shipper is the controlling party and may transfer the right of control to the consignee named in the transport document by transferring the document to that person without endorsement. If more than one original of the document was issued, all originals shall be transferred in order to effect a transfer of the right of control; and

   (b) In order to exercise its right of control, the controlling party shall produce the document and properly identify itself. If more than one original of the document was issued, all originals shall be produced, failing which the right of control cannot be exercised.

3. When a negotiable transport document is issued:

    (a) The holder or, if more than one original of the negotiable transport document is issued, the holder of all originals is the controlling party;

    (b) The holder may transfer the right of control by transferring the negotiable transport document to another person in accordance with article 57. If more than one original of that document was issued, all originals shall be transferred to that person in order to effect a transfer of the right of control; and

    (c) In order to exercise the right of control, the holder shall produce the negotiable transport document to the carrier, and if the holder is one of the persons referred to in article 1, subparagraph 10 (a) (i), the holder shall properly identify itself. If more than one original of the document was issued, all originals shall be produced, failing which the right of control cannot be exercised.

4. When a negotiable electronic transport record is issued:

    (a) The holder is the controlling party;

    (b) The holder may transfer the right of control to another person by transferring the negotiable electronic transport record in accordance with the procedures referred to in article 9, paragraph 1; and

    (c) In order to exercise the right of control, the holder shall demonstrate, in accordance with the procedures referred to in article 9, paragraph 1, that it is the holder.

Article 52 Carrier's execution of instructions

1. Subject to paragraphs 2 and 3 of this article, the carrier shall execute the instructions referred to in article 50 if:

    (a) The person giving such instructions is entitled to exercise the right of control;

(b) The instructions can reasonably be executed according to their terms at the moment that they reach the carrier; and

(c) The instructions will not interfere with the normal operations of the carrier, including its delivery practices.

2. In any event, the controlling party shall reimburse the carrier for any reasonable additional expense that the carrier may incur and shall indemnify the carrier against loss or damage that the carrier may suffer as a result of diligently executing any instruction pursuant to this article, including compensation that the carrier may become liable to pay for loss of or damage to other goods being carried.

3. The carrier is entitled to obtain security from the controlling party for the amount of additional expense, loss or damage that the carrier reasonably expects will arise in connection with the execution of an instruction pursuant to this article. The carrier may refuse to carry out the instructions if no such security is provided.

4. The carrier's liability for loss of or damage to the goods or for delay in delivery resulting from its failure to comply with the instructions of the controlling party in breach of its obligation pursuant to paragraph 1 of this article shall be subject to articles 17 to 23, and the amount of the compensation payable by the carrier shall be subject to articles 59 to 61.

Article 53 Deemed delivery

Goods that are delivered pursuant to an instruction in accordance with article 52, paragraph 1, are deemed to be delivered at the place of destination, and the provisions of chapter 9 relating to such delivery apply to such goods.

Article 54 Variations to the contract of carriage

1. The controlling party is the only person that may agree with the carrier to variations to the contract of carriage other than those referred to in article 50, subparagraphs 1 (*b*) and (*c*).
2. Variations to the contract of carriage, including those referred to in article 50, subparagraphs 1 (*b*) and (*c*), shall be stated in a negotiable transport document or in a non-negotiable transport document that requires surrender, or incorporated in a negotiable electronic transport record, or, upon the request of the controlling party, shall be stated in a non-negotiable transport document or incorporated in a non-negotiable electronic transport record. If so stated or incorporated, such variations shall be signed in accordance with article 38.

Article 55 Providing additional information, instructions or documents to carrier

1. The controlling party, on request of the carrier or a performing party, shall provide in a timely manner information, instructions or documents relating to the goods not yet provided by the shipper and not otherwise reasonably available to the carrier that the carrier may reasonably need to perform its obligations under the contract of carriage.
2. If the carrier, after reasonable effort, is unable to locate the controlling party or the controlling party is unable to provide adequate information, instructions or documents to the carrier, the shipper shall provide them. If the carrier, after reasonable effort, is unable to locate the shipper, the documentary shipper shall provide such information, instructions or documents.

Article 56 Variation by agreement

The parties to the contract of carriage may vary the effect of articles 50, subparagraphs 1 (*b*) and (*c*), 50, paragraph 2, and 52. The parties may also restrict or exclude the transferability of the right of control referred to in article 51, subparagraph 1 (*b*).

Chapter 11 Transfer of rights

Article 57 When a negotiable transport document or negotiable electronic transport record is issued

1. When a negotiable transport document is issued, the holder may transfer the rights incorporated in the document by transferring it to another person:
   (*a*) Duly endorsed either to such other person or in blank, if an order document; or
   (*b*) Without endorsement, if: (i) a bearer document or a blank endorsed document; or (ii) a document made out to the order of a named person and the transfer is between the first holder and the named person.

2. When a negotiable electronic transport record is issued, its holder may transfer the rights incorporated in it, whether it be made out to order or to the order of a named person, by transferring the electronic transport record in accordance with the procedures referred to in article 9, paragraph 1.

Article 58 Liability of holder

1. Without prejudice to article 55, a holder that is not the shipper and that does not exercise any right under the contract of carriage

does not assume any liability under the contract of carriage solely by reason of being a holder.

2. A holder that is not the shipper and that exercises any right under the contract of carriage assumes any liabilities imposed on it under the contract of carriage to the extent that such liabilities are incorporated in or ascertainable from the negotiable transport document or the negotiable electronic transport record.

3. For the purposes of paragraphs 1 and 2 of this article, a holder that is not the shipper does not exercise any right under the contract of carriage solely because:

    (a) It agrees with the carrier, pursuant to article 10, to replace a negotiable transport document by a negotiable electronic transport record or to replace a negotiable electronic transport record by a negotiable transport document; or

    (b) It transfers its rights pursuant to article 57.

Chapter 12 Limits of liability

Article 59 Limits of liability

1. Subject to articles 60 and 61, paragraph 1, the carrier's liability for breaches of its obligations under this Convention is limited to 875 units of account per package or other shipping unit, or 3 units of account per kilogram of the gross weight of the goods that are the subject of the claim or dispute, whichever amount is the higher, except when the value of the goods has been declared by the shipper and included in the contract particulars, or when a higher amount than the amount of limitation of liability set out in this article has been agreed upon between the carrier and the shipper.

2. When goods are carried in or on a container, pallet or similar article of transport used to consolidate goods, or in or on a vehicle, the packages or shipping units enumerated in the contract particulars as packed in or on such article of transport or vehicle are deemed

packages or shipping units. If not so enumerated, the goods in or on such article of transport or vehicle are deemed one shipping unit.

3. The unit of account referred to in this article is the Special Drawing Right as defined by the International Monetary Fund. The amounts referred to in this article are to be converted into the national currency of a State according to the value of such currency at the date of judgement or award or the date agreed upon by the parties. The value of a national currency, in terms of the Special Drawing Right, of a Contracting State that is a member of the International Monetary Fund is to be calculated in accordance with the method of valuation applied by the International Monetary Fund in effect at the date in question for its operations and transactions. The value of a national currency, in terms of the Special Drawing Right, of a Contracting State that is not a member of the International Monetary Fund is to be calculated in a manner to be determined by that State.

Article 60 Limits of liability for loss caused by delay

Subject to article 61, paragraph 2, compensation for loss of or damage to the goods due to delay shall be calculated in accordance with article 22 and liability for economic loss due to delay is limited to an amount equivalent to two and one-half times the freight payable on the goods delayed. The total amount payable pursuant to this article and article 59, paragraph 1, may not exceed the limit that would be established pursuant to article 59, paragraph 1, in respect of the total loss of the goods concerned.

Article 61 Loss of the benefit of limitation of liability

1. Neither the carrier nor any of the persons referred to in article 18 is entitled to the benefit of the limitation of liability as provided in article 59, or as provided in the contract of carriage, if the

claimant proves that the loss resulting from the breach of the carrier's obligation under this Convention was attributable to a personal act or omission of the person claiming a right to limit done with the intent to cause such loss or recklessly and with knowledge that such loss would probably result.

2. Neither the carrier nor any of the persons mentioned in article 18 is entitled to the benefit of the limitation of liability as provided in article 60 if the claimant proves that the delay in delivery resulted from a personal act or omission of the person claiming a right to limit done with the intent to cause the loss due to delay or recklessly and with knowledge that such loss would probably result.

Chapter 13 Time for suit

Article 62 Period of time for suit

1. No judicial or arbitral proceedings in respect of claims or disputes arising from a breach of an obligation under this Convention may be instituted after the expiration of a period of two years.
2. The period referred to in paragraph 1 of this article commences on the day on which the carrier has delivered the goods or, in cases in which no goods have been delivered or only part of the goods have been delivered, on the last day on which the goods should have been delivered. The day on which the period commences is not included in the period.
3. Notwithstanding the expiration of the period set out in paragraph 1 of this article, one party may rely on its claim as a defence or for the purpose of set-off against a claim asserted by the other party.

Article 63 Extension of time for suit

The period provided in article 62 shall not be subject to suspension or interruption, but the person against which a claim is made may at any time during the running of the period extend that period by a declaration to the claimant. This period may be further extended by another declaration or declarations.

Article 64 Action for indemnity

An action for indemnity by a person held liable may be instituted after the expiration of the period provided in article 62 if the indemnity action is instituted within the later of:

(a) The time allowed by the applicable law in the jurisdiction where proceedings are instituted; or

(b) Ninety days commencing from the day when the person instituting the action for indemnity has either settled the claim or been served with process in the action against itself, whichever is earlier.

Article 65 Actions against the person identified as the carrier

An action against the bareboat charterer or the person identified as the carrier pursuant to article 37, paragraph 2, may be instituted after the expiration of the period provided in article 62 if the action is instituted within the later of:

(a) The time allowed by the applicable law in the jurisdiction where proceedings are instituted; or

(b) Ninety days commencing from the day when the carrier has been identified, or the registered owner or bareboat charterer has rebutted the presumption that it is the carrier, pursuant to article 37, paragraph 2.

Chapter 14 Jurisdiction

Article 66 Actions against the carrier

Unless the contract of carriage contains an exclusive choice of court agreement that complies with article 67 or 72, the plaintiff has the right to institute judicial proceedings under this Convention against the carrier:

(a) In a competent court within the jurisdiction of which is situated one of the following places:
(i)   The domicile of the carrier;
(ii) The place of receipt agreed in the contract of carriage;
(iii) The place of delivery agreed in the contract of carriage; or
(iv) The port where the goods are initially loaded on a ship or the port where the goods are finally discharged from a ship; or
(b) In a competent court or courts designated by an agreement between the shipper and the carrier for the purpose of deciding claims against the carrier that may arise under this Convention.

Article 67 Choice of court agreements

1.   The jurisdiction of a court chosen in accordance with article 66, subparagraph *b*), is exclusive for disputes between the parties to the contract only if the parties so agree and the agreement conferring jurisdiction:
(a) Is contained in a volume contract that clearly states the names and addresses of the parties and either (i) is individually negotiated or (ii) contains a prominent statement that there is an exclusive choice of court agreement and specifies the sections of the volume contract containing that agreement; and

(b) Clearly designates the courts of one Contracting State or one or more specific courts of one Contracting State.

2.   A person that is not a party to the volume contract is bound by an exclusive choice of court agreement concluded in accordance with paragraph 1 of this article only if:

   (a) The court is in one of the places designated in article 66, subparagraph *(a)*;

   (b) That agreement is contained in the transport document or electronic transport record;

   (c) That person is given timely and adequate notice of the court where the action shall be brought and that the jurisdiction of that court is exclusive; and

   (d) The law of the court seized recognizes that that person may be bound by the exclusive choice of court agreement.

Article 68 Actions against the maritime performing party

The plaintiff has the right to institute judicial proceedings under this Convention against the maritime performing party in a competent court within the jurisdiction of which is situated one of the following places:

   (a) The domicile of the maritime performing party; or

   (b) The port where the goods are received by the maritime performing party, the port where the goods are delivered by the maritime performing party or the port in which the maritime performing party performs its activities with respect to the goods.

Article 69 No additional bases of jurisdiction

Subject to articles 71 and 72, no judicial proceedings under this Convention against the carrier or a maritime performing party may be instituted in a court not designated pursuant to article 66 or 68.

Article 70 Arrest and provisional or protective measures

Nothing in this Convention affects jurisdiction with regard to provisional or protective measures, including arrest. A court in a State in which a provisional or protective measure was taken does not have jurisdiction to determine the case upon its merits unless:

(a) The requirements of this chapter are fulfilled; or

(b) An international convention that applies in that State so provides.

Article 71 Consolidation and removal of actions

1. Except when there is an exclusive choice of court agreement that is binding pursuant to article 67 or 72, if a single action is brought against both the carrier and the maritime performing party arising out of a single occurrence, the action may be instituted only in a court designated pursuant to both article 66 and article 68. If there is no such court, such action may be instituted in a court designated pursuant to article 68, subparagraph *(b)*, if there is such a court.

2. Except when there is an exclusive choice of court agreement that is binding pursuant to article 67 or 72, a carrier or a maritime performing party that institutes an action seeking a declaration of non-liability or any other action that would deprive a person of its right to select the forum pursuant to article 66 or 68 shall, at the request of the defendant, withdraw that action once the

defendant has chosen a court designated pursuant to article 66 or 68, whichever is applicable, where the action may be recommenced.

Article 72 Agreement after a dispute has arisen and jurisdiction when the defendant has entered an appearance

1. After a dispute has arisen, the parties to the dispute may agree to resolve it in any competent court.
2. A competent court before which a defendant appears, without contesting jurisdiction in accordance with the rules of that court, has jurisdiction.

Article 73 Recognition and enforcement

1. A decision made in one Contracting State by a court having jurisdiction under this Convention shall be recognized and enforced in another Contracting State in accordance with the law of such latter Contracting State when both States have made a declaration in accordance with article 74.
2. A court may refuse recognition and enforcement based on the grounds for the refusal of recognition and enforcement available pursuant to its law.
3. This chapter shall not affect the application of the rules of a regional economic integration organization that is a party to this Convention, as concerns the recognition or enforcement of judgements as between member States of the regional economic integration organization, whether adopted before or after this Convention.

Article 74 Application of chapter 14

The provisions of this chapter shall bind only Contracting States that declare in accordance with article 91 that they will be bound by them.

Chapter 15 Arbitration

Article 75 Arbitration agreements

1. Subject to this chapter, parties may agree that any dispute that may arise relating to the carriage of goods under this Convention shall be referred to arbitration.
2. The arbitration proceedings shall, at the option of the person asserting a claim against the carrier, take place at:
    (a) Any place designated for that purpose in the arbitration agreement; or
    (b) Any other place situated in a State where any of the following places is located:
        (i)   The domicile of the carrier;
        (ii) The place of receipt agreed in the contract of carriage;
        (iii) The place of delivery agreed in the contract of carriage; or
        (iv) The port where the goods are initially loaded on a ship or the port where the goods are finally discharged from a ship.

3. The designation of the place of arbitration in the agreement is binding for disputes between the parties to the agreement if the agreement is contained in a volume contract that clearly states the names and addresses of the parties and either:
    (a) Is individually negotiated; or
    (b) Contains a prominent statement that there is an arbitration agreement and specifies the sections of the volume contract containing the arbitration agreement.

4. When an arbitration agreement has been concluded in accordance with paragraph 3 of this article, a person that is not a party to the volume contract is bound by the designation of the place of arbitration in that agreement only if:

(a) The place of arbitration designated in the agreement is situated in one of the places referred to in subparagraph 2 (*b*) of this article;

(b) The agreement is contained in the transport document or electronic transport record;

(c) The person to be bound is given timely and adequate notice of the place of arbitration; and

(d) Applicable law permits that person to be bound by the arbitration agreement.

5. The provisions of paragraphs 1, 2, 3 and 4 of this article are deemed to be part of every arbitration clause or agreement, and any term of such clause or agreement to the extent that it is inconsistent therewith is void.

Article 76 Arbitration agreement in non-liner transportation

1. Nothing in this Convention affects the enforceability of an arbitration agreement in a contract of carriage in non-liner transportation to which this Convention or the provisions of this Convention apply by reason of:

(a) The application of article 7; or

(b) The parties' voluntary incorporation of this Convention in a contract of carriage that would not otherwise be subject to this Convention.

2. Notwithstanding paragraph 1 of this article, an arbitration agreement in a transport document or electronic transport record to which this Convention applies by reason of the application of article 7 is subject to this chapter unless such a transport document or electronic transport record:

(a) Identifies the parties to and the date of the charter party or other contract excluded from the application of this Convention by reason of the application of article 6; and *(b)* Incorporates by specific reference the clause in the charter party or other contract that contains the terms of the arbitration agreement.

Article 77 Agreement to arbitrate after a dispute has arisen

Notwithstanding the provisions of this chapter and chapter 14, after a dispute has arisen the parties to the dispute may agree to resolve it by arbitration in any place.

Article 78 Application of chapter 15

The provisions of this chapter shall bind only Contracting States that declare in accordance with article 91 that they will be bound by them.

Chapter 16 Validity of contractual terms

Article 79 General provisions

1. Unless otherwise provided in this Convention, any term in a contract of carriage is void to the extent that it:
    (a) Directly or indirectly excludes or limits the obligations of the carrier or a maritime performing party under this Convention;
    (b) Directly or indirectly excludes or limits the liability of the carrier or a maritime performing party for breach of an obligation under this Convention; or
    (c) Assigns a benefit of insurance of the goods in favour of the carrier or a person referred to in article 18.

2. Unless otherwise provided in this Convention, any term in a contract of carriage is void to the extent that it:

(a) Directly or indirectly excludes, limits or increases the obligations under this Convention of the shipper, consignee, controlling party, holder or documentary shipper; or

(b) Directly or indirectly excludes, limits or increases the liability of the shipper, consignee, controlling party, holder or documentary shipper for breach of any of its obligations under this Convention.

Article 80 Special rules for volume contracts

1. Notwithstanding article 79, as between the carrier and the shipper, a volume contract to which this Convention applies may provide for greater or lesser rights, obligations and liabilities than those imposed by this Convention.

2. A derogation pursuant to paragraph 1 of this article is binding only when:

   (a) The volume contract contains a prominent statement that it derogates from this Convention;

   (b) The volume contract is (i) individually negotiated or (ii) prominently specifies the sections of the volume contract containing the derogations;

   (c) The shipper is given an opportunity and notice of the opportunity to conclude a contract of carriage on terms and conditions that comply with this Convention without any derogation under this article; and

   (d) The derogation is neither (i) incorporated by reference from another document nor (ii) included in a contract of adhesion that is not subject to negotiation.

3. A carrier's public schedule of prices and services, transport document, electronic transport record or similar document is not a volume contract pursuant to paragraph 1 of this article, but a

volume contract may incorporate such documents by reference as terms of the contract.

4. Paragraph 1 of this article does not apply to rights and obligations provided in articles 14, subparagraphs (*a*) and (*b*), 29 and 32 or to liability arising from the breach thereof, nor does it apply to any liability arising from an act or omission referred to in article 61.

5. The terms of the volume contract that derogate from this Convention, if the volume contract satisfies the requirements of paragraph 2 of this article, apply between the carrier and any person other than the shipper provided that:

   (*a*) Such person received information that prominently states that the volume contract derogates from this Convention and gave its express consent to be bound by such derogations; and

   (*b*) Such consent is not solely set forth in a carrier's public schedule of prices and services, transport document or electronic transport record.

6. The party claiming the benefit of the derogation bears the burden of proof that the conditions for derogation have been fulfilled.

Article 81 Special rules for live animals and certain other goods

Notwithstanding article 79 and without prejudice to article 80, the contract of carriage may exclude or limit the obligations or the liability of both the carrier and a maritime performing party if:

   (*a*) The goods are live animals, but any such exclusion or limitation will not be effective if the claimant proves that the loss of or damage to the goods, or delay in delivery, resulted from an act or omission of the carrier or of a person referred to in article 18, done with the intent to cause such loss of or damage to the goods or such loss due to delay or done recklessly and with knowledge that such loss or damage or such loss due to delay would probably result; or

(b) The character or condition of the goods or the circumstances and terms and conditions under which the carriage is to be performed are such as reasonably to justify a special agreement, provided that such contract of carriage is not related to ordinary commercial shipments made in the ordinary course of trade and that no negotiable transport document or negotiable electronic transport record is issued for the carriage of the goods.

Chapter 17 Matters not governed by this convention

Article 82 International conventions governing the carriage of goods by other modes of transport

Nothing in this Convention affects the application of any of the following international conventions in force at the time this Convention enters into force, including any future amendment to such conventions, that regulate the liability of the carrier for loss of or damage to the goods:

(a) Any convention governing the carriage of goods by air to the extent that such convention according to its provisions applies to any part of the contract of carriage;

(b) Any convention governing the carriage of goods by road to the extent that such convention according to its provisions applies to the carriage of goods that remain loaded on a road cargo vehicle carried on board a ship;

(c) Any convention governing the carriage of goods by rail to the extent that such convention according to its provisions applies to carriage of goods by sea as a supplement to the carriage by rail; or

(d) Any convention governing the carriage of goods by inland waterways to the extent that such convention according to its provisions applies to a carriage of goods without transshipment both by inland waterways and sea.

Article 83 Global limitation of liability

Nothing in this Convention affects the application of any international convention or national law regulating the global limitation of liability of vessel owners.

Article 84 General average

Nothing in this Convention affects the application of terms in the contract of carriage or provisions of national law regarding the adjustment of general average.

Article 85 Passengers and luggage

This Convention does not apply to a contract of carriage for passengers and their luggage.

Article 86 Damage caused by nuclear incident

No liability arises under this Convention for damage caused by a nuclear incident if the operator of a nuclear installation is liable for such damage:

(a) Under the Paris Convention on Third Party Liability in the Field of Nuclear Energy of 29 July 1960 as amended by the Additional Protocol of 28 January 1964 and by the Protocols of 16 November 1982 and 12 February 2004, the Vienna Convention on Civil Liability for Nuclear Damage of 21 May 1963 as amended by the Joint Protocol Relating to the Application of the Vienna Convention and the Paris Convention of 21 September 1988 and as amended by the Protocol to Amend the 1963 Vienna Convention on Civil Liability for Nuclear Damage of 12 September 1997, or the Convention on Supplementary Compensation for Nuclear Damage of 12 September 1997, including any amendment to these conventions and any future convention in respect of the liability of the operator of a nuclear installation for damage caused by a nuclear incident; or

(b) Under national law applicable to the liability for such damage, provided that such law is in all respects as favourable to persons that may suffer damage as either the Paris or Vienna Conventions or the Convention on Supplementary Compensation for Nuclear Damage.

Chapter 18 Final clauses

Article 87 Depositary

The Secretary-General of the United Nations is hereby designated as the depositary of this Convention.

Article 88 Signature, ratification, acceptance, approval or accession

1. This Convention is open for signature by all States at Rotterdam, the Netherlands, on 23 September 2009, and thereafter at the Headquarters of the United Nations in New York.
2. This Convention is subject to ratification, acceptance or approval by the signatory States.
3. This Convention is open for accession by all States that are not signatory States as from the date it is open for signature.

4. Instruments of ratification, acceptance, approval and accession are to be deposited with the Secretary-General of the United Nations.

Article 89 Denunciation of other conventions

1. A State that ratifies, accepts, approves or accedes to this Convention and is a party to the International Convention for the Unification of certain Rules of Law relating to Bills of Lading signed at Brussels on 25 August 1924, to the Protocol to amend the International Convention for the Unification of certain Rules of Law relating to Bills of Lading, signed at Brussels on 23 February 1968, or to the Protocol to amend the International Convention for the Unification of certain Rules of Law relating to Bills of Lading as Modified by the Amending Protocol of 23 February 1968, signed at Brussels on 21 December 1979, shall at the same time denounce that Convention and the protocol or protocols thereto to which it is a party by notifying the Government of Belgium to that effect, with a declaration that the denunciation is to take effect as from the date when this Convention enters into force in respect of that State.

2. A State that ratifies, accepts, approves or accedes to this Convention and is a party to the United Nations Convention on the Carriage of Goods by Sea concluded at Hamburg on 31 March 1978 shall at the same time denounce that Convention by notifying the Secretary-General of the United Nations to that effect, with a declaration that the denunciation is to take effect as from the date when this Convention enters into force in respect of that State.

3. For the purposes of this article, ratifications, acceptances, approvals and accessions in respect of this Convention by States parties to the instruments listed in paragraphs 1 and 2 of this article that are notified to the depositary after this Convention has entered into force are not effective until such denunciations as may be

required on the part of those States in respect of these instruments have become effective. The depositary of this Convention shall consult with the Government of Belgium, as the depositary of the instruments referred to in paragraph 1 of this article, so as to ensure necessary coordination in this respect.

Article 90 Reservations

No reservation is permitted to this Convention.

Article 91 Procedure and effect of declarations

1. The declarations permitted by articles 74 and 78 may be made at any time. The initial declarations permitted by article 92, paragraph 1, and article 93, paragraph 2, shall be made at the time of signature, ratification, acceptance, approval or accession. No other declaration is permitted under this Convention.
2. Declarations made at the time of signature are subject to confirmation upon ratification, acceptance or approval.
3. Declarations and their confirmations are to be in writing and to be formally notified to the depositary.
4. A declaration takes effect simultaneously with the entry into force of this Convention in respect of the State concerned. However, a declaration of which the depositary receives formal notification after such entry into force takes effect on the first day of the month following the expiration of six months after the date of its receipt by the depositary.
5. Any State that makes a declaration under this Convention may withdraw it at any time by a formal notification in writing addressed to the depositary. The withdrawal of a declaration, or its modification where permitted by this Convention, takes effect on the first day of the month following the expiration of six months after the date of the receipt of the notification by the depositary.

Article 92 Effect in domestic territorial units

1. If a Contracting State has two or more territorial units in which different systems of law are applicable in relation to the matters dealt with in this Convention, it may, at the time of signature, ratification, acceptance, approval or accession, declare that this Convention is to extend to all its territorial units or only to one or more of them, and may amend its declaration by submitting another declaration at any time.
2. These declarations are to be notified to the depositary and are to state expressly the territorial units to which the Convention extends.
3. When a Contracting State has declared pursuant to this article that this Convention extends to one or more but not all of its territorial units, a place located in a territorial unit to which this Convention does not extend is not considered to be in a Contracting State for the purposes of this Convention.
4. If a Contracting State makes no declaration pursuant to paragraph 1 of this article, the Convention is to extend to all territorial units of that State.

Article 93 Participation by regional economic integration organizations

1. A regional economic integration organization that is constituted by sovereign States and has competence over certain matters governed by this Convention may similarly sign, ratify, accept, approve or accede to this Convention. The regional economic integration organization shall in that case have the rights and obligations of a Contracting State, to the extent that that organization has competence over matters governed by this Convention. When the number of Contracting States is relevant in this Convention, the regional economic integration organization does not count as a Contracting State in addition to its member States which are Contracting States.

2. The regional economic integration organization shall, at the time of signature, ratification, acceptance, approval or accession, make a declaration to the depositary specifying the matters governed by this Convention in respect of which competence has been transferred to that organization by its member States. The regional economic integration organization shall promptly notify the depositary of any changes to the distribution of competence, including new transfers of competence, specified in the declaration pursuant to this paragraph.

3. Any reference to a "Contracting State" or "Contracting States" in this Convention applies equally to a regional economic integration organization when the context so requires.

Article 94 Entry into force

1. This Convention enters into force on the first day of the month following the expiration of one year after the date of deposit of the twentieth instrument of ratification, acceptance, approval or accession.

2. For each State that becomes a Contracting State to this Convention after the date of the deposit of the twentieth instrument of ratification, acceptance, approval or accession, this Convention enters into force on the first day of the month following the expiration of one year after the deposit of the appropriate instrument on behalf of that State.

3. Each Contracting State shall apply this Convention to contracts of carriage concluded on or after the date of the entry into force of this Convention in respect of that State.

Article 95 Revision and amendment

1. At the request of not less than one third of the Contracting States to this Convention, the Secretary-General of the United Nations

shall convene a conference of the Contracting States for revising or amending it.

2. Any instrument of ratification, acceptance, approval or accession deposited after the entry into force of an amendment to this Convention is deemed to apply to the Convention as amended.

Article 96 Denunciation of this Convention

1. A Contracting State may denounce this Convention at any time by means of a notification in writing addressed to the depositary.
2. The denunciation takes effect on the first day of the month following the expiration of one year after the notification is received by the depositary. If a longer period is specified in the notification, the denunciation takes effect upon the expiration of such longer period after the notification is received by the depositary.

DONE at New York, this eleventh day of December two thousand and eight, in a single original, of which the Arabic, Chinese, English, French, Russian and Spanish texts are equally authentic.

IN WITNESS WHEREOF the undersigned plenipotentiaries, being duly authorized by their respective Governments, have signed this Convention. * * *

Bill of lading copy

Code Name: "MULTIDOC 95"

MT Doc. No.

Consignor

Reference No.

Negotiable

MULTIMODAL TRANSPORT BILL OF LADING

Issued by The Baltic and International Maritime Council (BIMCO), subject to the UNCTAD/ICC Rules for Multimodal Transport Documents (ICC Publication No. 481).

(revised 1995)

Consigned to order of

Notify party/address

Place of receipt

Ocean Vessel

Port of loading

Port of discharge

Place of delivery

Marks and Nos.

Quantity and description of goods

Gross weight, kg. Measurement, m³

Particulars above declared by Consignor

Freight and charges

RECEIVED the goods in apparent good order and condition, as far as ascertainable by reasonable means of checking, as specified above unless otherwise stated.

The MTO, in accordance with and to the extent of the provisions contained in this MT Bill of Lading, and with liberty to sub-contract, undertakes to perform and/or in his own name to procure performance of the multimodal transport and the delivery of the goods, including all services which are necessary from the place and time of taking the goods in charge to the place and time of delivery and accepts responsibility for such transport and such services.

One of the MT Bills of Lading must be surrendered duly endorsed in exchange for the goods or delivery order.

IN WITNESS whereof the original MT Bill(s) of Lading have/has been signed in the number indicated below, one of which being accomplished the other(s) to be void.

Consignor's declared value of .....

subject to payment of above extra charge.

Note:

The Merchant's attention is called to the fact that according to clauses 10 to 12 of this MT Bill of Lading, the liability of the MTO is in most cases limited in respect of loss of or damage to the goods.

Freight payable at

Place and date of issue

Number of original MT Bills of Lading

Signed for the Multimodal Transport Operator (MTO) as Carrier

by

As agent(s) only to the MTO

Printed by the BIMCO Charter Party Editor

MULTIMODAL TRANSPORT BILL OF LADING

CODE NAME: "MULTIDOC 95"

I. GENERAL PROVISIONS

1. Applicability

2. Definitions

3. MTO's Tariff

4. Time Bar

5. Law and Jurisdiction

II. PERFORMANCE OF THE CONTRACT

6. Methods and Routes of Transportation

7. Optional Stowage

8. Delivery of the Goods to the Consignee

9. Hindrances etc. Affecting Performance

III. LIABILITY OF THE MTO

10. Basic Liability

11. Defences for Carriage by Sea or Inland Waterways

12. Limitation of Liability

13. Assessment of Compensation

14. Notice of Loss of or Damage to the Goods

15. Defences and Limits for the MTO, Servants, etc.

IV. DESCRIPTION OF GOODS

16. MTO's Responsibility

17. Consignor's Responsibility

18. Return of Containers

19. Dangerous Goods

20. Consignor-packed Containers, etc.

V. FREIGHT AND LIEN

21. Freight

22. Lien

VI. MISCELLANEOUS PROVISIONS

23. General Average

24. Both-to-Blame Collision Clause

25. U.S. Trade

J

Lloyd's salvage agreement copy

LLOYD'S STANDARD FORM OF SALVAGE AGREEMENT

(Approved and Published by the Council of Lloyd's)

LLOYD'S STANDARD SALVAGE AND ARBITRATION CLAUSES

1   **Introduction**

1.1   These clauses ("the LSSA Clauses") or any revision thereof which may be published with the approval of the Council of Lloyd's are incorporated into and form an integral part of every contract for the performance of salvage services undertaken on the terms of Lloyd's Standard Form of Salvage Agreement as published by the Council of Lloyd's and known as LOF 2011 (or its predecessor LOF 2000) ("the Agreement" which expression includes the LSSA clauses and Lloyd's Procedural Rules referred to in Clause 6).

1.2   All notices communications and other documents required to be sent to the Council of Lloyd's should be sent to:

Salvage Arbitration Branch
Lloyd's
One Lime Street
London EC3M 7HA

Tel: +44 (0) 20 7327 5408/5407
Fax: +44 (0) 20 7327 6827
E-mail: lloyds-salvage@lloyds.com

2   **Overriding Objective**

In construing the Agreement or on the making of any arbitral order or award regard shall be had to the overriding purposes of the Agreement namely:

a   to seek to promote safety of life at sea and the preservation of property at sea and during the salvage operations to prevent or minimise damage to the environment;

b   to ensure that its provisions are operated in good faith and that it is read and understood to operate in a reasonably businesslike manner;

c   to encourage cooperation between the parties and with relevant authorities;

d   to ensure that the reasonable expectations of salvors and owners of salved property are met and

e   to ensure that it leads to a fair and efficient disposal of disputes between the parties whether amicably by mediation or by arbitration within a reasonable time and at a reasonable cost.

3   **Definitions**

In the Agreement and unless there is an express provision to the contrary:

3.1   "Award" includes an interim or provisional Award and "Appeal Award" means any Award including any interim or provisional Award made by the Appeal Arbitrator appointed under clause 10.2.

3.2   "personal effects or baggage" as referred to in Box 2 of the Agreement means those which the passenger, Master and crew member have in their cabin or are otherwise in their possession, custody or control and shall include any private motor vehicle accompanying a passenger and any personal effects or baggage in or on such vehicle.

3.3   "Convention" means the International Convention on Salvage 1989 as enacted by section 224, Schedule II of the Merchant Shipping Act 1995 (and any amendment of either) and any term or expression in the Convention has the same meaning when used in the Agreement.

3.4 "Council" means the Council of Lloyd's

3.5 "days" means calendar days

3.6 "Owners" means the owners of the property referred to in box 2 of the Agreement

3.7 "owners of the vessel" includes the demise or bareboat charterers of that vessel

3.8 "special compensation" refers to the compensation payable to salvors under Article 14 of the Convention

3.9 "Scopic Clause" refers to the agreement made between (1) members of the International Salvage Union (2) the International Group of P&I Clubs and (3) certain property underwriters which first became effective on 1st August 1999 and includes any replacement or revision thereof. All references to the Scopic Clause in the Agreement shall be deemed to refer to the version of the Scopic Clause current at the date the Agreement is made.

4 Provisions as to Security, Maritime Lien and Right to Arrest

4.1 The Contractors shall immediately after the termination of the services or sooner notify the Council and where practicable the Owners of the amount for which they demand salvage security (inclusive of costs expenses and interest) from each of the respective Owners.

4.2 Where a claim is made or may be made for special compensation the owners of the vessel shall on the demand of the Contractors whenever made provide security for the Contractors' claim for special compensation provided always that such demand is made within 2 years of the date of termination of the services.

4.3 The security referred to in clauses 4.1. and 4.2. above shall be demanded and provided in the currency specified in Box 4 or in United States Dollars if no such alternative currency has been agreed.

4.4 The amount of any such security shall be reasonable in the light of the knowledge available to the Contractors at the time when the demand is made and any further facts which come to the Contractors' attention before security is provided. The arbitrator appointed under clause 5 hereof may, at any stage of the proceedings, order that the amount of security be reduced or increased as the case may be.

4.5 Unless otherwise agreed such security shall be provided (i) to the Council (ii) in a form approved by the Council and (iii) by persons firms or corporations either acceptable to the Contractors or resident in the United Kingdom and acceptable to the Council. The Council shall not be responsible for the sufficiency (whether in amount or otherwise) of any security which shall be provided nor the default or insolvency of any person firm or corporation providing the same.

4.6 The owners of the vessel including their servants and agents shall use their best endeavours to ensure that none of the property salved is released until security has been provided in respect of that property in accordance with clause 4.5.

4.7 Until security has been provided as aforesaid the Contractors shall have a maritime lien on the property salved for their remuneration.

4.8 Until security has been provided the property salved shall not without the consent in writing of the Contractors (which shall not be unreasonably withheld) be removed from the place to which it has been taken by the Contractors under clause A. Where such consent is given by the Contractors on condition that they are provided with temporary security pending completion of the voyage the Contractors' maritime lien on the property salved shall remain in force to the extent necessary to enable the Contractors to compel the provision of security in accordance with clause 4.5.

4.9 The Contractors shall not arrest or detain the property salved unless
   (i)   security is not provided within 21 days after the date of the termination of the services or
   (ii)   they have reason to believe that the removal of the property salved is contemplated contrary to clause 4.8. or
   (iii)   any attempt is made to remove the property salved contrary to clause 4.8.

5 Appointment of Arbitrators

5.1 Whether or not security has been provided (and always subject to Clause 6.6 and 10.8 below) the Council shall appoint an arbitrator ("the Arbitrator") upon receipt of a written request provided that any party requesting such appointment shall if required by the Council undertake to the Council's reasonable satisfaction to pay the reasonable fees and expenses of the Council and those of the Arbitrator and the Appeal Arbitrator

5.2 The Arbitrator, the Appeal Arbitrator and the Council may charge reasonable fees and expenses for their services whether the arbitration proceeds to a hearing or not and all such fees and expenses shall be treated as part of the costs of the arbitration.

6 Arbitration Procedure and Arbitrators Powers

6.1 The arbitration shall be conducted in accordance with the Procedural Rules approved by the Council ("Lloyd's Procedural Rules") in force at the date of the LOF agreement.

6.2 The arbitration shall take place in London unless (i) all represented parties agree to some other place for the whole or part of the arbitration and (ii) any such agreement is approved by the Arbitrator on such terms as to the payment of the Arbitrator's travel and accommodation expenses as he may see fit to impose.

6.3   The Arbitrator shall have power in his absolute discretion to include in the amount awarded to the Contractors the whole or part of any expenses reasonably incurred by the Contractors in:

(i)   ascertaining demanding and obtaining the amount of security reasonably required in accordance with clause 4.5

(ii)   enforcing and/or protecting by insurance or otherwise or taking reasonable steps to enforce and/or protect their lien

6.4   The Arbitrator shall have power to make but shall not be bound to make a consent award between such parties as so consent with or without full arbitral reasons

6.5   The Arbitrator shall have power to make a provisional or interim award or awards including payments on account on such terms as may be fair and just

6.6   The Arbitrator shall be entitled to satisfactory security for his reasonable fees and expenses, whether such fees and expenses have been incurred already or are reasonably anticipated. The Arbitrator shall have the power to order one or more of the parties to provide such security in a sum or sums and in a form to be determined by the Arbitrator. The said power may be exercised from time to time as the Arbitrator considers appropriate.

6.7   Awards in respect of salvage remuneration or special compensation (including payments on account) shall be made in the currency specified in Box 4 or in United States dollars if no such alternative currency has been agreed.

6.8   The Arbitrator's Award shall (subject to appeal as provided in clause 10) be final and binding on all the parties concerned whether they were represented at the arbitration or not and shall be published by the Council in London.

7   Representation of Parties

7.1   Any party to the Agreement who wishes to be heard or to adduce evidence shall appoint an agent or representative ordinarily resident in the United Kingdom to receive correspondence and notices for and on behalf of that party and shall give written notice of such appointment to the Council.

7.2   Service on such agent or representative by letter, e-mail or facsimile shall be deemed to be good service on the party which has appointed that agent or representative.

7.3   Any party who fails to appoint an agent or representative as aforesaid shall be deemed to have renounced his right to be heard or adduce evidence.

8   Interest

8.1   Unless the Arbitrator in his discretion otherwise decides the Contractors shall be entitled to interest on any sums awarded in respect of salvage remuneration or special compensation (after taking into consideration any sums already paid to the Contractors on account) from the date of termination of the services until the date on which the Award is published by the Council and at a rate to be determined by the Arbitrator.

8.2   In ordinary circumstances the Contractors' interest entitlement shall be limited to simple interest but the Arbitrator may exercise his statutory power to make an award of compound interest if the Contractors have been deprived of their salvage remuneration or special compensation for an excessive period as a result of the Owners' gross misconduct or in other exceptional circumstances.

8.3   If the sum(s) awarded to the Contractors (including the fees and expenses referred to in clause 5.2) are not paid to the Contractors or to the Council by the payment date specified in clause 11.1 the Contractors shall be entitled to additional interest on such outstanding sums from the payment date until the date payment is received by the Contractors or the Council both dates inclusive and at a rate which the Arbitrator shall in his absolute discretion determine in his Award.

9   Currency Correction

In considering what sums of money have been expended by the Contractors in rendering the services and/or in fixing the amount of the Award and/or Appeal Award the Arbitrator or Appeal Arbitrator shall to such an extent and insofar as it may be fair and just in all the circumstances give effect to the consequences of any change or changes in the relevant rates of exchange which may have occurred between the date of termination of the services and the date on which the Award or Appeal Award is made.

10   Appeals and Cross Appeals

10.1   Any party may appeal from an Award by giving written Notice of Appeal to the Council provided such notice is received by the Council no later than 21 days after the date on which the Award was published by the Council

10.2   On receipt of a Notice of Appeal the Council shall refer the appeal to the hearing and determination of an appeal arbitrator of its choice ("the Appeal Arbitrator")

10.3   Any party who has not already given Notice of Appeal under clause 10.1 may give a Notice of Cross Appeal to the Council within 21 days of that party having been notified that the Council has received Notice of Appeal from another party

10.4   Notice of Appeal or Cross Appeal shall be given to the Council by letter, e-mail or facsimile.

10.5 If any Notice of Appeal or Notice of Cross Appeal is withdrawn prior to the hearing of the appeal arbitration, that appeal arbitration shall nevertheless proceed for the purpose of determining any matters which remain outstanding.

10.6 The Appeal Arbitrator shall conduct the appeal arbitration in accordance with Lloyd's Procedural Rules so far as applicable to an appeal.

10.7 In addition to the powers conferred on the Arbitrator by English law and the Agreement, the Appeal Arbitrator shall have power to:
    (i)   admit the evidence or information which was before the Arbitrator together with the Arbitrator's Notes and Reasons for his Award, any transcript of evidence and such additional evidence or information as he may think fit;
    (ii)   confirm increase or reduce the sum(s) awarded by the Arbitrator and to make such order as to the payment of interest on such sum(s) as he may think fit;
    (iii)   confirm revoke or vary any order and/or declaratory award made by the Arbitrator;
    (iv)   award interest on any fees and expenses charged under clause 10.8 from the expiration of 28 days after the date of publication by the Council of the Appeal Arbitrator's Award until the date payment is received by the Council both dates inclusive.

10.8 The Appeal Arbitrator shall be entitled to satisfactory security for his reasonable fees and expenses, whether such fees and expenses have been incurred already or are reasonably anticipated. The Appeal Arbitrator shall have the power to order one or more of the parties to provide such security in a sum or sums and in a form to be determined by the Appeal Arbitrator. The said power may be exercised from time to time as the Appeal Arbitrator considers appropriate.

10.9 The Appeal Arbitrator's Award shall be published by the Council in London.

11   **Provisions as to Payment**

11.1 When publishing the Award the Council shall call upon the party or parties concerned to pay all sums due from them which are quantified in the Award (including the fees and expenses referred to in clause 5.2) not later than 28 days after the date of publication of the Award ("the payment date").

11.2 If the sums referred to in clause 11.1 (or any part thereof) are not paid within 56 days after the date of publication of the Award (or such longer period as the Contractors may allow) and provided the Council has not received Notice of Appeal or Notice of Cross Appeal the Council shall realise or enforce the security given to the Council under clause 4.5 by or on behalf of the defaulting party or parties subject to the Contractors' providing the Council with any indemnity the Council may require in respect of the costs the Council may incur in that regard.

11.3 In the event of an appeal and upon publication by the Council of the Appeal Award the Council shall call upon the party or parties concerned to pay the sum(s) awarded. In the event of non-payment and subject to the Contractors providing the Council with any costs indemnity required as referred to in clause 11.2 the Council shall realise or enforce the security given to the Council under clause 4.5 by or on behalf of the defaulting party.

11.4 If any sum(s) shall become payable to the Contractors in respect of salvage remuneration or special compensation (including interest and/or costs) as the result of an agreement made between the Contractors and the Owners or any of them, the Council shall, if called upon to do so and subject to the Contractors providing to the Council any costs indemnity required as referred to in clause 11.2 realise or enforce the security given to the Council under clause 4.5 by or on behalf of that party.

11.5 Where (i) no security has been provided to the Council in accordance with clause 4.5 or (ii) no Award is made by the Arbitrator or the Appeal Arbitrator (as the case may be) because the parties have been able to settle all matters in issue between them by agreement the Contractors shall be responsible for payment of the fees and expenses referred to in clause 5.2. Payment of such fees and expenses shall be made to the Council within 28 days of the Contractors or their representatives receiving the Council's invoice failing which the Council shall be entitled to interest on any sum outstanding at UK Base Rate prevailing on the date of the invoice plus 2% per annum until payment is received by the Council.

11.6 If an Award or Appeal Award directs the Contractors to pay any sum to any other party or parties including the whole or any part of the costs of the arbitration and/or appeal arbitration the Council may deduct from sums received by the Council on behalf of the Contractors the amount(s) so payable by the Contractors unless the Contractors provide the Council with satisfactory security to meet their liability.

11.7 Save as aforesaid every sum received by the Council pursuant to this clause shall be paid by the Council to the Contractors or their representatives whose receipt shall be a good discharge for it.

11.8 Without prejudice to the provisions of clause 4.5 the liability of the Council shall be limited to the amount of security provided to it.

12   **Awards**

12.1 The Council will ordinarily make available the Award or Appeal Award and Reasons on www.lloydsagency.com (the website) except where the Arbitrator or Appeal Arbitrator has ordered, in response to representations by any party to the Award or Appeal Award, that there is a good reason for deferring or withholding them. Any party may make such representations to the Arbitrator provided a written notice of its intention to do so is received by the Council no later than 21 days after the date on which the Award or Appeal Award was published by the Council and the representations themselves are submitted in writing to the Arbitrator or Appeal Arbitrator within 21 days of the date of the notice of intention.

12.2   Subject to any order of the Arbitrator or Appeal Arbitrator, the Award, or Appeal Award, and Reasons will be made available on the website as soon as practicable after expiry of the 21 day period referred to in clause 12.1.

12.3   In the event of an appeal being entered against an Award, the Award and Reasons shall not be made available on the website until either the Appeal Arbitrator has issued his Appeal Award or the Notice of Appeal is withdrawn subject always to any order being made in accordance with clause 12.1.

Special Provisions

These Special Provisions shall apply to salved cargo insofar as it consists of laden containers.

13   The parties agree that any correspondence or notices in respect of salved cargo which is not the subject of representation in accordance with Clause 7 of these Rules may be sent to the party or parties who have provided salvage security in respect of that property and that this shall be deemed to constitute proper notification to the owners of such property.

14   Subject to the express approval of the Arbitrator, where an agreement is reached between the Contractors and the owners of salved cargo comprising at least 75% by value of salved cargo represented in accordance with Clause 7 of these Rules, the same agreement shall be binding on the owners of all salved cargo who were not represented at the time of the said approval.

15   Subject to the express approval of the Arbitrator, any salved cargo with a value below an agreed figure may be omitted from the salved fund and excused from liability for salvage where the cost of including such cargo in the process is likely to be disproportionate to its liability for salvage.

General Provisions

16   **Lloyd's documents:** Any Award notice authority order or other document signed by the Chairman of Lloyd's or any person authorised by the Council for the purpose shall be deemed to have been duly made or given by the Council and shall have the same force and effect in all respects as if it had been signed by every member of the Council.

17   Contractors' personnel and subcontractors

     17.1   The Contractors may claim salvage on behalf of their employees and any other servants or agents who participate in the services and shall upon request provide the Owners with a reasonably satisfactory indemnity against all claims by or liabilities to such employees servants or agents.

     17.2   The Contractors may engage the services of subcontractors for the purpose of fulfilling their obligations under clauses A and B of the Agreement but the Contractors shall nevertheless remain liable to the Owners for the due performance of those obligations.

     17.3   In the event that subcontractors are engaged as aforesaid the Contractors may claim salvage on behalf of the subcontractors including their employees servants or agents and shall, if called upon so to do provide the Owners with a reasonably satisfactory indemnity against all claims by or liabilities to such subcontractors their employees servants or agents.

18   Disputes under Scopic Clause

Any dispute arising out of the Scopic Clause (including as to its incorporation or invocation) or the operations thereunder shall be referred for determination to the Arbitrator appointed under clause 5 hereof whose Award shall be final and binding subject to appeal as provided in clause 10 hereof.

19   Lloyd's Publications

Any guidance published by or on behalf of the Council relating to matters such as the Convention the workings and implementation of the Agreement is for information only and forms no part of the Agreement.

304

CPSIA information can be obtained
at www.ICGtesting.com
Printed in the USA
BVHW032145200121
598295BV00009B/31